JOAN,
Maid of Orléans

Other books by Henri Guillemin

Napoléon tel quel

La Première Résurrection de la République, 24 février 1848

L'Arrière-pensée de Jaurès

Pas à pas

Le "converti" Paul Claudel

JOAN,
Maid of Orléans

❖ ❖ ❖

HENRI GUILLEMIN

Translated by Harold J. Salemson

Saturday Review Press

NEW YORK

God does not need our lies.
—POPE LEO XIII

Contents

JOAN,
Maid of Orléans

I

To Find Her

It had been bothering me for a long time. Was there any way, in this day and age, to get to the true story of that mysterious Joan, known as "Joan of Arc"?

There we are! Only the third line, and the quotation marks appear: my favorite failing, what has been called my awful, characteristic "quotation quotient." Well, the dictionary says quotation marks indicate something the author is relating but cannot necessarily vouch for. When I used them in the title of my book, *The "Conversion" of Paul Claudel*, it was because, although Claudel had used the word himself, it did not seem to me quite the appropriate one to designate the ready return of a "child" (again Claudel's own word) to the faith of his early years. And if I write "Joan of Arc" it is because the girl whose tale I am trying to untangle would have been most disconcerted to hear herself so called. No one in her day ever called her Joan of Arc; it is an artificial name, invented after the fact by some sixteenth-century poet of Orléans. So quotes are called for; they are indispensable.

The work at hand calls first for study, for reconstruction if possible of the ambience in which Joan's story unfolded. What was happening at the time Joan appeared on the scene? What was the atmosphere in which she breathed? Since she would play a role in the affairs of France, what condition were they in when she became involved? It is only after we reconstruct this background that we can try to get at the facts about her origin, her makeup, her thoughts, her actions. First, we have to know the context into which she fitted.

When Joan spoke of "France," she did not mean our present-day hexagon. Not only did she say she was going "to France" when she left Vaucouleurs (for neither Vaucouleurs nor Domrémy were in France as she saw it), but later, when the King sent her to attack La Charité-sur-Loire in the fall of 1429, she quite clearly said she would have preferred to "come to France." To her, Saint-Pierre-le-Moutier and La Charité-sur-Loire were not "in France," either. France, in her eyes, was the Île-de-France, in other words, the small province of which Paris was the capital, and which today, in addition to Paris and its environs, includes the departments of the Aisne, Oise, Seine-et-Marne, and part of the Somme.

Let us look at a map showing the limits of the "Kingdom of France" in the fifteenth century. Within them were the Artois in the north, Normandy in the northwest, Brittany, Maine, Anjou, Poitou, and Saintonge in the west, Guyenne in the southwest, Berry and Auvergne in the center, Languedoc in the south, Champagne, Burgundy, and the Dauphiné at the east. Not included were Lorraine, Franche-Comté, and Bresse, nor Savoy or Provence. Cambrai, Metz, Besançon, and Marseilles were not under the French crown. All of those regions belonged to the Germanic Holy

NORMANDY

ARTOIS

CHAMPAGNE

BRITTANY

MAINE

ANJOU

BURGUNDY

POITOU BERRY

SAINTONGE

GUYENNE AUVERGNE DAUPHINÉ

LANGUEDOC

FRANCE IN 1429

Roman Empire; Macon was a border city.[1]

The descendants of Hugh Capet, who called themselves "Kings of France," had been having all kinds of trouble since 1328. The last son of Philip the Fair had died without male issue, and a Valois nephew had stepped in to succeed him, as Philip VI. He had been ruling since 1322 when, in 1328, the new King of England, Edward III, made the claim that a grandson was a more direct heir to the crown than a nephew. His father, Edward II, had married a daughter of Philip the Fair; so he was French on his mother's side and felt no qualms about proclaiming himself "King of France and England," in defiance of the usurper, Philip VI. This was what "respectable" history (see Joseph Calmette's *Jeanne d'Arc*, 1946) likes to describe as "armed litigation between two branches of the Capetian line," or, to put it more succinctly, the heirs having it out, a showdown between the claimants. The English got the advantage: Crécy, Poitiers; then the wind changed, and Charles V, with Du Guesclin, reversed the situation. He took all of it back from the semi-Capetians in London—all except Guyenne, where the conquerors had planted solid roots and enjoyed strong support.

What made matters much more difficult for the Valois was the behavior of their vassals, those powerful barons who recognized them only theoretically as suzerains. On that score, things were shamefully chaotic; it was hopelessly "every man for himself." The Duke of Brittany was impossible (it was while on his way to deal with that rebel that Charles VI suddenly went mad in 1392 in the forest of Le Mans); but the worst was Burgundy, who more and

---

[1] I well remember my father, who was born in 1865, telling me how in his childhood he heard the boatmen on the Saône River working to cries of "Pull Kingdom! Pull Empire!" These archaic terms carried over to the end of the last century, to designate the bank of the river the barge should be headed toward, since it had once separated the Kingdom of France from the Holy Roman Empire.

more often took it upon himself to pose as "Grand Duke of the Occident." John the Good had had an unfortunate idea when he gave Burgundy as a protectorate to his son Philip—Charles V's brother—known to history as Philip the Bold! Since he had annexed Flanders through his marriage to Margaret, Philip had begun taking himself for a quasi-king. He detested his cousin Louis of Orléans—the son of Charles V, brother of Charles VI, not to mention lover of his sister-in-law, Isabeau of Bavaria—for Louis, with designs on Luxembourg, entertained unspeakable ambitions which, had they been realized, would have thwarted the plans of the lord of Dijon and Bruges most odiously. So John the Fearless, who in 1404 succeeded his father "the Bold," found that the best solution for getting rid of cousin Louis was simply to have him killed (1407).

In all of these historical accounts, the word "Armagnac" appears as a synonym for "French." (The English later referred to Joan as the "Witch of the Armagnacs.") This is because Charles of Orléans, son and heir of the Louis murdered by John, married a daughter of the Count of Armagnac, creating a Valois-Orléans line that was to become a powerful support of the crown in the tussles with the Anglo-Burgundians. But that was not to happen right away.

In 1412, we had the pretty sight of the killer, John the Fearless, and the son of the man he had killed, Charles, riding together on the same horse, in the most brotherly of embraces; and in order to make this reconciliation palatable to the English, both Burgundians and Valois-Orléans agreed to permit a column of reinforcements to be sent into Guyenne by the King of England to pillage the Périgord and Saintonge provinces along their way and take hostages for ransom. Such was the "sense of nationhood" displayed by the great feudal vassals.

There were troubles in England, too. The grandson of Edward III, Richard II, had been on the throne in London since 1377 until he was overthrown, deposed, imprisoned, and finally killed by his cousin Lancaster, who became Henry IV. When Henry's son, Henry V, came to power in 1413, he felt that it would be just too stupid to fall asleep on the job with France in the hands of a crazy king. Forward to the attack! And on to the victory at Agincourt (1415), where French knighthood was cut to shreds by English archers. Things took a turn for the worse between Armagnacs and Burgundians at that time, and when they reached the breaking point, John the Fearless became master of Paris. The presumptive heir to the unfortunate Charles VI was the young Count of Ponthieu, born in 1403, who tried to come to an understanding with John the Fearless; but in 1419 at Montereau, under circumstances that remain unclear, John was killed by the Dauphin's men.

This Montereau incident drove Burgundy even more strongly toward the English pretender, especially since Flanders, in order to remain prosperous, needed British wool for its looms. The second Philip of Burgundy (this one was known as "the Good") was concocting a terrible revenge against the "criminal" of Montereau with Queen Isabeau. A perfect Franco-English entente was worked out at the Peace of Troyes in 1420: Charles VI (emulating Philip the Fair) married one of his daughters to the King of England and another to Duke Philip. The son who, it was hoped, would be born of the royal union would officially be recognized as "King of France and England," with a claim far stronger than that of Edward III a hundred years before, since this time the King of France personally had sanctioned it.[2] Yet, what about the Ponthieu "Dauphin"?

---

[2]Charles VI, the "Mad King," was insane only in fits, and had long periods of lucidity, as he amply proved at Vincennes in 1417, unexpectedly bursting in on one of the sex orgies for which Queen Isabeau used that country place. He killed two of his wife's partners with his own hands and for a time kept her locked up there. Was he "mad" when he signed the treaty at Troyes? I am not sure of it.

Forget him! After all, he had been repudiated even by his parents, and the treaty itself described him as "the so-called Dauphin."

But it is not easy to accept rejection. He would not take it lying down. No sooner had his unworthy father died, in 1422, than he had himself crowned under the name of Charles VII. But by that time, Heaven be praised, a son had been born to Henry V, King of England, and even though the baby was only ten months old, he was considered the true King of France (and of England, as well) by the terms of the Treaty of Troyes. So, it was not, as it had been a century before, grandson (Edward III) against nephew (Philip VI); it was son (a scandalously proscribed son: Ponthieu, known as "Charles VII") against grandson (Henry VI of England). And the son was additionally handicapped by the fact that the English held Paris, thanks to their Burgundian alliance, while he, poor wretch, had been forced to retire to Mehun-sur-Yèvre, where he had been crowned.

France therefore had two kings at once, one in Paris, the other at Bourges; and the ridiculous "King of Bourges" was Charles VII. Philip of Burgundy stood behind the English King, who was his nephew, being the son of his sister-in-law Catherine. The bonds were to grow even stronger between him and the English, for Bedford, the Regent (there had to be a Regent for such an infant King: he was the brother of the late Henry V, thus little Henry VI's uncle), had married Burgundy's own sister.

It was a bad start for Charles, who, at nineteen, could do nothing but protest that he was going to tear up the perfectly legal treaty his own family had signed and demand recognition of a claim that neither his father nor his mother had seen fit to preserve for him.

The reader by now may have grown dizzy with this

whirlwind of proper names, this free-for-all of highnesses. Perhaps we can boil it all down to three essentials:

1. The "Kingdom of France" was pretty much a fiction, made up merely of divergent local particularities. The idea of French unity had not yet been dreamt of. The kingdom was a thing of bits and pieces; there was total anarchy.

It has become fashionable, especially since 1940, to compare the English occupation to the Nazi occupation, but in reality it was nothing like it. The occupation was sporadic. Garrisons were implanted here and there. There is no point in speaking of "resistance," for there was no such thing. The intruders were referred to as *Goddams* (from their frequent use of the oath) or *queue-ies* (as if they had tails, or *queues*, like devils), and were certainly not popular. There was even scornful talk of some "renouncing Frenchmen" such as the Bishop of Beauvais, Cauchon, who had wormed his way up into the English Council. But the University of Paris was resolutely Anglophile, and in the southwest, in Guyenne, where sales of alcoholic beverages to the English were booming, the notables felt nothing but friendship for these good customers, and even worked out some profitable arrangements with them. Militiamen from Bordeaux assisted the English in subduing the towns of La Réole and Bazas in 1427–1428. In Normandy, there were groups of adventurers who specialized in attacking the military convoys, but the population did not take kindly to them, as evidenced by their nickname: *la merdaille* (the shitlets).

2. The noblemen fighting each other were all relatives, it was a bloodletting within the family. Richard II was executed in the Tower of London on the orders of his cousin, who replaced him; his ancestor Edward II, the one who married the French princess, met with violent death before him. Louis X, called the Quarreler, the first successor to Philip the Fair, choked his wife, and we have already

noted that Louis of Orléans was knocked off by John the Fearless, who in turn was taken for a ride. A wise historian, Louis Salembier, pointed out in his *Le Grand Schisme d'Occident* (The Great Schism of the West), a classic work written in 1902, that the burning at the stake of Jan Hus at Constance, in the same year as the battle of Agincourt, was doubtless a rough measure. Yet, he added, one should always try to put such an act into the context of the period before passing judgment on it. "Lesiglation in the Middle Ages was incomparably stricter and more bloody than it is today," he wrote, with capital punishment administered not only for homicide but also for "theft, sex offenses," and so on. Which is true, though with this reservation: if these severe measures were applicable to the common people, they ceased to operate where princes were concerned. Kings and dukes indulged in murder, breaking and entering, adultery, and sodomy with almost utter impunity. Justice merely lowered her eyes, and then smiled. Great lords disemboweled each other, in France as well as in England, but such excessive familiarities were the custom of the day, especially within the ruling families. Henry II of Trastamara killed his brother Pedro with his own hands, and Joanna I of Naples had her first husband butchered before being done in herself by her nephew.

The crowned heads were in fact a bunch of cutthroats; royal gangsterdom was in full bloom, and it was above the law.

3. Finally, to return to the affairs of France, the problem with the "litigation" among the Capetians was that the well-to-do antagonists were able to purchase mercenaries to do battle in their stead; when one of them coveted the holdings of another, he had all sorts of "enforcers" he could call on. And since what they coveted were usually inhabited and food-producing lands, who, do you suppose, "took it in the neck"? The people, naturally, the inhabitants,

whose exploitation was what the fight was all about. So the common people unfortunate enough to be living in the theater of operations always turned out to be the first victims, prey to the pillaging mercenaries while the fighting was going on, and during the respites left to the mercy of free-lances in search of a job. They treated the country folk to a diversified bag of tricks: these ranged from torture over a slow fire to the kidnapping of children, when some of the peasants were so stubborn as not to show them quickly enough where the cattle had been secreted or the nest egg hurriedly buried at the approach of the highwaymen.

When Joan came on the scene, rascals such as these had been marauding about the kingdom for a good century or more.

In 1429, Charles VII still held sway over only a very slight portion of his kingdom. Everything north of the Loire was gone, except for Anjou and three tiny loyalist islets, Tournai, Mont-Saint-Michel, and Vaucouleurs. In the south, the whole area from Blaye to Bayonne, even on the right bank of the Garonne at Libourne and Castillon, was also out of his hands. As for his Court at Bourges (and other unimpressive places), it was a festering "poison sac." His mother-in-law, Yolande of Aragon, widow of the King of Sicily since 1417, was a domineering woman, always meddling in the affairs of state, and not averse to manipulating favorites in a sort of courtly musical chairs. Many violent incidents occurred because of the consequent jockeying. One Peter de Giac, having poisoned his first wife to replace her with one of her ladies-in-waiting, was betrayed by this second spouse (who preferred George de La Trémoille) and then sewn into a wineskin and drowned. Arthur, Count de Richemont, a brother of the Duke of Brittany and a relative of

Yolande's (like Bedford, he was to become a brother-in-law of Philip of Burgundy), had plotted this crime with La Trémoille so that together they might win the King's privileged confidence. But once the deed was done, La Trémoille dumped Richemont and became the sole favorite. Whereupon, the Breton, who had once been friends with the English but who had turned to Charles VII after being disappointed by them, now veered again and went back into the camp of the Goddams.

So the "King of Bourges" was perplexed, suspicious, afraid, hesitant—and with good cause. He was twenty-six in 1429; and he was not attractive. See Fouquet's painting: with his lifeless eyes, weak lips, and drooping nose that bulged at the end, he looked like a real idiot. Yet this appearance was deceptive; under the stupid look, which he perhaps learned to affect for his own protection, there was a great deal of shrewdness. He was pious at this time. His wife, Marie of Anjou, had little charm, but he was faithful to her and, in 1423, they had a little boy, the future Louis XI, who had already been promised in marriage to Margaret of Scotland. Was he financially pinched? Mainly, he pretended to be, so as to increase the subsidies he could extract from the provincial assemblies, and Yolande had her own resources. Nevertheless, Charles borrowed, notably from La Trémoille, who asked to be paid back in châteaus, and from Regnault of Chartres, Archbishop of Reims and Chancellor. In 1429, La Trémoille and Regnault were the two biggest bloodsuckers of the French Treasury.

There had been an attempt at an armed operation against the English in 1424, but it had led only to the disaster of Verneuil. Now Charles was counting primarily on secret negotiations. La Trémoille and Regnault were both excellent at this kind of undertaking, always profitable to go-betweens, and La Trémoille was particularly useful at this point, for he had a close relative in Philip's court.

In October, 1428, the English appeared determined to annihilate the man they considered the pseudo-King of France, the illegitimate pretender who had taken the title of Charles VII. They besieged Orléans. If they could take that city, all of the Berry region would then be open to them, leading to the south. On All Saints' Day, Charles, in desperation, beseeched heaven that, should things go badly for him now, he might find refuge in Dauphiné, or at worst in Scotland. But Yolande did not share his defeatism. The English had still not captured Orléans, and she was paying —and paying—to keep the besieged "comforted" and get supplies in to them.

Now, what about the Church? How can we discuss Joan the believer without first investigating religious life and ecclesiastical affairs as they stood at the early part of the fifteenth century?

I would here remind the reader of the epigraph to this book, the sentence from Pope Leo XIII's 1899 "Letter to the Bishops of France": "God does not need our lies." He was alluding to the rose-colored glasses, the heavy veils, and other obscurantist devices that are the usual arsenal of Catholic historians. Leo XIII had little use for the deployment of ready-made piety. So, let us follow his advice and tell things the way they were.

The accepted picture is this: In that happy time known as the Middle Ages, Christianity was alive and vibrant, all fervor and crusades. The Vicar of Christ in Rome, "successor to Saint Peter," ruled over all souls; temporal powers existed only by virtue of his consecration.

While the period of Saint Louis, two centuries before, may have had some remote resemblance to this simplistic representation, by the fifteenth century, certainly, everything had changed. The princes were out to grab for themselves the moral prestige that the papacy still enjoyed, and the relations between the sovereigns and Rome consisted mainly of sordid quarrels over the amounts of ecclesiastical taxes and the bestowing of benefices. The word "benefices," echoing deafeningly throughout the whole era, designated the financial income of the higher charges of the Church, archbishoprics, bishoprics, canonries, abbeys, and even lesser charges such as priories that also entailed revenues. There were perpetual arguments between the Roman Curia and the lay courts over the division of these dispensations, for the benefices were not awarded without something being given in return, and thus they constituted a strong bargaining capital. One can readily see how the Pope, on the one hand, and the masters of those territories that had cathedrals or monasteries, on the other, would be at each other's throats to come out on top in the negotiations over these high-priced gifts.

First to kick over the traces was Philip the Fair of France. He sent William of Nogaret to Rome with the specific intention of making the Pope see reason, even if that meant putting him under arrest. Nogaret let it go at slapping His Holiness' face. Far from proving prejudicial to this uncivil dynasty, the successors of Philip the Fair found that such persuasive conduct, which would not stop at sacrilege to defend its financial interests, created a situation they had every reason to be delighted with: the Popes left Rome to set themselves up at Avignon, where they might act as almoners or chaplains to the Kings of France. It was wondrous. There followed a whole series of French Popes over the next seventy years. Out of 134 cardinals created during that happy time, 113 were French; not one was German. It was a triumph; but one can imagine how the Germanic Holy Roman Emperors felt about it. There was euphoria in the country of the *fleur-de-lis,* but the dark side was that the "religious" tax establishment grew more and more greedy.

After all, something had to be done to compensate the

Holy See for what it was losing by being away from its Roman States, which, incidentally, were being chipped away. And the fortress-palace that the Popes built for themselves on the banks of the Rhone cost an arm and a leg. To say nothing of the expensive entertainments that the Lords of the Church enjoyed, or their predilection for sumptuous apparel, lustrous jewels, and conspicuous carriages. Where the Pontiffs were concerned, anything mediocre was out of the question.

Gregory XI, though a Frenchman (Peter Roger de Beaufort), allowed himself to be indoctrinated by a sister of the Order of Penitence, Catherine of Siena, a stupid creature, thirty years old, who might just as well have stuck to her ecstasies: insolently, without restraint, she took the Pope to task for the "stench" of his Court. He gave in; he left Avignon and reestablished the Apostolic See at Rome, where the religious had gone into decline during the time of the awful exile. Gregory died shortly after his arrival in Rome, and the ensuing conclave took place amid great tumult. Having been left out of the picture for decades, the Romans now insisted upon an Italian Pope. Had not Petrarch himself called Avignon Babylon? Had not Dante expressed the indignation of all Italy in the somewhat unexpected aphorism, "Christ is Roman"?

The aristocracy of the peninsula, finally able to demand vengeance, was definitely less subtle in expressing what it had in mind: "For seventy years, France has been growing fat on Roman gold. Now, let us have a go at French gold for a change!" So, the conclave had no choice but to select a local candidate, and Bartolommeo Prignani became Urban VI.

But, hold on! The King of France now was Charles V. And, while it was true that his father, John the Good, had not been fortunate in his struggle with the English, Charles was of a different stamp. He was not about to let his cardinals make a fool of him just because they had been over-whelmed in Rome. The conclave would simply have to be held all over again. And hold it they did, under the dictates of the powerful voice booming at them from France. They changed their minds. After having elected an Urban VI, they decided to kick him out—they had simply made a mistake. So, pardon them, but on reflection Prignani was not the true "successor to Peter"; it was Robert of Geneva, and he became Clement VII. Well aware of where his duty lay and why he had been elevated, Clement, as anticipated, headed directly for Avignon and the service of the King of France.

Though dismissed, Urban VI was still vehemently supported by both the Emperor and the English, and he still held on to his Roman throne (Clement had gone to Avignon, so Urban could sit in Rome with impunity). And thus occurred a schism, the Great Schism of the West, which, with all of its dramatic twists and turns, would last for the next thirty-nine years.

Things were just fine for the French as long as Clement carried on at Avignon as he was expected to. But Charles V's successor went insane in 1392, so the next conclave could not have come at a worse time than it did, two years later, when Clement died. Instead of the foreordained French Pope, it chose a Spaniard, Pedro de Luna, who passed himself off as Benedict XIII. But the French refused to accept this, and created a super-schism, a schism raised to the second power. Still disdaining and scorning the so-called Pope of Rome, whom they refused to recognize (now Pietro Tomacelli, who called himself Boniface IX), they now also broke with the Pope of Avignon, for the good reason that he had this great defect: he was not French. In the high-flown terms of the period, this was called "subtraction of obedience." In less formal language, it could be stated: I refuse to acknowledge you, bad Pope, noncon-

forming false Pope; I shall no longer allow my subjects to
pay tribute to you; you no longer exist in my eyes.

And France got along very well with no Pope at all,
while the Royal Treasury collected and retained the
Church taxes which, obviously, could not be abolished for
so insignificant a reason. The King was able to take over
in toto (what a windfall!) the advowson of benefices, the
naming of bishops. This lasted for five years. But then a
compromise was struck and the smaller schism disappeared, while the great one remained.

In 1409—we are coming to Joan, her birth is just a short
time in the future—things were different. A shrewd
Neapolitan, Baldassare Cossa, called a Council of Church
dignitaries at Pisa to try to cure the Church of its disunity
by unexpectedly naming a new Pope whom everyone
might recognize. What a joke! Could anyone imagine old de
Luna at Avignon, called Benedict XIII, and now Angelo
Corrario in Rome, called Gregory XII, politely stepping
aside in order to accommodate Baldassare? He must be
pulling their legs! The outcome was what it had to be: no
longer two Popes but three! For, after having gone through
the motions of getting moribund old Petros Philargos
elected at Pisa (to serve only over the turn of the year, as
Alexander V), Baldassare set himself up as Pope. True, he
was not a priest, but what did that matter? He corrected
that shortcoming immediately, on the double, all flags
flying, minor holy orders, major orders, the whole thing.
And Baldassare Cossa, now an ordained priest, took the
name of John XXIII. It is common knowledge that the
Holy Spirit must *ipso facto* descend and inhabit the candidate elected by a conclave. So one wonders how the Third
Person of the Holy Trinity was able to survive those dark
hours without making any mistakes, when faced with this
triple whirligig and a sky perpetually crisscrossed by the
anathemas and excommunications that the three rival
Popes kept hurling at one another.

There had to be a way out, and to find it was the goal set for a huge ecclesiastical assemblage called under the benevolent eye of His Majesty, the Holy (Roman) Emperor, King of Rome, on his own ground. Twenty-nine cardinals, 33 archbishops, 150 bishops, 100 abbots, 300 doctors of theology, and others—a crowd of some 10,000 members of the clergy—gathered together as the Council of Constance. Their meeting sprouted some intricate rhetoric about how the Pope simply had to be subject to the opinions and counsel of the sacred Council, which henceforth, it was decreed, would convene every five years.

The first matter of priority, of course, was, one way or another, to get Their Three Holinesses to step down. It was not possible to proclaim the current Pope of Rome, Gregory, as the true Pope, since he was just as suspect as his two competitors. After that, the Fathers of Constance would assume the power to elect—for the Roman See, of course —a Pope of their own choosing, who, owing his elevation to them, would be properly grateful.

Gregory XII presented no great problem, for when he saw the financial indemnity he was being offered, he was more than happy to trade his pontificate for a simple bishopric. But Cossa, known as John XXIII, was another matter: he would not listen to reason, argued back, was hypocritical, then rebellious, and in May, 1415, they were obliged to depose him formally. As for Benedict XIII, the Spaniard, he refused to listen or agree to anything, and when he was finally declared "divested," on July 26, 1417, he continued to hold out and claim his position as Pope from his refuge in the château of El Cid at Peñíscola.

Once the members of the Council had gotten together, they were in no great hurry to conclude their business. All sorts of intrigues were working at cross-purposes. The University of Paris insisted that there must be a Pope who could continue its usual assortment of benefices, even adding to them, if possible. The King of France had his men speak up, too; but he was now Charles VI, and his power after Agincourt was nothing compared to that of the earlier Charles V (Charles the Wise). For two whole years, Catholicism remained without a leader.

However, that dilemma did not keep things from humming at Constance: there was a constant round of festivities, receptions, and tournaments. Each of the Lords of the Church had come there escorted by his "household," and each tried to show that he could outdo the others. The laurels went to the Archbishop of Mainz, whose retinue included five hundred persons—counselors, secretaries, and servants. The Council may have erred a bit in its show and pomp, but it did not make light of questions of orthodoxy. The Emperor was irked by Jan Hus, the good theologian who in 1402 had been named Rector of the University of Prague, but who now, under the doleful influence of the English priest John Wycliffe, was presenting immoderate demands that constituted a threat to the established order. Between entertainments, the Council, deciding it was not obligated to honor the safe-conduct guarantee in which the good man had put his trust, locked up Hus and then sent him to the stake (July 6, 1415). A second pyre ten months later (May 23, 1416) rid the Emperor and the Church of Hus' friend and disciple, Jerome of Prague. As Salembier put it, the Council was watching out "for the rights of the Church and the interests of the State, by striking down the troublemakers and rebels."[3]

On November 11, 1417, a Pope was finally elected. He was an Italian and a Colonna—the honored traditions were reappearing. It is true that this Martin V was no more an ordained priest than Baldassare Cossa had been. But, no matter. Little obstacles like that, when necessary, are straightened out with divine promptness. The day after his

---

[3]Louis Salembier, in *Le Grand Schisme d'Occident* (1902), p. 350.

election, Martin received a deaconate; the next day, ordination; and on the third day he was crowned. Martin V, practically speaking, was the handpicked candidate of the Emperor, and the Court of France expected no good to come of him. Nevertheless, he tried to be friendly and, "moved by a feeling of pious sympathy"[4] *(sic)*, showed consideration for those vanquished at Agincourt by temporarily reducing the size of the pontifical taxes they had to pay.

This new single Pope never risked stating which earlier Popes during the period of the Great Schism were to be revered as having been incontestable true sons of the Paraclete. Never did Martin V refer to Gregory XII as "Our Predecessor." It was only later that the Church, as quietly as possible, validated the Roman Popes of the Schism; she deemed the rest not to have existed and their designations were declared unused, so that they might later again appear on the true list. And that is why, after five and a half centuries, it was possible for us to have a new John XXIII, so completely different from the first.

Now, what about the clergy? Hardly impressive, was it? In the higher circles, everyone was spying on everyone else, arguing, fighting, using vile ruses to obtain the richest benefices, which the wiliest gathered hand over fist; for multiplicity of livings was not forbidden and it was not unusual to find certain operators with more vicarages than they knew what to do with. Did this not require being resident in a number of different places? Not at all; many of these prelates did not "reside" at all, but merely collected the revenues. And Salembier, in the work already mentioned, quite seriously points out that in Joan's time we

---

[4] *Ibid.*, p. 385.

find, "on the most venerated of seats, prelates who might have been more at their place behind a counter."[5] Winchester, the English cardinal whom we will have occasion to see at work, was a banker before being transmogrified into a Prince of the Church; and, in fact, this scarcely represented any change in occupation. As for the run-of-the-mill clergy, Gerson[6] himself rendered this harsh judgment: "Convents today [I trust he meant 'all too often' and was only letting his anger carry him away] are prostitutes' cribs; monasteries look like traders' shops, and cathedrals have become thieves' dens." Out in the countryside, on the other hand, many priests were doing the best job they could, though they were usually extremely poor and had only a minimal education.

Can we really speak of the "faith" of most of the faithful? To the huge majority of peasants, faith revolved around superstitions, worship of relics, and pilgrimages. To them, God was above all the invisible tyrant hidden up in the sky, and the allocation of rain or sunshine was his main occupation. From this belief arose the practice of religious processions as entreaties for the protection of crops. Among the rich and among the courtiers, disbelief was rife. While it was not yet fashionable to say so, "religion," to many of the privileged, was simply nonsense fit for the gullible masses. The fables of Christendom did not mean much any more, what with the mercenaries equally at ease wearing the sign of the cross and disemboweling each other (the English and the Armagnacs wore the same Greek cross—though red for the former and white for the latter—while the Burgundians wore the X-shaped Saint Andrew's cross). The King of France was "very Christian," the King of England "most Christian"; but Regent Bedford acted in

---

[5] *Ibid.*, p. 19.
[6] John de Gerson, French theologian (d. 1428), who tried to reform the Church in his (and Joan's) time. *(Translator's note)*

conquered France just as Bonaparte would do much later in Italy, and he carried off the stained-glass windows of Coucy.

Salisbury, heading the expeditionary force against Or-léans, lost no time in sacking the opulent chapel of Notre-Dame-de-Cléry on his arrival in that city. To these realists, even the age-old laws of chivalry were ridiculous outmoded nonsense. It had once been forbidden to honorable men to attack a city whose master was unable to defend it. The Duke of Orléans was a prisoner of the English, but this did not deter His "Most Serene and Christian" Majesty's Council from sending its troops to storm the city in his absence.

It was in this "deep mire," as Michelet called it, that Joan was to appear, at the very time when the remains of feudal paternalism were beginning to give way to the burgeoning capitalism of the Renaissance.[7]

Joan, the rustic little Christian girl, was completely out of place, totally anachronistic in the corrupt world into which fate threw her. From the very start, it was obvious she must inevitably come to a bad end.

---

[7]On this score, see Michel Bataille's *Gilles de Rais*, 1967, p. 28.

II

To Describe Her

What is so puzzling about Joan's whole story is that, unlikely though it seems, it is true. It could not have happened, and yet it did. Or at least that is the way it looks, on the face of it. Just imagine: a seventeen-year-old country girl comes along and says she is going to do what all the King's soldiers have been unable to—drive out the English and save the kingdom. And then she does it. What's more, she never for a second believes there is a chance she can fail, because God sent her; He spoke to her, she says, through His angels, whom she saw with her very own eyes. She will let them burn her at the stake in the end, rather than admit she was wrong, that it was only a dream, that she was just the victim of an illusion. No, she will cling to her belief in the reality of her visions and her divine mission, cling to it for dear life, as the expression goes, or to the death—ready to face death itself rather than say it wasn't so. And it does appear that there were a number of strange and wonderful events in that life of hers. Alain, the philosopher, the unbeliever, himself called it "perhaps the most beautiful of all human stories."

I wanted to find out for myself. Surely there is a fabulous element in the tales told about Joan. So let us see what we can make of them. It's all very well for Thierry Maulnier[1] to turn disgustedly away from the musty old "document collectors" and rely on the mind's "creative virtues." I, for my part, shall pursue my inquiry slowly, painstakingly, step by step, without trying to call upon the intuitions of a genius I am afraid I do not have.

Paul Claudel says of Joan that she has "more or less disappeared within her legend,"[2] and Bernard Shaw refers to "the whitewash which disfigures her beyond recognition."[3] These are proper appraisals. The accumulated generations of commentators have created real obstacles between us and the truth. What is needed now is a thorough pruning and clearing job. What is definitely not needed is the kind of thing Michelet does in his standard treatment. A thesis by Gustave Rudler[4]—amazing how little attention has been paid to it, but then, some people are untouchable! —shows us what that is. Michelet totally disregarded the original documents; he had full access to the works of his predecessors, and lifted from them at will; he transposed and rewrote, but with only one thing in mind: dramatic effect. From the viewpoint of historical methodology, or simple honesty, his approach was nothing short of scandalous.

But Michelet was to give himself away by a real slipup.

[1]See section by Thierry Maulnier in *Mémorial*, collected tributes on the fifth centennial of Joan's "rehabilitation" (1956), p. 5.
[2]See Paul Claudel, *Cahiers du Rhône* (1942), p. 2. In his *Journal* (1929), he had also discussed the layers of "platitudes and inanities" that have to be penetrated in order to get to the real Joan, and the "mouldering manure" to be turned over and swept aside so that one may feel close to her.
[3]Bernard Shaw, *Saint Joan* (Penguin ed.), 1951, "Preface," p. 11.
[4]Gustave Rudler, *Michelet historien de Jeanne d'Arc* (Presses Universitaires de France, 1925).

L'Averdy had misread the Latin text (proving at least that he had referred to it), and he thought that a tailor who had come to take Joan's measurements in prison had put his hand a little too suggestively on her hand *(manum)*, for which she slapped him. And of course Michelet, who never bothered to check anything, repeated this story, taking advantage of the tale to go into one of his most animated numbers. Was he not supposed to be democratically inclined? No matter. For the time being, his political persona went by the board and he exclaimed indignantly, "To think a tailor's hand should touch the hand that had borne the flag of France!" How right Joan was to put the scoundrel in his place!

I had always thought this was a strange anecdote, that Joan's reaction appeared a bit extreme, to say the least. Rudler cleared it up. There was no *manum* in the original at all, but *mammum* (breast)—which is quite a different story . . . Pitiful, foolish Michelet! That time his cribbing cost him. He should get a zero for his *Jeanne d'Arc.* Or maybe not a zero, but a very poor mark. That's what happens when you try to cut corners.

Rudler warns us that "there are few subjects so hard to establish on sound critical bases as the story of Joan," and again, that in the preparatory stages the importance of "negative criticism" is "enormous."[5] We are fortunate as far as documentation is concerned. Between 1841 and 1849, Jules Quicherat, a prime example of the conscientious scholar, published in five volumes everything he had been able to find about Joan in the writings of her times, and his work remains irreplaceable. After him, other researchers dug up supplementary material, often of great value: in particular, the "Morosini chronicle" and the account books of the city of Orléans. Each of these texts, then, has to be

---

[5]Rudler, *op. cit.*, vol. I, pp. 81 and 89.

evaluated as to origin, date, and degree of credibility. This is the ABC of "historical history," as Charles Péguy used to call it, as opposed to the fictitious, made-up, respectable, conventional version of history (such as we have recently seen in such staggering profusion on the subject of Napoleon).[6] Now, the minute you begin to acquaint yourself conscientiously with the official history of Joan of Arc, you bump into flagrant falsehoods at every step. And all of them have been accepted, passed along, and imperturbably enshrined as one hundred percent authentic. Of course, we have all heard how Joan magically recognized Charles VII at Chinon, even though he tried to fool her, how she saw through his trick, and went straight to him. We know that at Beaurevoir, she slid down a rope in trying to escape, but unfortunately the rope did not hold. We have been told (Anatole France, for one, did not fail to emphasize this) that Joan bought herself a building at Orléans. All of which is totally false, though currently taught and accepted. But if details like these were the only kinds of nontruths circulating about Joan, it would be a small matter!

At the very start of his career, Émile Zola thought of writing a life of the Maid. He would tell it, he said, "without exclamation marks." Too bad he never got around to it. When I think of his *Lourdes,* and the striking picture of Bernadette he left us, I am even more regretful that he did not carry through with his plan about Joan. But he had to publish in order to live, and he was warned off by the amount of research he would have to do before feeling competent to write the book. Zola was not cut from the same stuff as Michelet; he was principled about the truth, and never wrote until he felt informed.

I know how dangerous it can be to try again "to stir

---

[6]In connection with the 200th anniversary of his birth, 1969, and the 150th anniversary of his death, 1971. *(Translator's note)*

through these ashes which so many hands have sifted."[7]
And I am also aware that Jacques Madaule was correct in
referring to the "persistent mystery that surrounds Joan."[8]
Régine Pernoud, to whom we are so deeply indebted for
her several books, warns, "No, everything is not clear
about Joan, and the historian must be the first to recognize
this," for Joan "will never cease putting questions to us."[9]
But, as Rudler says, it remains a "fascinating" story. And,
calling on all the conscientiousness and good will that an
old literary warhorse could muster, I thought I might in
turn try to find her, to understand.

   Herewith my report.

   Even Joan's vital statistics—name, ancestry, parentage,
date and place of birth—are lost in the fog.

   What *was* her name? At the trial, she was to state that
"back home they called her Jeannette," but "in France, she
was called Jeanne [Joan]." When Cauchon asked for her
"surname," her answer was that "she had no idea." Nobles
had family names, not plebeians: first names were enough
for them, as for servants. There was nothing vaguer in the
fifteenth century than the last names of common people.
Joan's "uncle," the one who would help her get away from
Domrémy, appears in some papers as "Lassois," in others
as "Laxart"[10] and yet he was actually just a plain and simple
"Durand." Joan's brother John, although ennobled at the
same time as she, and entitled to call himself "Du Lys"—
with its suggestion of the royal *fleur-de-lis*—simply referred

---

[7]Claudel, *Cahiers du Rhône.*
[8]Jacques Madaule, *Histoire de France*, vol. I, p. 204.
[9]Régine Pernoud, *Vie et Mort de Jeanne d'Arc* (Hachette, 1953); *Telle fut Jeanne d'Arc*
(Fasquelle, 1956); *Jeanne d'Arc* (Seuil, 1959); *Jeanne d'Arc par elle-même et par ses témoins*
(Seuil, 1962); *La Libération d'Orléans* (Gallimard, 1969).
[10]Easily mistaken for each other when phonetically transcribed from the pronun-
ciation of the period. *(Translator's note)*

to himself as "Dalie."[11] On interrogation, Joan herself said that in the village her father was sometimes called "Tarc" (or "Darc" or "Dare").[12] The document known as the "Orléans manuscript" reads: Joan, "daughter of a farmer named Jacques [that is, James] Tart." It must be understood that there were a number of Jameses in Domrémy, each of whom had some "last name," occasionally used to distinguish him from the others, and her father's sounded something like Dar or Tar. The royal secretaries, in the letters of nobility, were to prefer "Day"[13] (perhaps because the terminal *y* seemed more elegant?). So we can scarcely refer to her as "Joan of Arc," for obviously that name is quite fictitious.

Who were her parents? I would not lightly dismiss the idea that Joan was the daughter of Isabeau of Bavaria and Louis of Orléans, and therefore a half-sister to Charles VII, or perhaps even his sister, if Charles, too, was a son of Louis. Régine Pernoud treats this whole suggestion as a joke, but that seems too cavalier a conclusion.

The theory does have a regrettable origin: it first appeared in 1805 in a tragedy in five acts, for which one Peter Caze, Napoleon's under-prefect at Bergerac, was responsible. But in 1819, this same Caze, departing from the poetic license he had used in his play, brought out two fully documented volumes, ambitiously titled *La Vérité sur Jeanne d'Arc* (The Truth about Joan of Arc), in which he marshaled his facts. Now Jean Bancal is planning to publish a

---

[11]His descendants would write it "De Dallye."

[12]Per the French version of the minutes of the interrogations of Joan of Arc, published by Father Paul Doncoeur in 1952: ". . . that her father was named Jacques Tarc." (Again allowing for phonetic transcription.—*Translator's note*)

[13]A copy of the "letters of nobility" conferred on Joan and her family was recently sold at auction in Paris, and her father Jacques is called *Darcq* in it. But the copy was made in 1610 (and its translation into French in the eighteenth century). So the spelling cannot be considered conclusive; it simply more or less follows the custom established by that time.

very learned and in no way negligible work with the same thesis, publicly or privately endorsed by Maurice Druon and André Castelot.

Jean Bancal was good enough (and I am most grateful for his generosity) to enumerate for me the eighteen reasons that seem to him to prove Joan's high-placed parentage beyond the shadow of a doubt. On examination, none of them seemed really valid to me. However, there remains what Bancal rightly calls Joan's extraordinary devotion to Charles of Orléans; the fact that she so strangely stated at her trial that her "voices" had given her, about the Duke, "many revelations, more than about any man living, save the King"; and it is hard to understand the reason for the Maid's passion for so petty, so libertine and weak an individual, who was quite content to stay in London and even, in 1432, went so far as to hail Henry VI outright as "King of France and England." Yet I think it is best to adopt the position of Philippe Erlanger as to the heart of the matter, and follow the conclusions which, after wise and patient analysis, he presented in March, 1963, in the *Revue de Paris*.

The fact that this theory would make it so much easier to explain the "ease" with which a simple country girl was able "to approach the King and convince his entourage" is what really attracted Caze and his disciples, and what made Thierry Maulnier as recently as 1965 describe the idea as "appealing."[14] Though it might seem amazing that an illiterate peasant girl was able to gain access to the sovereign, it would have been simple and natural if Joan were indeed "of royal blood." However, on one hand, many men and women, often of the humblest birth, both before and after Joan, had had entrée to Court if they were supposed to have supernatural connections; and on the other, we shall soon

---

[14]Maulnier, *op. cit.*

see that, contrary to the legend about the "ease" of Joan's access, one obstacle after another barred her path, both at Vaucouleurs and at Chinon, and it was only with the greatest difficulty that she succeeded either in seeing the King or in gaining his partial confidence. I am convinced that that theory is purely imaginary: Joan was without doubt the daughter of the "farmer" James and his wife Zabet (or Zabillet), sometimes nicknamed Rommée.[15]

Were her parents penniless? No. They had some small holding, and her father even seems to have been a sort of village notable, albeit a very minor one. Nevertheless, he was the one delegated by the village, in March, 1427, to go to see the Sire of Vaucouleurs, Baudricourt, about a dispute with the Lord of Montigny. We have no idea how old James and Zabet may have been when Joan left them. They had three sons, Jacquin, John, and Peter, all born before Joan. There was also another daughter, Catherine, who may have been either older or younger than Joan, but who was no longer alive in 1429. The father died in 1439 (age unknown). His wife was a widow in 1440 when she moved to Orléans, where the city helped support her until her death in 1458.

We are equally in the dark about the exact date of Joan's birth. From two contemporary, though not too trustworthy, documents, some have claimed that Joan was born on January 6, 1412. Why 1412? Because at the trial she was to give her age in 1431 as, "it seems to her, about nineteen." There were no parish records at the time. The lords alone

---

[15]Rommée or Romée (Rome-ish) was a common nickname of the period for women who had made a pilgrimage to Rome. But the Pope recognized in the Duchy of Bar since 1378 was the one at Avignon. Had she made a pilgrimage to the Holy Father, it would have been there (not to Rome). But just across the Meuse from Domrémy the Pope of Rome was taken as the true Pastor. So it is all quite muddled. Joan, it should be noted, was "from Greux," though "reared at Domrémy." The King's dispensation of taxes in July, 1429, applied to Greux as well as to Domrémy.

had record books in which they kept the birth dates and death dates of family members. The common people—of whom Joan was one—had little use for knowing the dates of the month. Their year was figured by the religious holidays and local fairs. And January 6 was an important religious holiday: the Epiphany, or the Feast of Kings, also known as Twelfth Night. Had Joan indeed been born on "the twelfth day of Christmas," she would surely have known it. Her parents would have told her. So, we must rather conclude she was born on some nameless day, probably in 1412, but perhaps in 1411.

Was she really *là bonne Lorraine* that François Villon would call her in his ballad about the "snows of yesteryear"? Strictly speaking, Joan was not from Lorraine at all. In the fifteenth century, Lorraine was part of the Holy Roman Empire, which ended at the boundary of the Meuse. Joan was born on the west side of the river, in the Duchy of Bar, not on the east side in Lorraine. And neither her father, who seems to have come from Champagne, nor her mother, from Vouthon, would properly have been called Lorrainers.

What do we know of her "secret life," that is, what she did before she became known in 1428? Not much. And I am hard put to share the excitement of Régine Pernoud and Father Paul Doncoeur at the depositions of the "childhood witnesses" at her rehabilitation trial. We will later go into detail about this 1456 inquiry; neither civil nor religious authorities made any secret of what it was they were looking for then. And what they got was fulsome detail, tailored to fit. It is truly black comedy, when you place the testimony at this inquiry alongside the vicious slanders of Joan that the Rouen inquisitors so readily elicited in the same area just twenty-five years earlier.

It is best to take these flowery bouquets and honeyed words with the greatest reserve. They don't really amount to much. To say that Joan was religious and a churchgoer in her earliest days, as she was to be later during her "public life," is no great revelation. We need look no further: a good little girl; an uneventful childhood. I would dwell on only one such detail—precisely because it did not originate in that 1456 inquiry, but was contained in a letter about her written by Perceval de Boulainvilliers to the Duke of Milan in 1429. That is: there were athletic contests, footraces among the little girls of Domrémy, in which Joan excelled. She was what today we might call a tomboy: she liked fresh air, action, and perhaps also being a standout, a leader.

On the other hand, in 1428, when she was about sixteen, there are some dependable facts that are worth consideration. In July of that year, the Sire of Vergy led an attack on Vaucouleurs; the population of Domrémy retreated to Neufchâteau (some six miles higher up the Meuse), and Joan worked briefly at an inn in the town. It was kept by a woman known locally as *La Rousse* (the Redhead). We may judiciously suppose that Joan's parents, holed up at the hostelry until the bandits withdrew (leaving their home in who knows what condition), let their teenage daughter help the innkeeper, thus cutting down a bit on the cost of their lodgings.

And now Joan attracted public notice for the first time. She was brought before the officialdom of Toul by a young man who took an action against her for breach of promise. We may conclude that she loved the young man; she wanted to be taken in his arms; she probably did not even balk at the idea of marrying him. Her parents approved of the marriage plans (as she would testify later at Rouen). But then, she changed her mind. She took back her promise, to her parents' chagrin; she stood up to them—and there were, we can assume, the usual family quarrels as a result.[16]

Why this turnabout? In saying yes, or almost saying yes, to this boy she liked, who had aroused her, attracted her, Joan was committing a breach of promise far greater than the one he accused her of. Joan was able to date quite precisely when it was that she first heard her "voices." She did not say, "it seems to me," or "approximately," but clearly stated they had first spoken to her "when I was thirteen." Her words are well known and have often been repeated: ". . . came this voice about noon, in the summer-time, in my father's garden. . . . I heard the voice coming from near the church"; and, at the same time, "light," a "great light." This is not the place to try to analyze this phenomenon; we will do that in our final chapter. For the moment, let us just consider one fact, for which I have borrowed Father Yves Congar's wording: "People of that period lived simultaneously in the visible world and also in a supraterrestrial world. The reality of the latter was greater and more compelling to them than that which our senses can perceive."[17] So, for the moment, let us stick to the facts alone.

In 1428, when the flight to Neufchâteau took place, Joan had been carrying the secret of "divine communications" within her for years. The voice was God's; she never doubted that for a second; in fact, she would use the plural

---

[16]Joan stated at her trial that she had stayed at Neufchâteau "about two weeks" —which is a short time, if she actually went from there to Toul, appeared in court, and then came back. (I would rather place the trip to Toul some time after she was at the Redhead's.) The 1456 witnesses, quite obviously well aware of the kind of accusations made against Joan back in 1431, were unanimous in lauding the innkeeper as the most respectable kind of woman, and insisting that Joan stayed at the inn only "four or five days" at the most; so one can see how dependable their testimony may be considered.

[17]Yves Congar, *Ecclésiologie du Haut Moyen Âge* (1968), p. 104. The author is dealing with an earlier period, but what was true of everyone around the year 1000, while it might apply less broadly in the fifteenth century, would still be true of the common people, the country folk. And Joan belonged to the country folk.

"my voices" at her trial, because she was sure that several of her "brothers in Paradise," as she called them, had been talking to her. At first, the voices only told her, over and over, to stay as she was: a good girl, loving God, and behaving according to His will. But then later, they gave her an order, a directive, a commandment coming from the Master. And Joan told how dumbfounded she was at first by what she was ordered to do, for it was so unheard of, so unseemly: no less than to go and fight, like a man, "in France," in the service of the Dauphin. For he was being persecuted by wicked people, Englishmen and Burgundians, who were keeping him from doing his job as King. They were devastating the kingdom, torturing, robbing, killing the poor people, and the whole thing was "a pity." But how, up there in Heaven, could they expect this child, who did not even know how to sit a horse and knew nothing of war, to turn suddenly into a warrior, procure arms (where?), and lead soldiers (which ones?)? She lived far out in the country; she knew no one among the great; soldiers have to be paid, and she didn't have a blessed sou. What the voices wanted didn't make sense. Yet "the voices" were adamant. We want you, Joan, and no other. Go to the Dauphin; he will give you soldiers. "Go, daughter of God," Saint Michael said to her, "I will be helping you. Go! Go! Go!"

And that was what had finally convinced Joan that she had to obey the obsessive command (which, in her heart, she had known she would do all along). How wonderful, if indeed she were able to accomplish that mad mission! Yet for a long time she had gone on thinking she could not, that it was a practical impossibility for her—all because of the confused predictions that had been circulating and that she had gotten wind of.

Everybody knew that if the Anglo-Burgundians had the upper hand at present, it was because of that awful woman,

the traitorous wife of poor King Charles VI. But the country folk adapted Christian mythology to present circumstances: the evil done by woman, they prophesied, could be
repaired only by a virgin. Isabeau was cast as Eve. Why,
then, could not Joan, fantastic as it seemed, be the little
virgin meant by the King of Heaven to play the role of
Holy Mary? The girl who was later imprisoned at Rouen
would swear during the trial that she put no faith in these
local prophecies, but by that very fact she was admitting
that she knew of them. Some who were less cautious, at the
time of her rehabilitation, doing what they believed to be
right, would point out that Joan often referred to these
popular beliefs so that she might be taken seriously, and
that she convinced her "Uncle Durand" (the "first believer
in Joan," as Lamartine[18] would call him) to help her with
her schemes by making use of them.

It was he, her mother's cousin (truly fond of little Joan,
who could twist him around her finger), who, without even
her parents knowing, agreed to chaperone her on her trip
to Vaucouleurs to see the King's representative. Durand
lived at Burey; Joan would go to visit him and then, secretly, they could go together to see Baudricourt. She was
a reasonable person and she figured her best chance was to
go through channels. She could hardly carry out her commandment without agreement and support from the re-
gional authority; the Sire of Vaucouleurs alone could make
it possible for her (with a horse, money, and an escort) to
reach the Dauphin and let him know that, "sent by God,"
she had come to save him. But what about the "uncle"?
How would it sound when he started to tell the governor
all this about his niece?

This was in the spring of 1428, before Anthony de Vergy's raid—and what was bound to happen, happened.

---

[18]See Alphonse de Lamartine, *Le Civilisateur* (1852), first installment.

The noble sire felt he had been magnanimous enough in granting audience to this bumpkin with some kind of cock-and-bull story to relate. But when Baudricourt heard the poor man, embarrassed and stammering, come out with his tale of a divinely inspired niece who needed an escort to take her to Chinon, to see His Majesty, no less, in order to tell him that celestial voices had sent her, if you please, to save the kingdom, milord the governor turned on poor Durand. Did the man really think his royal functions left him time to waste listening to this kind of madness? Away with it! And as for that crazy niece, or second cousin, or whatever she was, he'd better take her home to her parents posthaste "with a couple of good cuffs" to remember him by. The deluded idiot girl could do with a good spanking; and, after that, forget the whole matter. Understood?

And now, what about the unknown lad who almost saw to it there could be no "Joan of Arc"? He appeared in the spring of 1428, which may have been the best time, since in the spring the sap is rising. Joan was terribly upset by her rebuff at Vaucouleurs. She had finally come to believe in the "mission" she had dreamt about for so long. What inconceivable, fantastic happiness, to have been chosen "among all other women," to experience being "in God's hand." And what a future lay ahead of her, what adventure! Quite different from living out her life in the backwoods of Domrémy, as all her friends would do . . . And then—catastrophe!—it all came crashing down. She had run up against the impossible. Now, she could see that she could never make it; it was over, through no fault of hers. She had been ready, more than ready, itching to go. But now, forget it! The whole idea was destroyed, doomed! Her "brothers in Paradise" would surely not hold it against her. They could see she was not being allowed to, that a wall had been put up, barring her road, and how awful she felt about it!

In a transport of joy, she had promised God that she

would do nothing but her mission until it was accomplished. No love, no marriage. And now she was empty-handed, useless. So here was this boy who wanted her, who offered to marry her and whom she had, so to speak, not even looked at until now because her mind had been on the other thing. Well, why not, O Lord, why not? She gave in; she looked at him and welcomed him; he was a good match. They went out together. She must have even kissed him.

But, then, everything changed. Domrémy had never actually experienced war before, but this was it. Vergy's villainous column swooped down on the countryside. Alarum! Run for your lives! They fled to Neufchâteau. The fires lighted up the sky, back where their deserted village was. When they got back, they found their church in ruins and their house pillaged. And Joan was ashamed, saying to herself, All of this is my fault. She was being rudely reminded: If you had listened to us, if you had gone to Chinon, no matter how, but gone there—the villains would already be routed. Just one obstacle, and you give up and throw in the towel! We were counting on you! God was counting on you! But instead of doing the job cut out for you, what did you do? You let us down, Joan! You followed another path, because he appealed to you, admit it, because you liked having that boy kiss you.

Charles Péguy was wrong, I am sure, in imagining that Joan was caught in some dilemma out of a Corneille tragedy. He conceived of her as torn between two duties: whether to obey her voices or her parents, and as being tortured by how it would hurt her people if she left them for an undertaking which they saw as senseless and revolting. But that is not so. Rather, listen to what she said, clearly, categorically: "Had I had a hundred fathers and a hundred mothers, I should still have gone!" It was Baudricourt who stopped her through his refusal to listen to her, absolutely not her parents, nor fear of disobeying them or making them unhappy. Joan was completely resolved to disregard her parents' opposition. On the other hand, giving up that boy, and their budding love and the inkling it gave her of what it was simply to be a woman in the arms of her man, meant that she would be torn apart inside.

She made up her mind. She told her near-fiancé that she was taking back her word; she would not be his, could no longer think of marrying him—because she was responsible for the tragedy that had befallen all of them. She did not help him understand what she was saying. She never spoke to him of her "voices."[19] That was none of his business. Besides, it was a secret on which she had quietly turned the page. But the wind of destiny had blown back the page that she had not wanted to continue reading. There it was again, before her, demanding her total attention. You must! You must! And the original temptation came back. Of course, she might have been happy, a vibrant, lively girl, possessed by a male whose eyes and body so appealed to her. But then what? Afterward, inevitably, sooner or later, life would turn drab again: she would remain in one place forever, working in the fields, tending the house. Instead, she would seek the highways, adventure, Chinon, the King, war, battle, with the certainty she would win, since her sword was the sword of God. That was a wild and heady way to live! Joan's heart had to break a little—but not all that much. The only choices people ever make are between temptations, and it is always the greater one that wins. Temptation: we usually use the word with a sexual connotation. Yet some temptations, which have nothing to do with the flesh, sweep everything before them.

---

[19] At her trial, she would specify that she had never mentioned the "voices" to anyone back home, not even her priest.

Once back in Domrémy, Joan had only one thought: to get away at any cost, to break through the barrier. Was it impossible? Of course not! For heaven was on her side, God the Father, Our Lord, and all the legions of angels. She had been silly to give in last spring, to let go because of one refusal. A refusal can always be reversed. She was still going to find out whether the great sire at Vaucouleurs who held the key to her departure (or the surest key, at any rate) would not end up by giving it to her. She had to have that key; and she was going to get it.

Enguerrand de Monstrelet would later say in his *Chronicle* that it was while serving at the Redhead's at Neufchâteau that Joan had learned to ride. Was he guessing, or did he have something to go on? We have no way of knowing. I tend to feel this is an authentic detail, and that headstrong Joan must have ridden as much as possible in the fall of 1428. That would be one more trump in her hand. But how could she manage to appear before Baudricourt again and get him to give his consent?

Fortunately, Uncle Durand was still around, and she could still twist him around her finger. In order to allow her a second try at Vaucouleurs, Durand was ready to burden his soul with a great lie: that he needed Joan at his house because his wife was nearing her time, and he would really appreciate it if father James and Romée, his cousin, could let him have their Joan for a while. The parents believed him, and said yes. But I would presume they also made sure to tell the "uncle" to keep an eye on her. For her father had had "a dream" (as Joan would testify at her trial, using the Biblical terminology she often resorted to, in her special way of presenting things): he had seen his daughter running off with some soldiers. And he had been overcome with such anger that he swore that if his brainless daughter (who had already greatly irritated him by turning down a proper marriage) were to do anything so monstrous as to dishonor her parents by going off like a strumpet, Heaven knows where, with a gang of men-at-arms, he would go after her, drag her back, and drown her in the Meuse with his own bare hands.

To tell the truth, Joan had not been very discreet. She had found it hard to keep to herself, and was finding it harder now toward the end of 1428. It came out later, through several of the witnesses who testified in 1456, that at the time, without giving herself away, she dropped a hint here and there among her friends that they would see what they would see, that she was working on something, something that would astonish everyone, and that the predictions that were going around (remember?) were not all that wrong.

And a few good souls, always happy to be of service to their neighbors, had put in a word or two about these startling conversations to Joan's father. If "farmer" James agreed to let cousin Durand have Joan to take care of his house, it was certainly because Durand had never breathed a word to him of their escapade to Vaucouleurs last spring to see Baudricourt. At any rate, Joan was off for Burey, with the blessing of her folks, who had been taken in; and from there, still in complicity with her "uncle," on to a second try at the governor, absolutely determined, this time, that she would succeed. How? Who knows?

And Baudricourt would agree. It must surely have been a strange thing, an outlandish, suspicious thing, to obtain such a reversal from an administrator who, I am sure, we can safely assume was a top-level bureaucrat: a self-assured man, not inclined to sudden impulses, having little use for the supernatural, and concerned above all not to stick his neck out. There were reports, later, that there had been something trumped up about it. Du Haillan, the historiog-

rapher of Charles IX, offered the explanation that some
thought the most likely: namely, that some "politicians,"
Baudricourt being one of the foremost, "decided that [for
the good of the kingdom] they should make use of the
fabricated miracle." "Fabricated," meaning forged, faked.
Guillaume du Bellay, in his *Instructions sur le fait de guerre*
(Instructions on the waging of war), reached somewhat the
same conclusion: the start of Joan's "public life" was a wily
machination set in motion by the King's councillors at the
instigation of the Sire of Vaucouleurs. And less than thirty
years after Joan's exploits, Pope Pius II[20] mentioned in his
Memoirs that perhaps (as the Bishop of Arras had told him
in 1459) a plot had been hatched at Vaucouleurs to bring
Joan forward, since the sire of the place had found it "expedient" to help his sovereign by "producing a virgin who
would say she had been sent by Heaven." But then Étienne
Pasquier in his *Recherches sur la France* would in turn disgustedly refute what he had heard on the subject: that
Baudricourt, "having misled" Joan and "found her capable
of understanding"—in other words, cunning, and not stupid—"had had her play out a whole deception." Whence
the thesis, which has its adherents even today, that Joan
was put together out of whole cloth by Charles VII's "secret services."[21]

Personally, I do not believe a word of this; yet things are
more complicated than the beatific legend would have us
think.

Joan was later to claim at Rouen that Baudricourt "on
two occasions refused and rejected her," but that "the third

---

[20]Piccolomini (d. 1464), known as the writer Aeneas Silvius, who had become
Pope in 1458, the year Joan's mother died.
[21]See Jehanne d'Orliac, *Yolande d'Aragon* (1933); Paul Lesourd and Claude Paillat,
Dossier secret (L'Église de France) (1967), vol. I.

time he received her and gave her some men [the escort she was asking for]." But what three times? She had gone to Vaucouleurs only twice, first in the spring of 1428 (in May, it would seem), then right at the start of the next year. I believe from Joan's remark we may draw the inference that her uncle, trembling at his own temerity but totally under her spell, did try a second time and was turned away, doubtless none too gently, but that Joan hung on and finally succeeded in gaining an audience and recognition as someone who might eventually be put to use.

Determined to stick it out in Vaucouleurs, Joan made no secret of what Heaven intended for her. People now came to see her, to admire her: there were the beginnings of a groundswell. The time was not the twentieth century, but the fifteenth, and what might not "take in" anyone today, unless it had to do with medical miracles, was perfectly acceptable to the common people of that time. Her simple "red dress" appealed to them. She in no way seemed crazy. She was quiet, well behaved, intelligent; she looked you straight in the eye; she went to church regularly; the curé heard her confession. And she kept telling everyone that it was true, she was not lying, she knew what she was saying —God had given her the mission of saving the kingdom.

It was well known at Vaucouleurs that the English were outside Orléans and posed a real threat to the King. And Joan affirmed, with the greatest conviction, that if the governor sent her to Chinon she would free Orléans, drive the British out, and have the Dauphin crowned at Reims. What was more, she said far and wide that she was going to Chinon anyway, alone if need be, and on foot, "were she to wear her legs down to the knees." ("A hundred fathers and a hundred mothers"; "legs down to the knees"; we begin to detect a consistency of style, not averse to hyperbole.)

The governor might, of course, have cut all that off with

a flick of his hand, turned away the "madwoman" or at least have shunted her out of the limelight. But would that have settled things? It is doubtful. People were becoming aroused; and two noblemen had by now taken an interest in her, John of Metz and Bertrand de Poulengy. She had gotten to them, to John especially. They found her amazing, with a sincerity beyond suspicion, and contagiously enthusiastic. She was tough; she was sharp. It was impossible not to like her. What a courageous girl! So fiery, so determined, sitting her mount like a seasoned horseman! They were ready to go with her to watch over her, if she were allowed to go to Chinon. And by now, she was being fed and housed free of charge at Vaucouleurs.

Baudricourt must certainly have ordered an investigation, and the result was not bad. Except for her wild ravings, the girl seemed normal. Headstrong, to be sure; she had turned down a very attractive marriage offer, approved by her parents, but she had won her case before the court at Toul, where her "betrothed"—as he claimed to be—had sued her. The court found that there had been no real commitment on her part; she had not given herself to the young man; she was therefore free to change her mind, as far as the marriage was concerned. Nothing wrong with her conduct, on that score.

All of a sudden, perhaps while he was still investigating, Baudricourt learned of a new, interesting fact. The Duke of Lorraine himself wanted to see the peasant girl and asked that she come to visit him at Nancy. Obviously, the governor could not object to that. The truth was that the Duke was not asking to see her in her capacity of "divine" warrior, but simply because he was sick and hoped this girl whom people were talking about might have talent as a "healer." Joan had no business in Nancy, which was in the opposite direction from Chinon, but the invitation, the summons sent her by this noble lord, might help her in her

endeavor. At Nancy, with only one aim in mind, she unabashedly asked the old prince to direct his son-in-law to
take her to Chinon and present her to the King. As for her
host's health, alas, there was nothing she could do for it and
she did not hesitate to tell him she knew nothing of benefi-
cent witchcraft. All that she did advise him (shyness was
never one of her strong points, and her hearing was sharp)
was that he ought to stop living in sin, as he was, with a
woman who was not his wife. The Duke, obviously less
than happy with this advice, sent her away with a mere
four francs for her trouble, the miser.

The son-in-law in question, whose protection Joan had
audaciously asked for, was René of Anjou. The Bar territory came under his overlordship, and he was a brother of
the Dauphin's wife and son of the formidable Yolande of
Aragon. Perhaps he was visiting his father-in-law at Nancy
when Joan was there; perhaps, indeed, it was he who had
called the Duke's attention to the strange girl who was
creating the furor at Vaucouleurs. René of Anjou was in
constant touch with Baudricourt, who was not just any-
body, not just some country squire of no importance, but
a personage with the highest family ties, and René was full
of deference toward him. Baudricourt and he, we may be
sure, had discussed Joan and what use might eventually be
made of her. She was so far known only locally, but her
fame was beginning to spread, and this was a matter worth
considering. It is quite probable that René had also mentioned her to his mother, and we know how deeply Yolande
was involved in matters of state. The strange girl, Heaven-
sent or not, was beginning to figure in politics, high politics, in fact, with her prognostications about Orléans, the
English, the coronation.

While it is wrong to think that Joan was created,
"brought into being," by some shrewd operators—for she
brought herself into being, obeying a commandment that

did not originate at Court—it is a fair bet that there were operators working for her in the wings. They approached her case, thinking, Let's see what this is all about. How can we use her? Why not take a chance? What have we got to lose?

I am quite willing to believe that some discreet instructions may have gone forth from Chinon to Vaucouleurs, not too obvious, of course, but similar to: Let's not overlook anything. Don't turn up your noses. One can never know. So send her along and we'll make the decision here.

Out of precaution (and perhaps also on specific instructions), the governor first made sure that Joan was exorcised. With this kind of sybil, whether real or only alleged, it was better to determine at once that she was not a creature of the devil. Joan agreed to this official demand, though not very gracefully—the whole thing was offensive, and ridiculous, seeing that the exorcist was the very curé who regularly heard her confession—but, if this was the way it had to be, so be it.

Baudricourt then finally agreed to grant Joan an audience. We know nothing of what passed between them, except for the nonsense that the prosecution was to attribute to Joan two years later at her trial, with the promoter-prosecutor alleging it had come from Baudricourt himself, or rather from third parties to whom Baudricourt had repeated it.

But the governor allowed himself to become only half involved. He let Joan go, rather than commissioning her to go. He gave her no document signed by him commending her to the King, and the courier Colet, a Court messenger who was returning to Chinon and could therefore travel with her, was not given any introductory letter either. That was the better part of wisdom, for there was no guarantee that Joan would reach her destination; the lands she had to cross, for more than a hundred leagues, were in the hands of the King's enemies; should the Burgundians take her, it would be better if she had nothing on her to provoke their anger, nothing to identify her with the "French" authorities.

Also, there was no problem in paying for her trip, since private individuals had volunteered to defray all expenses. Uncle Durand would be able to boast later, in 1456, that he himself—with one "James Alain, of Vaucouleurs," of whom we know absolutely nothing else—had advanced the twelve francs needed for the purchase of a horse for his "niece," and that a collection was taken up to get her the necessary clothes. It was unanimously decided that she should wear men's attire, in view of the dangers en route —better that it not be apparent right off that this horseman was a woman. And finally, John of Metz declared he would pay all costs on the way.

John of Metz and Bertrand de Poulengy each had a servant along. They were to go with the courier Colet, who knew the road well; and one "Richard Larcher" (or should that be read *l'archer*, "the archer named Richard"?) would also travel with the party.

Then came the time to leave. "Come what may!" had been the governor's only word of godspeed when the little band set out. Joan was not about to go by way of Domrémy and have to stop and say farewell to her parents.[22] That would have been going right into the lion's jaws. They would grab her and lock her up for good. Instead, she would write and "beg their pardon." She could not be concerned about the shouting, the curses, and the weeping that would take place at home when they found out that, after all, she *had* taken off with a group of men-at-arms. Being sure of success, unalterably sure of it, it made no

---

[22]How would Durand-the-doublecrosser ever convince his cousins that this was none of his doing?

difference whatsoever to her. God was in charge, and her parents would calm down soon enough; they would make the best of the situation.

We would like to be able to visualize little "Jeannette," who became Joan; but, in all likelihood, we will never really know what she looked like. No portrait of her has come down to us; at most, only a few concrete details of her physical appearance that we can glean here or there.

Not one of the few trustworthy documents gives any quick sketch of her, and none makes reference to her beauty. Little Laval saw her on June 6, 1429, and it is hard to believe he would have said nothing of her prettiness or grace, had he been struck by them. We have every reason, then, to think that Joan was not beautiful. *Rusticana facie*, Philip of Bergamo would write of her. Translate that: "a rustic face," in other words, a heavy-featured peasant girl. *Toto corpore praevalida*, he added, meaning well structured, muscular. We might think there would be at least a word about the light in her eye. Nothing. Her eyes were in all likelihood not very large. She was rather small (*brevi statura*, according to Bergamo); the length of fabric for the dress ordered for her in June by the Duke of Orléans' treasurer was only two ells, so she could not have been more than about five-foot-four. Her hair was black (*nigro capillo*); and it was a black hair that Quicherat was able to touch as recently as the last century in the wax of the seal still appended to the bottom of the hand-signed letter that Joan addressed to the municipality of Riom. The contemporary Hungarian visionary Engelide, who claimed to have seen Joan in spirit, depicted her as stocky, short of neck, with a "port-wine stain" behind the right ear. All the evidence agrees about her voice: high, pleasing, and feminine. It seems to have been a somewhat surprising characteristic in this otherwise rather mannish girl.

That is all we have to go on to paint her picture: a peasant type, not tall, not striking, solid and stocky; with a voice that did not really fit her physique, but contrasted with it because of its delicacy. Before leaving Vaucouleurs, she had had her hair cut, since she had to look like a man. The "Joan of Arc bob" was the nineteen-twenties name that Paris gave to what is now called a "pageboy hairdo." But the modern style comes down over the ears, while hers did not. Her hair was cut "with a bowl," above the ears,[23] to accommodate the helmet she would have to wear.

Was she illiterate? There is a habitual misunderstanding on this point. We always hear quoted the fact that Joan once said at Poitiers, during the ecclesiastical investigation we will discuss later, that she "did not know A nor B," and this has been the basis for saying that she could neither read nor write. But I think there is a mistake in interpretation here. It was about theology, about those abstruse subjects in which the doctors interrogating her were so well versed, that she actually was perfectly ignorant. True, she did not know one word about all that; she knew "neither A nor B." But Joan was to sign by hand (albeit awkwardly, unsteadily) several letters of which we still have the originals; and at Rouen she would ask the court please to put the charges against her in writing, so that she might ponder them. Maybe she really could not read or write when she left Vaucouleurs in 1429; nothing proves the point, one way or the other. But she certainly was able to read in 1431.

Just two more notes before we begin following the short trajectory that was to lead her from Vaucouleurs to Compiègne, and from there on to the stake at Rouen.

---

[23]Article 5, of the twelve in the (corrected) bill of charges at her trial specified "hair cut round above the ears," and the "clerk of La Rochelle," in his *Chronicle*, "hair round and black." The curious statue of Joan, dressed in real armor, that stands in the cathedral of Strasbourg is the only one, to my knowledge, that reproduces the Maid's true hairdo; it is a somewhat pudgy version of Joan, without physical allure, and I have never seen it reproduced. Yet it seems interesting to me, though I have not been able to ascertain its date.

In a matter of days, in just a few weeks, she would be impatient for action, and at the Court of the King she would literally demand, Hurry! Come on! Move! Let's get going! "I will last but a year, barely more." Her "voices" had clearly told her that she would not "last" long. It is important for us to understand that she knew this. And this is not the first nor the last time that we will find such surprising facts in Joan's career. But we have to learn to live with them. We might as well forget about her if from the outset we exclaim at everything that stumps us in her story, Out of the question, we won't accept it!

Secondly, to whom did she attribute her "voices"? After Saint Michael, the original contact, to "Saint Catherine" and "Saint Margaret," who were heroines of her own private folklore. She really knew very little about them, other than the fact that she had been told both were martyrs, both died for their faith, let themselves be killed rather than renounce it. They were the ones she had promised to obey, the ones she wanted to be like, so as to be worthy of the great favor they had done her: the favor of singling her out, although she was so insignificant, to speak to her familiarly. So, naturally, Joan knew what she was headed for—the same fate as her two big sisters.

The little horsewoman with the tough arms under her gray tunic, with the thick sinewy thighs beneath black gaiters (a sharp-visored "riding-hood" on her boyish head, behind it the shaved nape visible), the little girl who was so delighted to have pulled it off and to have won the governor over, now sat chest out, eye aflame, lips laughing. Yet, at the same time she was a young woman well aware of the fact that she was headed for a death not too far in the future, at the end of a "martyrdom" for God, for "Our Lord." And that was all right with her. Joan had agreed to it.

III

Joan Meets the King

It was quite a way from Vaucouleurs to Chinon: some four hundred-odd miles, through dangerous country.

There were not only the Burgundians to worry about—the English were not conspicuous in the area, and the route the party took would be as direct as possible, through Joinville, Bar-sur-Aube, Bar-sur-Seine, and Auxerre, toward Gien, where they would be back in the King's territory—but also bands of wandering highwaymen, who could mean trouble. The little squad of six men plus Joan felt it would be better to ride by night. Just what the date of the long trip was is uncertain. Historians cannot get together on this and we have nothing decisive to pin it down.

Joan had never stopped repeating at Vaucouleurs that it was necessary (why?) for her to be with the Dauphin "before Mid-Lent"—which, since Easter in 1429 fell on March 27, meant that she wanted to be at Chinon before March 7. So in February she was marking time, as the days went by without her getting any closer. At any rate, she did get to Chinon before Easter, for her famous "Letter to the

English," dictated in the presence of several important personages, is very clearly dated "Tuesday of Holy Week,
March 22." But that gives us no information as to the actual
date of her arrival. All that we can be sure of is that they
rode for eleven days. Whether that was during the last
fortnight of February or the last days of that month and the
first days of March, it could not have been very warm
during those nights of slow progress, always remaining on
the lookout. (There are plenty of references to Joan's doublet, her gaiters, and her little hat; but never to any topcoat.
Yet, she must surely have had some outer garment in this
still wintry weather, some greatcoat or warm hooded cape.)

Could the healthy, alluring young girl, surrounded by
six young males day and night, never have had to fend them
off, never have had any problem with them? There are two
invaluable references on this count. One is from the lady
known as La Touroulde, with whom Joan was to spend
several weeks. Called to testify at the "revision trial" of
1456, she stated, "I heard the men who escorted her to the
King. They said that at the beginning they had wanted to
gain carnal knowledge [the phrase is as transcribed by the
secretaries, who probably polished the plain expression
they heard], but they had not dared." We have every reason
to believe this was true. This was no ordinary girl they
were dealing with. She called herself a "daughter of God,"
and calmly said she talked with angels. Desirable though
she might be, and well built at sweet seventeen, there was
an aura about her. Intangible? Imaginary? None the less
effective. To try to get intimate with her (against which she
would undoubtedly react violently) would be something
like a sacrilege.

The other statement, from Dunois, goes even further.
When you were with Joan, he would say (and he was only
twenty-six when he first saw her), "you did not think of
women any more." Note that he uses the plural. Dunois

was not just saying that on looking at Joan, one did not think of the enjoyment there might be in making love to her; he said more: that she cleansed your heart, made your male obsession vanish. She was of another atmosphere, another world. When she was there, you changed; you became better.

So, there need have been no problem in the relations between Joan and her traveling companions for the eleven days they were constantly together. There was a true feeling of camaraderie. It was not really that they "had not dared"; they had simply ceased to lust after that body.

Where did they sleep by day, since they traveled at night? In some abandoned barn, some shack, or a natural hiding place, while one stood guard. Joan never got undressed. She slept between John and Bertrand, fully clad. She was in good spirits; and since they looked on her as a comrade, they played tricks on her. Two or three times, they pretended to panic: There! Ahead! An ambush! And the fellows would spur their horses to rear and wheel around wildly. Joan peered into the shadows. Where were the enemy? Where? She didn't see them.

She never got scared. So they gave in. She laughed. And they pushed on, humming. At Auxerre, she really did something daring. It was Sunday, and she insisted on going to mass. Absolutely; she would hear no arguments against it. The group must have broken up, I assume. They could not have gone to mass, all seven of them, together. That would be too noticeable. But, nevertheless, to venture that far into a "Burgundian" city was a great chance to take! Which, fortunately, led to no mishap. She heard her mass, all right, and they were off again, toward Gien.

From the last layover, near Sainte-Catherine-de-Fierbois, Joan sent a message to the King asking to be received—

which proves that she was carrying no letter of introduction. She had, of course, hoped that somehow Baudricourt would have found a way of advising the Dauphin of her arrival. And the governor had, in fact, written, but Charles, at this point, knew nothing about it. Before her judges, at Rouen, Joan tried to make it seem that all had gone perfectly smoothly for her, that she arrived at Chinon, stopped at a hostelry, advised the King of her presence, and saw him that very afternoon. Dunois, in 1456, trying not to contradict the Maid too blatantly, conceded that there was some time lapse between Joan's arrival at Chinon and her access to the sovereign—say, forty-eight hours. Had it been only that! In truth, it took an elaborate production for Joan to reach the feet of His Royal Highness. The prelude seemed interminable.

However, Joan was not arriving at Chinon like a bolt from the blue. Word had preceded her. Once at Gien, in "French" territory, she repeated to everyone what she had said at Vaucouleurs: that God had sent her to save the kingdom, drive out the English, then go to Reims and turn the Dauphin into a real King. The "Bastard of Orléans,"[1] the very day after Joan had been through Gien (word traveled fast along the Loire River), heard about the appearance of this girl on horseback, a real little saint, people said, who had come from Vaucouleurs and was going "to France" to work wonders, according to her. Dunois lost no time in sending his agents to Chinon to gather information. Just who was she? What was this all about?[2]

Still chaperoned and funded by John of Metz, Joan

---

[1] That is, the one we know as Dunois, who at the time did not yet have that name; he was John, son of Louis and one of his mistresses, therefore a half-brother to Charles, Duke of Orléans, the prisoner of the English; he commanded the armed forces of the besieged city.

[2] Jean Bancal believes that Dunois announced Joan's salutary arrival to the people of Orléans as early as February 12, the very day of the defeat at Rouvray. That would be most interesting, but I can really see nothing to back it up.

waited at the hostelry for the royal reply to her request for an audience. She grew impatient waiting. Yolande may well have intervened for her, but the mother-in-law did not have as much influence over her son-in-law's mind as she might have wished. The Council stood between them, and particularly Chancellor Regnault of Chartres, as well as La Trémoille, two VIP's who did not much care for her. (La Trémoille, who had once plotted with her and Richemont, had broken with her immediately after they did away with Giac.)

One of the most consequential depositions at the rehabilitory investigation (a quarter-century after the events we are trying to reconstruct) would be that of Simon Charles, then former presiding officer of the Audit Chamber, who was at Chinon when Joan arrived. This witness was explicit: "There was deliberation at Court as to whether or not the King should see her."

This was the first hopeful sign for Joan—she was not being scornfully turned away, she was not being ignored. The King sent an emissary to the hostelry so Joan could clearly state what she wanted and the "mission" she claimed to have been given. Following that: physical and moral examinations. It was, of course, not out of the question that this peasant girl might be "inspired." Charles V, the Wise, had had his royal astrologer at Court, who was none other than the father of the poetess Christine de Pisan, and he had granted audience to one Guillemette of La Rochelle, also "sent by God," who was supposed to be the bearer of secrets she would reveal to him. And Charles VI had not disdained, at least twice during his reign, to receive "mystics," whom he did not joke about: first, Marie de Maillé, and then Marie Robine, known as the "Gasque of Avignon." The first thing to do with this girl of Bar was to make sure she was a virgin. If she were not, she would be sent away—or, indeed, arrested. A girl claiming to be a virgin when she was not, and boasting that God was with her, might well have been selected by the devil to perform his evil deeds. (The King probably did not know she had been exorcised.) Who would perform the physical examination? Any worthy matron could have done this. But no, it was undertaken by the King's mother-in-law, assisted by her daughter, the Queen. So it is not wrong to believe that Yolande was interested in Joan; indeed, greatly so.

Very well, the girl was intact. Now the moral test, to be given by churchmen. Later, at Rouen, Bishop Cauchon spoke of "three weeks" for this examination. Where did he get this detail that he passed off as established fact? We can be certain there were two successive ecclesiastical commissions to look into Joan's case, for we know the names of some of the "commissioners," not all the same at Poitiers as at Chinon. At Chinon, Joan had benefited from a fortunate accident which, by her own admission, got her away from what she called "those clerics who argued against me." Whatever the duration of this first series of questions, regardless of its extent, it must have held up the royal audience considerably more than the delay of a few hours that Joan suggested, or even the two days mentioned by Dunois. Simon Charles is once again our source for the following specification: "The King was hesitant to receive Joan until it was reported to him that Baudricourt had written that he was sending" him the girl. A sovereign (or a chief executive officer) does not have time to read all the mail that comes in addressed to him. He has assistants for that. They open it, sort it out, and "lose" what they wish, if they feel it is worth taking the risk. Baudricourt's note had been lost in that way. Who talked? A mystery. Yolande kept worrying, inquiring, and perhaps that was what coaxed the paper out of its hiding place. The King knew Baudricourt well; if this man took it on himself to let Joan come, it was because, at the very least, she was worth a conversation.

There was a bit of excitement at Court when the news got out. The King was about to see the girl-dressed-as-a-man who was the curiosity of the day. I would not swear that all the comments made about the event at the château were necessarily on the serious side, and I suspect some of the ladies of the Court smiled suggestively as they talked of the virgin girl. Her presentation to the King was something not to be missed.

Yet everything went off as scheduled in the crowded great hall. It was an evening affair, with candles and torchlights in great profusion, sending up a cloud of smoke and creating oppressive heat. Joan did not come forward all by herself; she was surely accompanied and guided—perhaps by Milady Yolande. She followed where she was led, straight toward His Majesty. Later, the gossips would tell the wonder of it: Imagine, an illiterate country girl, yet never an awkward movement, she did everything just right, spontaneously performing all the proper curtsies. The Lord knows Joan had been waiting so long for this moment that she had had more than enough time to prepare for it, rehearsing twenty times, if she did it once, all the motions called for by the ritual.

Without any fear whatsoever—was not Our Lord standing behind her, even though invisible?—she went toward the prince, steady of leg and sharp of eye. And we need not doubt that she was surprised, and shocked, when finally she saw the Dauphin in his human reality. The puny runt before her was nothing like the archangel she had imagined. But, no matter. He was the one Heaven had destined for the throne, the one criminals were keeping from his rightful rule, and she had come to set it right.

Charles took her aside. All witnesses agree on that. She was able to speak to him freely, privately. There was one thing she wanted to tell him, which would be the formal guarantee of her credibility. Legend has it that Charles VII was not sure he was the son of Charles VI, and this worry haunted him. But Joan is reported to have said to him, "Doubt no more! You are truly the son of a King."

It certainly seems likely that Charles VII may have been eating his heart out about his paternity (Charles VI or Louis of Orléans?),[3] but where did the statement, attributed to Joan, come from? Pasquerel alone is the authority for it; and who was he? An insidious monk who suddenly moved in on Joan as her personal chaplain at Chinon. He claimed to come from Le Puy-en-Velay, where he had met Joan's mother on Good Friday, during that year's great pilgrimage. The devout woman, he said, was deeply concerned for her "Jeannette," and with a mother's tears, she had implored him to go and join her daughter at Court, to give her his religious counsel and not leave her side. Now, nothing is less certain than that "Romée" made a pilgrimage to Le Puy, and it could very well be that Pasquerel was, instead, foisted on Joan by a well-meaning Yolande, or on the other hand, by an intriguing La Trémoille. In his 1456 testimony, Pasquerel would make many categorical assertions: "Joan told me . . . I know from her own mouth . . ." But that definitive tone by itself need not convince us of his sincerity. In the present case, for instance, I can scarcely picture Joan uttering the words he attributes to her—for they would have been so presumptuous as almost to constitute lese majesty. And, besides, why would those words automatically have implied that she was possessed of divine information? Even if she swore "God told me so," that would not necessarily prove to the King that she knew whereof she spoke.

On the other hand, what Peter Sala was to write later,

---

[3]There is in existence an autograph copy of a confidential letter, written in Italian, by Louis XI, Charles VII's son, in which he says that he is not too sure who his grandfather really was, since, to quote him, his grandmother Isabeau had been *una putana* (a whore).

based on what he had learned from Charles VII's former chamberlain William Gouffier, seems much more likely to be authentic. Charles VII is reported one day to have confided to Gouffier that Joan, to his utter stupefaction, had repeated to him the very words he had spoken alone in his chapel on All Saints' Day of 1428. He was begging God, as we have already seen, to spare his life if Orléans should fall and he were forced to seek refuge in Dauphiné or Scotland. Now, *that* would be a proof, proof that Joan knew things that no one on earth could know, save him to whom she was talking. The King looked into Joan's eyes, and was shaken. Perhaps she may have begged his pardon for what she had just done; perhaps she knelt before him. Simon Charles assures us the King was "radiant" when he returned to the courtiers after his tête-à-tête with Joan. Radiant is hardly a word one would unthinkingly apply to a gentleman who watched his every motion, constantly aware that he must hide his true feelings. But Charles VII was visibly shaken. No question about it: this was no ordinary girl, but one with "second sight."

The soldier's tale was to cause a great stir shortly thereafter, and was additional proof. It would become known far beyond Chinon, as the Italian "Morosini chronicle" would attest. Joan was going into the château, when a soldier of the guard, showing off before his buddies, said in a loud stage whisper, "Is that the one they call the Virgin of Vaucouleurs? Just give me one night with her, and I swear she'd never be the same the next morning."

Joan stopped before the man, and said, "You are wrong, my friend, to hold such evil thoughts. *If you but knew how close you are to death!*"

Two hours later, the soldier fell into the Vienne River, and was drowned.

Joan was now no longer living at the hostelry, but in the château proper, in the building known as the Coudray wing.

However shaken the King had been, he was not yet ready to use this seeress for the military task she had said was to be hers. Hardly! There could be no question about her unquestionable and frightening "power," but what proved that it came "from Heaven"? Suppose it came from the devil? Charles, ever on the alert, may well have thought of that himself. But if not, there were plenty in the Council ready to suggest it to him, particularly since he had not confided to them any details of what Joan had told him. Regnault and La Trémoille, knowing how fully Yolande was for Joan, urged the sovereign to beware, not to do anything hasty, to be sure there were additional safeguards.

One thing is certain: the revelation Joan made to the King, which to her way of thinking should have settled everything immediately, did not have the overwhelming effect she had anticipated. It had so little effect, indeed, that, since he had to go to Poitiers, the Dauphin took her along to subject her to another ecclesiastical investigation there, more thorough than the first. She was a good girl, seemingly a devout Christian, but being from the country and unsophisticated, how could one be sure she had not unwittingly become the tool of demons? You needed specialists in this matter, who knew what precautions to take. And this time they would even have a well-known expert on their commission, a representative of the Inquisition, the Inquisitor of Toulouse, Preaching-Brother Turelure.

Joan obeyed. What else could she do, since this was the will of the Prince? But it seemed deplorable to her, a bitter pill indeed. What would make the Dauphin believe in her and understand she was here to save him? How could she make him realize that if, instead of stalling and inflicting these stupid miseries on her, he had given her the army she had so long dreamt of, the Dauphin would already be in Orléans, with the English scattered before him, and the way open to go to Reims and his coronation?

At Poitiers, the King saw to it that Joan was the guest of Advocate-General Rabateau, a most distinguished notable. That was thoughtful, of course. But what she wanted was to get into action! And she gave them a hard time, the monks, the bishops, the theologians who made her dizzy with their silly questions. Respect was not her forte. As one of the exasperating cross-examinations was about to begin, she familiarly slapped the shoulder of an equerry, Gobert Thibaut, and shamelessly announced, "Men like you are what I need and what I like: men of arms." Implying, obviously, "As for those others, well . . ."

Brother Séguin questioned her about the language her voices spoke: Was it French, proper French? And Joan burst out laughing, for the brother, who was from Limoges, had an accent as brittle as porcelain: "Certainly my saints didn't talk the way you do!"

One of the questioners asked her right out whether she believed in God, and the answer rang out: "More than you do!" More than that idiot who kept refusing to see what was quite plain. They had taken out their reference books, their treatises on what methods to use to distinguish good "spirits" from evil. Their guides to witchcraft! And Joan mocked them with, "The Lord's Book has more in it than all of yours put together!" For she was familiar with the Lord's Book; she herself was a page out of it. The theologians must have been startled. And for them not to take umbrage at such insolence, she must indeed have had powerful support.

She did have. First of all Yolande, and no doubt the Queen, as well as René of Anjou. And the young Duke d'Alençon had enthusiastically come over to her. He had been stunned with admiration when he saw the girl "run a lance" in tournament before his eyes with astounding mastery. (It would not be surprising if Joan had practiced this back at Vaucouleurs.) And then there was also public opinion in Poitiers, the simple people, the poor, the humble. The Court might disdain them, yet it knew they were the support of the régime, its nourishing substance; the life of ease the rich led was made possible only by the exploitation of the people. It would be foolish to pay no attention to their interests. And the way Joan had caught their fancy was something to see! They all wanted to get near her, to venerate her. This plebeian movement had to be taken into consideration, and Baudricourt had done so back in his area. It could come in handy.

Finally, there was the King. The clerics could sense there was nothing the King really wanted so much as to be reassured about Joan, that she represented the Good Cause— so that, as soon as possible, without fear, he might start playing this providential trump card.

The fly in the ointment was the man at the top. Regnault of Chartres had gotten himself named head of the Commission, and he was cold as ice where Joan was concerned. Was he the one who had insisted right from the start that it was indispensable to make further inquiries at Domrémy, Baudricourt notwithstanding? That was going on right now, and Domrémy of course was not just next door. Two monks had been sent out there; their round trip alone would require three weeks. And once there, they would need some time to carry out the minute investigations they had been charged with. Beyond that, it had seemed worthwhile to solicit several major opinions. Should she be accepted or not? What was the view of John Gerson, until recently pontiff of the University of Paris, who had taken refuge in Lyons since the Anglo-Burgundian occupation of the capital? What was the opinion of the venerable Jacques Gélu, Bishop of Embrun, who had a reputation for saintliness? Letters were sent to these authorities; now their answers were awaited.

Joan, in short, was finding out what it means to deal with established order and the powers-that-be.

In the end, it would be up to the gentlemen-priests of the Commission to decide, after their farcical interrogations and their closed-door discussions. The word from the Bar country was satisfactory. Joan's behavior at Poitiers had been carefully observed: no impediment there. She was seen to be pious, well mannered, and sober as well. She ate sparingly; often, just some bread soaked in wine. (Wine? This would not be held against her. Common wine "is the drinking water of France," says Bernard Shaw.[4]) Of course, there were those men's clothes she wore. But she dressed this way with good reason. She wore them because she planned to act like a man, fight like a man against the English; she had made that plain enough, day after day. And the letter that she intended to send the English proved that she was ready to pounce like a little lioness; she was only waiting for the chance. One could not climb ladders in skirts: that would truly be impropriety, even lewdness. So there was no objection to the masculine disguise.

The Commission's report, therefore, would prove favorable. Jacques Gélu would point out that this person was of very mean origin (coming, as he said, from "manure"). She must have truly exceptional virtues for God to send his angels to one of such low social standing. The clerics came to the conclusion that as far as they were concerned, from their supernatural point of view, they would not veto the decision. They limited their respectful daring to a suggestion taken from the Gospel, the very words of the Re-

---

[4]Bernard Shaw, *Saint Joan* (Penguin ed., 1951), "Preface," p. 11.

deemer about the tree and its fruit: there was nothing in religion to prevent giving Joan a try, and it could be hoped that her actions would bear excellent fruit. The applicant —for that was what Joan was: she was asking for a job— said she could do certain things. Why not give her the opportunity? She was not sent by the devil, that was certain; as for whether she truly came "from God," events would tell, that was all there was to it. It was a guarded opinion, one might even say a bit mealy-mouthed. The good doctors were not saying no; they were almost saying yes, yet leaving room, as was proper, for the "judgment of God."

Now, the Royal Council had to decide. It goes without saying that while the clerics were at their work, the Council had also been studying the subject deeply, with Regnault forming the link between Council and Commission. Regnault was an archbishop on one side, but a chancellor on the other; and if he had really been determined to get rid of Joan, we can be quite sure the Commission's report would not have been what it was. The Council was made up of technicians of the temporal sphere. They were not much concerned with religious considerations, for many of them, while they would not make a point of it, had personally outgrown these. They were realists, manipulators of the concrete, practitioners of hard fact, specialists at making the most of any situation. They were diplomats. Any altruistic impulse seemed to them immediately suspect— either a mask for something else, or a sign of mental debility. They were not the sort who could be fooled. Fantastically nearsighted characters, they believed they were the only ones with clear vision.

What was Joan's case to them? Well, times were hard; the general situation was alarming, what with the threat to Orléans. And here was this mystical "retardate," this visionary country girl, not ill intentioned, it would seem, certainly full of good will, and ready to lend a hand. The common people, of course, were all for her. Some reports even pointed out that at Orléans they were awaiting the girl as if she were the Messiah. Considering the way things stood, it might not be a bad idea to send her to Orléans to revive morale. Much more important things than Joan's so-called mission were taking place behind the scenes. Buying time would be a precious advantage, and that might be just what the madwoman from Domrémy could do. La Trémoille and Regnault both saw it that way. All Charles VII had to do was fall in line. And he did: it was decided to use Joan.

On April 22, 1429, the Royal Treasury reimbursed John of Metz one hundred *livres*[5] to cover the expenses he had incurred in bringing Joan from Vaucouleurs to Chinon. But only on April 22, whereas Joan had arrived at Chinon on March 6 at the latest, and perhaps as early as February 23. It had certainly taken long enough for her to be accepted. However, John of Metz was probably not paid the moment the decision was made; administrative reimbursements, then as now, were likely to be slow in coming. She was to leave for Orléans on April 28, and it would be necessary to have armor made for her at Tours before that and a standard (or even two) painted for her, so we can infer that the Council, after lengthy hesitations, consented to give its approval about mid-April, 1429.

Joan could breathe freely at last. She was wild with joy. This was it! Forward, to the fight! She had had a new "vision." She knew now where the sword was that she wanted: it was in the chapel of Saint Catherine, at Fierbois,

[5]The French *livre* at this time represented the value of a pound of silver (as in the case of the British pound sterling), and was subdivided into twenty *sous* (or *sols*) of twelve *deniers* each (equivalent to shillings and pence). *Livre* and *franc* are historically interchangeable, but rather than the twenty-cent value of the modern *franc*, the *livre* meant something closer to the classical five-dollar parity of the pound sterling. *(Translator's note)*

buried near the altar. Someone was sent there to dig for it, find it, and bring it back. Joan admitted later she never saw this messenger, but she had been brought a slightly rusty sword that two seconds of polishing made "like new."

She took a "surname," since she had none but had been known only as Jeannette or Joan. It never occurred to her to call herself Tart or Dare; that was only her father's occasional "surname"; she had no idea why. She decided she should be called the Maid *(La Pucelle)*. But let us not be misled. This must be read correctly, historically. It had nothing to do with virginity.

In the fifteenth century, no virgin of good family would have referred to herself as a "maid." That was a word strictly for the masses. A maid, or *pucelle* (from the Latin *puella*, meaning young girl), was a servant girl in common parlance. This would become perfectly clear when Inquisitor Bréhal, at the time of Joan's rehabilitation, described her as "Joan, simple maid, and virgin." One might even say that at the time the term "maid" would very likely carry a connotation quite the opposite of virginity because of the promiscuity it implied to everyone's mind. Which explains why Bréhal added his precise explanation, apparently almost in amazement. The term changed in meaning between the fifteenth and eighteenth centuries. That was why Voltaire decided to play it for the laughs it would elicit from his society constituency when he used it as the title of his satire of Joan.

The truth is that Joan, in declaring herself the Maid, was simply calling herself a servant, nothing more. She was the Little Servant of the Lord.[6]

---

[6]Michelet, ever ready to fall for misinterpretation, insisted that if at Rouen Joan did not use her assumed title of the Maid, it was out of modesty. According to him, she wanted to spare the members of the clergy a word that was so sexually suggestive!

Now we have a somewhat better picture of her, in those first weeks of her great adventure, and can see her more as her contemporaries did.

She was said to have *competentis elegantiae;* but here again we must beware. This Latin phrase did not mean elegance as we understand it today, but good manners and urbanity. The flattering adjective means to me that she excelled in them, which was, of course, surprising in this girl of the fields. She did not like social gatherings, and preferred the company of military men to that of women; small talk was anathema to her. She liked d'Alençon very much. He became very fond of her and invited her to his home at Saint-Florent, near Saumur, to introduce her to his wife. And Joan, sure of herself, promised her hostess that after the battles she would send her husband back to her, intact and handsomer than ever. According to Dunois, from time to time, when she was among military men, she would concoct tall tales of her fantastic past, full of all kinds of prowess and extraordinary exploits; then she would burst out laughing: It's not true! You know it's not true! I was only fooling!

She laughed easily, but she cried easily too. She wept at Vaucouleurs, and a great deal at Chinon and Poitiers, when things went against her or when people would not believe her. She could be insolent on that score, as we have seen. She could also lose her temper and be violent. That we shall see soon enough.

Since she was going to be a soldier, and be with her comrades as one of them, well, she would be like them and change her clothes in front of them, having her armor adjusted, from head to foot, without any prissiness whatsoever. D'Aulon and d'Alençon both mentioned that they had seen her breasts on several occasions, and that they were delightful.

IV

Orléans: Joan in Her Glory

Was Joan a soldier? She certainly wanted to be, with determination, with joyful conviction. But that was just where she was wrong. The execution of her "mission" started with a misunderstanding.

Let us first see how things stood, militarily and politically, on April 28, 1429, when Joan set out from Blois—as she believed, at least—to go and cut the English to bits (it would only take a minute!) and send the survivors scurrying off like rats.

The siege of Orléans was dragging on and on. The English had appeared before the city walls on October 12; they had been there, for almost seven months now, still without launching an attack. Misfortune struck when they had barely taken up positions at the fortress of Les Tourelles overlooking the bridge, that great nineteen-arched span that led from Orléans into Sologne: their general-in-chief, Salisbury, had been hit by a cannonball fired from the right bank. The shot tore away half his face and he died four days later. Then the besiegers divided their forces. How many were there, in all? Maybe four thousand, forty-five hundred at most. They set up three strong points along the river: upstream, at Jargeau; downstream, at Meung and Beaugency. On December 1, John Talbot, a good warrior, it was said, and Sir William Glasdale, whom Joan always referred to as Glassidas, joined them.

Their operations were unusually weak. They had built a number of "bastilles" or blockhouses around the city, yet they did not try to set up a blockade. There were three blockhouses to the south, on the left bank; six to the west and north, where the roads to Orléans lead in from Blois, Châteaudun, and Paris; and just one to the east, near the junction of the roads coming from Pithiviers and Gien. That last bastille was a good mile and a quarter away from the ramparts (as against a quarter to half a mile for the others), so access to the city was not cut off from any direction; entrance through the Burgundy Gate was virtually unimpeded. Since October, there had been only one significant encounter, at Rouvray on February 12, when the "Armagnacs" tried to crush John Fastolf's supply column that was coming in from Paris: a bitter defeat for the French. They had lacked coordination, they constantly had misunderstandings. The Count of Clermont, having quarreled with the other leaders, refused to join in, and two days later turned his back on the fight and left, taking several of his associates with him. It had been close to a rout, but the English had not been able to take advantage of it; in fact they had not even tried to. One gets the feeling there was no follow-through, and that far from being full of fire and fury, the English were at loose ends, without directives. We must take the few words that appeared in a report from Bedford, the English Regent, uncle of the boy King Henry VI, very seriously: this siege of Orléans, he would say in July, "undertaken on God knows whose decision. . . ." It had not been his idea, obviously, even though he was sup-

posed to be in charge of things at the time. The English
Court was experiencing stormy weather and was plagued
by dissension and intrigue. Winchester, the banker turned
cardinal, although a Lancaster, was at loggerheads with his
cousin Bedford. There were political overtones behind all
these disagreements. The Earl of Suffolk, William de la
Pole (or Guillaume de la Poule, which was Joan's way of
calling him "chicken"), who represented Bedford in the
expeditionary force, was not sure what was expected of
him. So he held off and carried on a "phony war" that
allowed for no attack, a do-nothing war which was all tor-
por and courtesy.

On Christmas day, Suffolk sent polite word to the Bastard (Dunois), in command of the royal military forces at
Orléans (where Gaucourt was civil governor), that he could
do with a touch of music. At your service, sir! And the
fiddlers were sent over to serenade the Goddams! Another
time, Suffolk had sent the generals and civil authorities a
basket filled with exotic fruits such as dates and figs. In
exchange, all he wanted was some black panne for a lining
for his dressing gown. No sooner said than done! So, obviously, the English were in no hurry to see the battle joined.

Charles VII did not care for battles either. The catastrophe at Verneuil, five years earlier, was a very bitter
memory, and he was seeking a way out through some
means other than armed combat. His goal, his real desire,
was to effect a friendly settlement with Philip of Burgundy. If he could only split him away from the English,
their hold on his crown and on a good half of his kingdom
would undoubtedly evaporate. There was frequent contact
between Bourges and Dijon, and Charles VII was quite
sure (not without good reason) that for his own interests,
the Duke of Burgundy had no wish to see the Lancasters
too powerful on the continent. If they got too strong, they
would soon attempt to take away his Flemish possessions

and the juicy revenues he got from them. One particular
incident had taken place in February. The municipality of
Orléans—rather significantly—had felt it might be oppor-
tune to turn to Philip and ask him to try to arrange an
armistice with Bedford in the city's name. And Philip had
not refused. He made the overture, but ran into a firm, not
to say rude, partner. Bedford answered that it was not his
habit to "beat the bushes" and then leave the "flushed
game" to others. Philip, thus rebuffed, had withdrawn the
three hundred Picards he had among the besieging troops.
That created a crack in the cement of the Anglo-Burgundian alliance; it might be widened, if one went about it
right.

With the English not attacking, the Duke of Burgundy
sulking, and the Court at London obviously unable to make
up its mind, Charles VII began to think it was not impossible that the English at Orléans might just pick up and leave,
without his having to risk trying to force them to do so.
Making Bedford and Henry VI lose face was an attractive
idea, and it might well be that Philip would have no objection to it. But the first condition for succeeding, of course,
was that the people of Orléans must not get discouraged,
but must hold out as long as necessary. That was why
Charles VII, along with his mother-in-law, had already
supplied the besieged with a few subsidies in kind, food and
munitions, especially food. The authorities in Orléans
needed food for the population, which had more than dou-
bled because of the retreat behind the city's ramparts of
those who had lived outside the walls, in the suburbs of
Saint-Pouair, Saint-Vincent, and Saint-Euverte, as well as
the evacuated villages of Fleury, Senoy, and Saint-Jean-de-
Braye. Combatants were not needed; the city was overflowing with them. They were at least as numerous as the
English, and if any additional mercenaries arrived they
would have to be paid. No, they had plenty of men; Orléans

had no desire to see its garrison swollen any further. This
was music to the ears of a sovereign given to thrift.

   No one had taken the trouble to fill Joan in on these
problems. They were beyond her, and she was not in accord with this thinking at all. To her, it was simple: attack
the English, "throw them out of all France," and then,
thanks to her, the Dauphin would become the King blessed
by God, and her job would be done. She might even—her
voices had suggested—bring the Duke of Orléans back
from England.

   So she sent her well-known letter to "Guillaume de la
Poule, comte de Suffort," and his commanders. It was a
dictatorial document, calling on them to fall back at once,
and then to go home. What they were doing was not right
at all, trying to deprive the Dauphin of his rightful heritage, seizing and "violating" all of those "good cities" which
were not theirs. They ought to be ashamed. Her letter was
a bit disorganized, with the same command stated three
times: Go home, Englishmen, that is your duty; and if you
do not leave of your own free will, then I, the Maid, will
drive you out, and how! ("The Maid will wait upon you
promptly and to your greatest woe. . . . If your men fail to
obey, I will have them all slaughtered. . . ." God has sent
me, hark to "that news," and "if you see not reason," be
sure that we will "strike upon you and make so great halloo
[in other words: send up such a war cry] that in a thousand
years in France will not have been the like.")

   She was still using her hyperbolic style. Did she really
think the English would listen to her? Not exactly. But she
thought it proper and necessary to try this measure first. It
was good, honest procedure, the kind that should prevail
among Christians. Before shedding blood and causing the
death of men (for that, too, was "great pity"), Joan felt she

should try, if possible, to make the English understand their guilt, the impious villainy of their behavior. And besides, something new had been added, as she was warning them: she was here now, she who was nothing less than the very arm of "God, King of Heaven, son of Holy Mary." That ought to give those Englishmen something to think about. Maybe they would finally open their eyes to the crime they were committing, when faced with such a threat.

But since there was every likelihood that those wicked men would not listen to her, Joan, at Blois, considered herself in her iron suit. Serious but content (she wore "plain" armor, without the inlaid decorations preferred by nobles), she got ready to mount her horse. This was the moment when she must first have begun to feel a bit of concern, even though she was still far from realizing the gap between what she wanted to do and what the King, or rather his Council, intended for her to do. She saw herself as a "warrior chief" (she had written to the English, "I am a warrior chief"), and yet not for one second did Charles VII, much less his councillors, to say nothing of his commanders, ever contemplate giving her such a role. Some of the stories tell us that she was given "a military household." Not at all. D'Aulon, whom the King assigned to her, never acted as her chief of staff; he was her quartermaster, at most, her secretary, or perhaps her equerry. She had two pages to wait upon and serve her, Louis of Coutes, and another whom we know only by his first name, Raymond. Plus her private chaplain, the monk Pasquerel. And the troops that Joan would lead to Orléans would not be a relief army; they were just another supply column, albeit the biggest yet.

Here is what John Chartier, chronicler of the reign, has to say about it: "There were loaded in the city of Blois cartloads of corn [food and arms] and brought together great many oxen, sheep, cows, and pigs. And Joan then took to the road."

Dozens of carts and hundreds of heads of cattle; the soldiers went along only as an escort, the armed protection for this wealth of nutrition meant to bolster the physical and moral stamina of the people of Orléans so they might continue to hold out. And Joan was part of the package. She was to be a different kind of support, a morale-booster such as they had never had. Faithful subjects of His Majesty, above all do not lose heart! See the gift that the King and the Lord are sending you—the same little saint you have been talking about for the past two months. Here she is! Here is the Maid: *Gott mit uns* made flesh! This is tangible proof that God is an Armagnac. That will make the English tremble.

That, then, was the way things stood, from the royal vantage point. No question of promoting Joan to commander-in-chief, with the power to make decisions. It would be ridiculous, facing a specialist like Talbot, to turn the French military command at Orléans over to a country girl of seventeen who knew no more of war than she did of theology: neither A nor B. With Dunois, Gilles de Rais, La Hire, and all the others in the field, all competent commanders, breveted strategists, graduates of the War School, the King never dreamt of humiliating them, insulting them, by making them answerable to the well-built, but still childlike, peasant girl.

As seen from the Royal Chancellery, Joan was a rare fetish, a good-luck charm, an incomparable mascot, who enjoyed powerful religious prestige in the minds of the common people. Charles VII, might even have volunteered personally: a good girl, not stupid at all, one hundred per cent pious, a visionary, she claimed, but at any rate gifted with a strange clairvoyant power, trying only to do good, sacrificial, and animated by a childlike and pathetic drive.

She was an unanticipated auxiliary they could not fail to make use of, and who ought to prove of great value in the short run.

Joan wanted priests along, a lot of military chaplains to give last rites to the men who would fall, perhaps that very evening; for she was convinced, beyond doubt, that that day, or the next at the latest, they would be engaged with the English. If the convoy were attacked en route, the carts would be formed into a circle, the livestock on the inside, while she and her horsemen, like a howling hurricane, burst on the assailants. And, what with God on their side, and Saint Michael the archangel and all the heavenly hosts, victory would be assured before they started!

Meantime, in the cloud of dust sent up by the caravan, Joan seemed like some early version of a cowgirl headed for the roundup. She insisted that *her* soldiers all be shriven before they left, as she herself had been. They set off singing hymns, with religious banners waving among the pikestaffs. The whole exodus, holy songs interspersed with mooing, seemed much more a move to new grazing ground, or a religious procession, than a relief column. The ladies of the Court must have smiled their tight little smiles: the farm girl had really found her place in that swarm of cattle.

Being unfamiliar with geography, Joan did not question the itinerary. A terrific wind was blowing out of the east, making the standards flap enthusiastically. And Joan was unaware that Orléans was on the north bank of the Loire, while her column kept moving forward on the south. Then all of a sudden, as they made a broad circle through Olivet, in order to go unnoticed by the English sentries of Champ-

Privé, Les Augustins, and Saint-Jean-le-Blanc, Joan realized they had bypassed Orléans, were now beyond the city,
and thus were evading confrontation with the English.

What did this mean? She wanted to fight, and they were
keeping her from it. They were making her sidestep the
enemy instead of heading straight into him. When Dunois
came to greet her at the port of Le Bouchet—still on the
south bank—Joan gave vent to her first outburst, to be
followed by others in a regular stream. What was she here
for, anyway? Was that her mission, to escort livestock, on
the sly, unbeknownst to the enemy? Dunois did his best to
calm her, pointing out how invaluable she was for the
morale of the besieged, how his duty was to make sure the
convoy was not exposed to either attack or robbery, and
especially to make sure that she, the divine envoy, had an
uneventful journey. Very well—if that was how it had to
be.

Joan quieted down, even though she was sad and humiliated at having been deprived of a possible fight which
might have proven her invincibility without further delay.
Then her irritation was rekindled by a totally exasperating
new complication. She had expected to go straight to her
destination. The direction of the wind would have made no
difference in that case. But they had stupidly gotten themselves on the opposite shore upstream of Orléans by a good
half a league. Now the supplies had to be put on barges to
float down to the city, and the east wind that had blown all
day was keeping the barges at Orléans; they could move
upstream only by sailpower, and the gale wind had immobilized them. It was perplexing and nerve-racking.
Dunois talked to the Maid. To be sure, she was something,
this straight-from-the-shoulder fiery kid, neither stupid nor
prim. She had personality and power. An unusual little
dame, hard to handle, yet she would have to be handled,
like a little wild mare, with the bit between her teeth,

pulling on it. For Dunois had immediately understood the total discrepancy between the part she saw herself playing and the one they had allotted her. No question, she would try to turn everything upside down, listen to no one, do as she pleased, and set off on the very next day to get at the English. Why delay? Wait for what? I'm telling you that I have brought all the power of Heaven to the rescue. But the instructions he had received about Joan left no possibility for any mystical improvisation.

Surrounded by the gusts of the storm, and the stampings and other noises of animals and soldiers, Dunois was becoming upset and worried. There was trouble on the horizon; she was too impatient and would not hold still. And then, suddenly, unbelievably, the tornado subsided in two minutes—and resumed in the opposite direction. Nothing like it had ever been seen! The wind, which had been roaring in from the east, was now equally strong from the west. Just what they needed. A real miracle. Joan? Could it have been Joan who . . . ? Was there really communication between her and Him Who commanded the winds? Dunois, along with a great many others marooned there on the river bank, must have turned toward the girl in armor, with questions in their eyes. Twenty-five years later, the Bastard would not try to hide the fact that that perfectly timed atmospheric phenomenon, coming when least expected with the suddenness of a miracle right after Joan appeared, had made him stop and think.

The barges arrived, practically flying across the water, and the victuals and stock were loaded. When that was done, the escorting soldiers fell into their formation at their commander's order, and turned their backs to the Loire. What could they be thinking of? Joan, dumbfounded, asked Dunois, What was all this? Just what was scheduled, he replied. You were told it was only an escort, and nothing else, weren't you, Joan? Well, now it is heading back to its cantonment. Back to Blois, now that its assigned task is completed.

The Maid was speechless, choking. She had been had, swindled! So they were not, as she had been allowed to believe, the army that was to relieve Orléans? Monstrous rascality. Unutterable treachery. Was that how it was? She was losing her men? Well, then she would leave with them. And she would give the Dauphin a piece of her mind, or, if he tried to hide, his councillors would hear from her, the foul double-dealers. Did they expect her to go into Orléans alone, without the warriors she was leading, or was supposed to be leading? Those diplomats hadn't had a good look at her! What did they take her for? An imbecile? A toy? This time, it would be the real showdown—she was livid with anger.

Dunois, in the face of this cyclone, tried to stay calm. Tried to find something to say, to clear his sovereign, to admit nothing, since she had not yet understood. He repeated over and over again that this was none of his doing, she was unfair to take it out on him this way, he was only obeying (orders are orders!), and she, like a devoted servant, a good little soldier, ought to obey, too. Of course, they would be going after the English, without delay, and she would be in on it, she could count on that. As far as he was concerned, his duty, what the King had expressly told him to do, was to meet Joan at Orléans, where everyone was awaiting her in a fever of hope and joy. She could not let down all those good people who were dying to acclaim her.

Joan gave in to Dunois' entreaties on one condition: that he would bring back the soldiers they had taken from her, go after them at Blois, and bring them back. She had to have those men-at-arms, the archers, the lancers she had spoken to along the way, whose souls were so well prepared, if need be, to meeet their Maker. She would have it no other way. Either Dunois promised to get her mercenaries back, or she was leaving with them. Dunois promised; there was no alternative. And he asked himself what in the world he would tell the Council members to justify this request and the change in plans. The girl was irresistible. Call it an act of God?

Obviously, he would be accused of spineless acquiescence, lack of authority. Well, he'd like to see Regnault and the others try to stop that girl once she got started! The promise he had had to make her bothered him even more because he knew that Orléans would be less than hospitable to these additional mouths to feed. Gaucourt, the civil governor, had already shrugged at the idea of Joan and the dubious honor the court was doing him in sending him the Maid with her halo. He would certainly not be happy with the added complications the Bastard was bringing him through his absurd promise.

So her men were leaving. Joan shook her head as she watched them. Was she to go on to Orléans? It was nighttime now, and Dunois told her that her formal entrance would take place the next day. They crossed the Loire to sleep on the right bank, at the château of Reuilly, near Chécy. And the whole of the next day, April 29, until sundown, went by without the Bastard feeling that it was the right time for doing the two leagues (an hour's ride) from Chécy to Orléans. Why the delay? So that the English at the Saint-Loup strongpoint would not have the opportunity to seize Joan as she went by? Not at all. They were no threat, a mere handful. "In order to avoid the tumult of the crowd," was the way the official *Journal of the Siege* stated it. Let us be clear about that. There would be "tumult," all right, of the most lively kind, when Joan, who was so ardently expected, finally entered at the Burgundy Gate. But it was another kind of "tumult" that Dunois was worrying about, especially since he had found out so unambiguously what it was like to deal with an incandescent Joan. All she dreamt of was bumps and bruises. He could see only too clearly what might be likely to happen if he were to take Joan into Orléans in the morning or too early in the day. She would be perfectly capable of calling the populace to arms in defiance of all good sense and leading them against the English blockhouses in the west, the ones closest to the ramparts, or even against Les Tourelles. She was impetuous, mad for action, and drunk with her "divine" assurance. As illiterate in strategy as she was in tactics, she might head straight for death, offering the English the chance for their biggest carnage ever. So the top priority was for Dunois, with appropriate fabrications and assorted specious reasonings, to keep control over the fiery lass and protect the city and its people from the wondrous, but terrifying, manias of the "little saint." Dunois had thought he was getting a sweet, docile, little God-fearing girl, but instead he had "been issued," as the quartermaster might say, a bombshell.

In those days, there was no night fighting. So Joan would not go into Orléans until after dark on that Friday, April 29, 1429. One day's respite. And, about eight o'clock that night, there was the oft-described reception: bells tolling, trumpets blowing, crowds cheering, weeping with joy and shouting hosannas, kissing Joan's stirrups, hands grasping for anything they could touch on her armor, and Joan on her white horse, at the Bastard's right, saying thank you, and beaming with happiness.

The lodgings that had been prepared for the Maid were at the home of James Boucher, treasurer to the Duke of Orléans, the captive duke.

On Saturday, April 30, since Dunois was afraid to go to see Joan, she went to him. What was the plan? When would they attack? Louis of Coutes, the page, reported later that

once again he had seen her come back "very irritated."
Joan's first stay in Orléans, which lasted only a little more
than a week, was an almost uninterrupted bout of tremen-
dous tension for her.

The fact was, she never simmered down. She was all
storm and fury. She could not tolerate the fine gentlemen,
the "captains" who claimed to know more about things
than she. For they did not seem to understand that her
presence had changed everything, that their ways, their
plans, and their precautions were of no interest any longer,
made no sense. Everything was settled, the English were
done for, all that was required was a little shove, a solid one,
of course, but there was no doubt as to the outcome. God
had told her long ago that she was meant to crush the
English.[1]

Dunois, on that April 30, did his best to explain to her
that they could not yet attack. He certainly did not tell her
the King was not anxious for an attack, was even opposed
to it. He surely had not sent Joan to Orléans so that her
martial fantasies might compromise his undercover diplomatic maneuvers, which, all things considered, seemed to
be going quite well. They could not attack, Dunois said,
because they were outnumbered—and he kept on exaggerating the strength of the besiegers. But Joan refused
to listen. She kept trotting out her childish "divine in-
spirations": no matter how many Goddams there were,
they meant nothing, they would not hold up, inasmuch
as ... All right. They had heard it all before! Granted, there
was the matter of the wind that shifted, which Dunois
remembered well, and the radiance that emanated from

---

[1]Gustave Rudler saw this perfectly: "The week in Orléans was just one struggle,
short but violent, between the army commanders and Joan ... systematic opposition of the professionals to an outsider, ... contempt of noblemen for a girl of
no social standing whom they were quite willing to exploit, even as they excluded
her from their councils." (*Michelet historien de Jeanne d'Arc* [Presses Universitaires
de France, 1925], vol. II.)

Joan. But the wind had probably been a coincidence. And as for the girl's magnetism, well, anyone could see she had a kind of charm, in spite of her coarse features, in fact she was truly a charmer, but still facts and orders came first. And the orders were crystal clear: take no risks such as they had at Vouvray, and surely none such as at Verneuil. In other words: hold off any offensive for the time being.

But Joan kept at it. You claim we are outnumbered? (Apart from the sin of disbelief, how stupid can you be? Didn't you see all those hundreds of men in the streets last night, all excited and itching to fight?) Well, then, keep your promise. You gave your word, your word as a knight. Go on, go to Blois, quick, and bring back the real soldiers! Go ahead!

There was nothing for Dunois to do but give in again; he promised that he would leave for Blois no later than the next day, Sunday, May 1, and bring back the archers and lancers who had left two days before.

That April 30, Joan had twice gone out to the English blockhouses to try to get back the two messengers who had carried her letter to Suffolk and whom the English, not content with just not answering her, had taken prisoner, in defiance of all the laws of war.

Outside the fortification at Croix-Basset, she heard the Goddams call her men-at-arms "mackerels" (pimps), but she did not understand what they meant. Then when she went to Les Tourelles, where Suffolk was, she was charmingly addressed in French as "witch."[2] She was warned she would be roasted if ever they laid hands on her, and she had to flee from the cannonballs that rained around her. She

---

[2]Many of the English officers spoke French, for most of the English nobility were of French descent. Winchester's original family name was Beaufort, and Warwick, who was to turn up at Rouen, was named Richard de Beauchamp.

was indignant. Witch, indeed! She, a witch? She shouted back at them, "Liars! Liars!" and the mortars answered back.

Then followed three days of horrible inactivity. Military Governor Dunois had made her promise that she would be good, await the reinforcements quietly, and not stir up any trouble, and she was also under the scrutiny of Civil Governor Gaucourt, who had been warned about her. Her hands were tied, her mouth taped; that was the truth of it. The city fathers poured wine in honor of Joan and her team (d'Aulon, the two pages, and the monk Pasquerel): seven pints of wine at two *sous* apiece; and the next day they presented her with an allice-shad. It cost the city twenty *sols*, so it must have been a good-sized fish. But had Joan come to Orléans to feast on shad?

Wednesday, May 4,[3] the sentinels on the ramparts announced the approach of squadrons of cavalry as well as foot soldiers. At last! Dunois, Gilles de Rais, and Marshal de Saint-Sévère were bringing back the men who had been shamefully dismissed on the twenty-eighth. And Joan, to her displeasure, noted that this time they were not coming by the route they had made her take, but were arriving straight from Blois on the north bank, merely making a short half-circle around the city so as to enter through the only free gate, on the east. The Englishmen must have seen the approaching French column, but they had stayed quietly in their bunkers, without trying to stop it.

This time, Dunois took the initiative and went to Joan. He said he had to warn her, the Maid was to have no illusions. Even now, with these reinforcements, they were

---

[3]It is hard to work out exact concordance for the ensuing events from the various indications contained in the *Journal of the Siege*, John Chartier's *Chronicle*, and the testimony of 1456. These are only details, but a historian cannot imply that he knows facts precisely when such is not the case. I have given here as close an approximation as we can make out, but we cannot be sure of an exact sequence.

still not strong enough; it was imperative that they wait and be patient. What he did not add—probably on orders —was that His Majesty was in no hurry for the fighting to begin in earnest; on the contrary, he assured her that the King had agreed to send more troops soon.

The Bastard knew all too well what Joan's reaction would be. This beat everything; what he was telling her really was the crusher. First they sent away the soldiers that she, as "war commander," had brought to free Orléans. Then Dunois said, Of course, if we had them here . . . And he had gone after them, and brought them back, only to tell her—what? That it was still the same, they were still not strong enough, they could not think of trying to raise the siege, the English were still much too strong. This was black humor, and it was beyond all endurance. What about God, the God of Hosts, Who was only awaiting a small sign, a little bit of God-helps-those-who-help-themselves so He could unleash His mighty thunder and bring them victory? Did He count for nothing? Had God never sent any message at all, or was He being denied, disregarded, declared null and void? Joan wondered aloud to Dunois: Why all this messing about? Whom were they thumbing their noses at—her, the kingdom, or the Lord?

Dunois had determined in advance how he would parry that one. There was one thing his fiery friend, his fighting little saint, did not know, however nice, however ardently devoted to doing right she might be. That was the serious news he was bringing back from Blois: Captain Fastolf, the victor of Rouvray, was marching on Orléans, coming from Paris. He might arrive at any moment now. In such circumstances, even Joan herself would have to admit, the most elementary wisdom would be to keep a sharp eye out, husband their resources, watch for Fastolf's arrival, and then pounce on him suddenly, all together, the minute he was sighted on the plain.

At the first intimation of fighting, taking chances, setting an example, Joan became human again. Yes, if an English army were truly approaching, then that was something else. But look, this isn't any trickery, is it, Dunois? She didn't want him, on the pretext of sparing her, to wait and let her know too late, so that she would not be able to get to the battlefield until the fighting was over. Friendly once more, but still champing at the bit, Joan warned Dunois, quite disrespectfully, that if he played that kind of trick on her she would "have his head." Just like that! She was giving the orders now. What about the local authorities, and the captains? There was a pretty clear threat in the intentional overemphasis of her tone, despite the way she tried to make a joke of it all. Joan by now was well aware of the enormous prestige she enjoyed in Orléans. She knew the people were with her. And no one else had better forget it!

On the afternoon of May 4, Joan was napping in her room when she was awakened by a great noise from outside. Shouting, hoofbeats on the street, the tocsin ringing. Was it a sortie, a sudden attack by the defenders on the Saint-Loup blockhouse? Not likely. A sudden English foray? No, it was a weak position, and the rest of the enemy strong points were not joining in.

My feeling is that it must have been a spontaneous unprepared operation by civilians of Orléans, "whipped up" by Joan's presence in their city as well as the reinforcements that had arrived that morning. They were a group of fanatics who, grabbing whatever was at hand—axes, knives, pikes, iron bars, swords borrowed or stolen from soldiers—had hit the little bunker with an energy redoubled by the knowledge that it was not very strong. A cheap little victory, but something they would be able to brag about. The one sure thing we know is that on that midafternoon of the fourth, when Joan suddenly jumped up, she swore at her page Louis ("bloody fellow!") for having let her sleep while the fighting was going on, shouted as loud as she could for d'Aulon to come and put her armor on her, had herself hoisted onto her horse (in such a rush that she forgot her standard: young Louis quickly passed it out to her through the window), and tore off in the middle of the mob heading for the Burgundy Gate.

When she reached the Saint-Loup bunker, it was all over. The blockhouse had been taken and the victors were indulging in the usual massacre. Rank-and-file prisoners, mercenaries whose pay was their only fortune, so that they could not be exchanged for anything, were having their throats slit. Only the leaders were set aside, possible objects of ransom. Joan watched. It was war, and this was how war was waged. Later on, in June, at Jargeau, the Maid would kneel near a prisoner whose head had been split open by one of the guards and hold the fractured head on her knee, calling for a priest to administer extreme unction. But that happened when the regular butchery was already over and such after-battle brutality seemed scandalous to her.

There is no evidence that at Saint-Loup she tried to have anyone spared. She was delighted: this unexpected venture was encouraging, a good sign. It was only too bad that she had missed being in on the action because of Louis' negligence.

Thursday, May 5, 1429, was Ascension Day. On religious holidays, a truce was habitual. After completing her devotions, Joan tried one last time to get the English to release her two messengers. She made sure that she stayed a safe distance from Les Tourelles for this final effort and delivered her request attached to an arrow shot by an archer. She was offering a man-for-man exchange, for, as she said (seeing nothing amiss in this), the prisoners from Saint-

Loup the day before had not been "all killed." But the only response she got was a call of "whore" in a stentorian voice. "Witch" had revolted her. Now "whore" destroyed her, and right there on the shattered bridge, unable to control herself, she burst into tears.

That Thursday, after vespers, the captains held a council of war. She was not invited. Nevertheless, at the end of the meeting, Dunois insisted, out of kindness and thoughtfulness, as well as caution, that Joan be asked to sit in with them for a moment, so as to be filled in on their plans, even if these had to be exaggerated a little in order to keep her happy. Several of them opposed the idea, saying she would be out of her element in dealing with military planning. The Sire of Gamaches was extremely vulgar in referring to her as "a girl from who knows where, who has been God knows what," most likely a sly allusion to Joan's brief service the year before at the Redhead's. There had been some gossip about that. However, Dunois did get the support of a few of those present, and Joan was sent for.

She was given a more or less honest "briefing," which she listened to with growing agitation. "She paced back and forth without sitting down," John Chartier reported. Convinced that they were lying to her—which was not wrong—and that they were keeping the real, no doubt meaningless, decisions from her, Joan finally burst out, "You want to hide your intentions from me? Well, I won't tell you what I intend to do either. But you'll see it, you'll be aware of it soon enough! You and your Council! *I have my own counsel* [meaning her voices]. And it is a good deal better than yours!"

They separated on an icy note, and no one had to warn Gaucourt that it would be a good idea to keep an eye out for anything impulsive or wild the crazy wench might be planning to try.

Yet the governor would still be caught short. Friday,

May 6, at dawn, Joan ordered her page Louis to blow his "buglet" in the street. She was already in the saddle and in armor. People came running—those who had taken part in the Saint-Loup affair two days before, and others who had been inspired by it. We will do the job ourselves, Joan told them, and they all rushed toward the only exit, the Burgundy Gate. The huge portal with its crossbeams was closed; and the guards had orders not to open it except on formal command from the authorities.

The governor came rushing up, with a squad of men. The way was barred, he said; absolutely no thoroughfare.

The way was barred, was it? Well, they'd see about that!

And Simon Charles, recounting what the governor himself told him, wrote that Joan lost control of herself to the point of calling Gaucourt *mauvais homme* (wicked man), which might today more truly approximate *salaud* (son of a bitch). I really thought, Gaucourt added, that she was going to have me cut to pieces. It was revolt, insurrection. An awful brawl. The governor was overwhelmed. The mob removed the beams, pulled back the bolts and pried off the huge lock with crowbars. And the stream of humanity flowed through, toward the Loire. Joan intended to seize Saint-Jean-le-Blanc, first of the English strong points upstream, by way of the Île-aux-Boeufs and the Île-aux-Toiles, and then storm the monastery of the Augustinian friars (Les Augustins), next to Les Tourelles, which the besiegers had turned into a fortress.

It took some time to cross the Loire, and the regular captains were frantic. To try to stop Joan's drive was inconceivable, with such a mob of overcharged men behind her. All they could do was fall in with her charge, perhaps organize it a little, and do their best at least to keep it from turning into a catastrophe. This was no longer a minor operation, the kind of ten-against-one no-risk fight there had been on the fourth at Saint-Loup. This was the major battle joined, the real breakthrough, direct, barbaric, without any preparation whatsoever, none of those elementary precautions that professionals understood so well: diversions, feints, with breathing spaces provided, movements to be executed, forces held in reserve. It was sheer sabotage, a mess, madness—in a word, just what might be expected from a brainless girl who believed that fervor was the answer to everything.

The English at Saint-Jean-le-Blanc, seeing the mob of madmen rushing at them, fell back toward Les Augustins. Joan now had the captains around her. They probably refrained from saying I-told-you-so, for they had succeeded in whipping the attacking force into a somewhat less shapeless mass. (I would imagine that by now civilians were no longer so prominent in it.) Once launched on this improvised assault, the best thing to do was give in, and carry it out as honorably as possible. But now there was a problem. The Augustinian monastery was a difficult position, and the English within it were defending themselves like devils. Men were falling, and no progress was being made. After several hours of futile struggle, the sun started to set and the captains urged Joan to give it up. But her courage did not flag. Hoarse and sweating, she still did not personally stop fighting, at the foot of the walls, among her men, amid the hail of arrows and cannonballs. The captains tried to reason with her, saying there was no further hope today, the men were dying in vain, and it was time to fall back across the river. The tacit looks they exchanged and the meaningful expressions on their faces confirmed their unanimity on this.

Where was the Maid's "God of Hosts" now that she needed Him? He should have been there from the start, to settle things at the first unsheathing of a sword, according to the understanding Joan had with Him. But there was no evidence of His presence. They had done their best, ripped holes in their forces, but still there was no trace of divine intervention. They were only thinking these things, not saying them, but Joan heard them as loud as if they had been dinning in her ears. She no longer looked so confident. Her eyes were downcast. She could not understand. Something had failed to work. But what? She had done everything she could.

Then, as they were folding back, limping, depressed, the English suddenly committed an unspeakable blunder. There was her divine manifestation, after all! The idiots, the asses—they had been fully sheltered behind their impregnable fortifications, and now they were coming out as if the field belonged to them. They seemed to think the Armagnacs were at their mercy because they were pulling back, that all they had to do now was to wipe them out. Long live God! Open-field combat, what luck! The Goddams no longer had a chance! La Hire knew that, too. His cavalry swung around. Joan and La Hire set the pace, followed by the charging squadrons. The English suddenly collapsed, caved in. In a few minutes, their Augustinian fortress had been taken.

Joan was back into her own; she had known victory was certain, all right, known it could not fail.

They spent the night in the newly-won position, at the foot of Les Tourelles, which Joan had decided to capture the next day. And that, indeed, was what they would do, although not without opposition. Joan would be wounded during the engagement; a whirling quarrel from a crossbow would bore into her flesh, between neck and shoulder. Knocked to the ground, she disdained the magical treatments the soldiers carried as first aid: parchments with hieroglyphics that were supposed to perform miracles when applied to a wound. Miracles of that kind smelled of sulphur, and Joan was not having any part of them. She was no believer in witches! She would have only classical medical treatment, with oil and fat. Besides, she was not all that unhappy at the wound; it was rather welcome, in fact, for back at Chinon she had categorically foretold that she would be wounded outside Orléans. This proved it! Did they think she didn't know what she was talking about? And there is proof positive that Joan made such a prediction, in the Giustiniani correspondence, a letter written from Lyons in April—and she was not wounded until May 7.

Her wound dressed, the Maid, in pain, retired for a moment "to a vineyard," out of range of the battle, to pray; but not for long, "half of a quarter-hour," in Dunois' words. Then she rushed back toward her men, in the smoke, and with her good hand raised her standard, shouting, "Charge! Charge! *It is all ours!*"

And at Glasdale (who, she was assured, had himself been the one who called her "whore"), " 'Render, 'render, Glassidas!"

They forced their way into the towers. The English leaders tried to escape over the bridge, where a makeshift crossover had been rebuilt, but the defenders of Orléans sent an incendiary barge beneath it, loaded with inflammable waste, old bones, and pitch. The planks caught fire and Glasdale was dumped into the Loire, along with more than twenty others. This, according to the *Journal of the Siege*, was an unhappy accident for the besieged who, "by ransoming them, might have come by great finance," and had already started counting the gold ducats they had expected to collect for the captured Goddams.

That was on Saturday, May 7, 1429. Capturing Les Tourelles was a splendid thing, a big step forward; but there were still the forces occupying the other six blockhouses, to the west and north, who had done nothing in the last two days and constituted an untapped enemy reserve of at least two to three thousand men.

Sunday morning, May 8, all of Orléans was up on the ramparts to watch the final encounter. Fastolf was nowhere to be seen. He had not even left Paris yet, and Dunois must have been well aware of this, even when he fed that rumor to Joan a few days before as a tranquilizer.

The English took up battle formation. The whole Armagnac army was facing them, with Joan in the forefront clad in a coat of mail, since her bandaged shoulder made it impossible to put on plate armor. Silence. Everyone held his breath. Then they heard the Goddam officers in the other camp start barking commands. Right about face! Could it be? Yes, it was! Absolutely!

This was it. The English were backing away. They admitted being outclassed. They were taking to their heels, raising the siege. They had been there seven months, and now in three days they had been persuaded to run. Who persuaded them? The captains? None of them would dare claim that. Joan, the little girl, had accomplished it, with her insubordination, her mad confidence, her furious determination. And as every bell in the city joined in tolling exultingly, as people hugged each other (it's over! we're saved!), the captains in their amazement looked askance at Joan. Intoxicated and serene, she was mumbling bits of prayers as she sat erect in her coat of mail, one shoulder thicker than the other.

V

Interval: The Cooling-Off Starts

❖ ❖ ❖

Was the King deliriously happy? Did Charles VII shower
Joan with blessings in grateful delight?

Quite the contrary. The Dauphin in all probability had
not especially appreciated Joan's caprice in forcing the Bastard into a deal. Nor had he been elated that she refused to
assume the position intended for her: the saint in her niche,
the visionary deep in prayer, bolstering the morale of all
Orléans with her tales of apparitions and the assurances
vouchsafed her by Heaven of His Majesty's brilliant future.
True, she had been given armor, but only because, if combat had to begin, she would unavoidably have to be allowed
to fight—but then, of course, only in the ranks. Submissive,
obedient, especially never challenging the captains in the
conduct of operations.

But she had kicked over the traces, refused her place in
the doghouse, insolently usurped functions she had no
right to, and led the whole affair as she saw fit, at breakneck
speed. One couldn't make head nor tail of it. What would
Philip think? This girl upset everything, respected noth-

ing, trampled around in the temporal sphere, when she was supposed to stick to her domain, the spiritual. And now, just because she had been lucky enough to pull it off, through a concurrence of circumstances due in great part to English passivity, inertia, and lack of daring, because she had made one hell of a big noise, people had eyes only for her. She was being vaunted to the skies!

We can readily assume that there were plenty within the Council who tried to open the sovereign's eyes, to "make a believer of him," concerning the excessive acclaim for his little helper, whom they had been foolish enough to let him take on. The city of Orléans, these days, was just waiting for him to come share its exaltation. Well, let it wait! Charles had no desire to go to Orléans and find that Joan was more popular there than he was.

In the circular the King sent to all his "good cities" on May 10, Joan's role was reduced to a minimum in the liberation of Orléans: the whole thing—a "marvel," to be sure— was credited to the royal armies and their generals under their master's directives. There was one incidental mention, to cover the obligation, of the Maid,[1] who "was always present in person at the execution of all these operations." She "was present"—implying watching, approving. The words were carefully chosen so as not to say, yet not flatly deny, that Joan had had any active participation in the events. She "was present" and that was all the inhabitants of the kingdom needed to know.

Simon Charles related, at the time of her later rehabilitation, that after lifting the siege at Orléans Joan joined the

---

[1] This mention of "the Maid" without further elucidation would seem to establish clearly that there had been some prior circular, no doubt presenting Joan as a divine helper who had suddenly appeared, proof that Heaven was on the side of the King. But no evidence of that document has ever been uncovered.

King at Loches, where it seems she stayed from May 11 to May 23, and the sovereign strongly urged her "to rest." In other words, he was asking her to hold her peace, to be good enough to stop mixing into things. If we need you, we'll call you, don't call us.

I am overcome with admiration for those who write that the chronology of Joan's activities in 1429, after Blois at least, is so clear to us. Truth to tell, her schedule remains obscure at the very least, and for the specific period from May 8 to the Loire campaign, undertaken on June 10, it is quite impossible to follow Joan closely. According to one German document (how dependable, we do not know), she stayed with the King in Loches (doing what?) until May 23. And then? A letter by Guy of Laval places her at Selles-en-Berry on June 6, preparing to leave on that day for Romorantin. But what was she doing at Selles, and why was she going to Romorantin? There is nothing specific about her activities between May 23 and June 6. However, there are a few clues to her actions and her attitudes at the end of this spring of 1429.

First of all, there was the sumptuous dress that the Duke of Orléans had ordered be given her. His English "gaolers" were as considerate as they could be of him, and he was allowed to correspond freely with his treasurer. The latter ordered for Joan "two ells of fine vermilion [crimson] Brussels [lace]" and "another of lost [dark] green fabric" for a short coat or mantle. So, the Maid did not always dress in men's clothing? Joan must have worn this magnificent garment at least once to honor its donor, quite a change from the shabby red dress she had worn to Vaucouleurs. And now that she was received at Court, she must have been quite gratified to appear different than a little black-and-gray pageboy.

When Guy of Laval met her at Selles-en-Berry, she was in her cuirass. She had a sense of social propriety. She had "wine brought" for my enjoyment, the young man told his mother, and Joan let him know she had made a gift of a small gold ring to the widow of the great Du Guesclin (young Guy's grandmother). A gold ring, even a small one? Joan, it would seem, now had the means to give presents. The King had not neglected to compensate her for the services rendered, and after all, she did have to support the members of her "household"—her steward, her chaplain, and the two pages.

Laval noted that when on horseback she held "a small axe" in her hand; a, ceremonial axe, a sort of marshal's baton. She liked fine armament as well as fine horses: *in equo et in armorum pulchritudine complacet*, Perceval de Boulainvilliers noted; *complacet*, she took pleasure in them.

Her brothers had appeared upon the scene. Laval, on June 8, noted that her "brother" had been there for several days. Just one brother, not three? The account books of the city of Orléans reveal that the municipality laid out "72 *sols* for three pairs of gaiters and three pairs of shoes for the Maid's brothers," which would indeed seem to indicate the presence of all three; and the same registers also later made note of four *livres* allocated to John, the middle brother, "to help him to live and maintain his station," that station, of course, being that of a gentleman-brother. All of which sounds a good deal like living off sister Joan. Obviously, the family had gotten over its anger at *la Jeannette*. She no longer put them to shame. See how well she had turned out, in fact! How could they help but rush to her, as fast as possible, to congratulate her on her success?

Quicherat, in the very remarkable *Aperçus* he published in 1850, smilingly suggests that there was some "bombast" about her, and Gerson, in his friendly account of her, indulgently avers that she had a bit of the "gift of gab." She knew how to give orders. "You, priests, go and organize processions," was her response, from the height of her charger, to the clergy of Selles who had come to the porch of the church to do her honor. She was authoritative and sure of herself. On that June 6, she had firmly extended a future invitation to young Laval to come and drink an even better wine with her "in Paris," where she promised she would pour it herself.

A lot had happened to her in the past three months. She had risen prodigiously and her station in life had undergone a spectacular metamorphosis: she had gone from the distaff to the sword, from the mud of the fields to the carpetry of royal mansions, from the patching of old clothes to raiment valued at thirteen pieces of gold. It would not be surprising if she were impressed with herself, if it had gone to her head somewhat. All those people in the streets venerating her, kneeling before her, staring open-mouthed at her as if she were an angel, and the women bringing medallions and rosaries for her to touch, as if to make them miraculous by her contact. Regnault of Chartres, in his bittersweet way, asked whether all the adoration surrounding her were not a danger to her Christian humility. And she ingenuously answered, yes, it was a danger, and if God did not continuously help her to keep a hold on herself, to remember she was but a fragile instrument in His hand, she might indeed be exposed to the perils of pride. But the archbishop need not worry; she was not going to become bigheaded or arrogant. She told her hostess, La Touroulde, with her good girlish laugh, "Go ahead, touch the medallions yourself. It'll do just as much good."

Wherever she was, she would ask what time the children's mass was celebrated. For it was among little children that she felt happiest. And when she was reproachfully told that she, who was now a member of Court, should not gladly suffer the presence of beggars, of ragged hangers-on, of ne'er-do-wells, she answered that they did not bother her, but rather that she felt at home among these poor people, for "she had been sent for the consolation of the wretched."

However, she was losing precious time, for the King was letting the days roll by, doing nothing. The freeing of Orléans, as he well knew, was only a prelude for Joan. The important thing, the principal object for which God had delegated her, was his coronation.

D'Alençon and a few others had suggested that Charles strike while the iron was hot. The English were retreating, demoralized; this was the time to launch an offensive against Normandy, cut them off from Paris, and throw them into the sea. The King was not unaware of d'Alençon's personal interest in returning to his domains, but he was not ready to countenance anything as vast as a military expedition toward Rouen. The English had suffered a setback, true; but nothing more. They were not crushed as Charles VII had been only five years before at Verneuil. He could not easily forget that!

The intelligence was clear: Fastolf's reinforcements would arrive sooner or later to strengthen the adversary. It would be pure madness to try an attack on Normandy now. Rouen was very far away; the distance from the Loire to Rouen was immense, the risks incalculable. As for Paris, which Joan dreamt about (thinking she was already there, the foolish girl!), Burgundy had been holding it for eleven years and Philip certainly enjoyed boasting about that. Orléans, well and good: Philip could not care less. There, he was even willing to let his allies down. But Paris! That was something else again. Just the suggestion of retaking the capital meant setting the Duke of Burgundy solidly against you. Any threatening gesture toward Paris was to be avoided like the plague. Especially now when Philip seemed to be turning reasonable.

There is a letter by Giustiniani, written from Bruges, in which that trader, fully cognizant of how the business of state affected business itself, whispered that Philip, as over-lord of Bruges, took subtle delight in the news coming from the Loire: "It is to his interest that the English be beaten a little." Just a little. Not too much. Philip had no desire to see England control all of France, but neither did he want a Charles VII without an English thorn in his foot. It was to his advantage that both sides have such problems as would make them consider him; then he could lean toward the highest bidder.

Charles VII therefore concluded that it was best to do nothing that might irritate his cousin, nothing to imply that with its success at Orléans the Court at Bourges had turned aggressive toward him. Maintaining the proper atti-tude was essential: esteem, consideration, no animosity, a program of both dignity and prudence, ready to extend a hand.

Joan could not bear the inaction that enveloped the King. (The inaction was only apparent, for the chancellery was busy, from morning till night, with discussions about the major issue—relations with Burgundy.) She kept pestering, harassing a King already disquieted by the boundless and truly irksome celebrity of this "Maid." The Duchess of Milan was begging Joan to help her reconquer her do-mains. The Count of Armagnac wanted her to inform him as to which was the true Pope. (He, for one, had never given in to the decisions of Constance; he had held out to the end with Benedict XIII in his Spanish retreat, and was still supporting his successor, Clement VIII.) And the *capi-touls* or consuls of Toulouse, with serious money troubles, were asking Joan to favor them with her financial advice! And now old Christine de Pisan was writing poems com-paring her to Judith, Esther, and Deborah, while Alain Chartier, equally extravagant in an epic vein, placed her alongside Hector, Alexander, and Hannibal!

Who was this girl, anyway? That was what the King wondered, whenever he thought of her, and I would not be surprised if most often he preferred thinking of something else. In 1456, Dunois was to tell how on one day in May, 1429, at Loches, Joan had gone to implore Charles VII to delay no longer, but to leave for Reims just as soon as possible. Christophe de Harcourt, who was also there, as were the Sire of Trier and His Majesty's confessor, Gérard Machet, Bishop of Castres, asked Joan, as she kept talking about "her counsel," to tell them "how he [the counsel] acted when he spoke to her." The King also insisted she try and describe it to them. Joan "blushed," Dunois reported, for she did not like doing what she was asked to do; it was a sort of violation. But the King was the King. His request was a command. So Joan complied, and explained: "When there was a problem, because they were not willing to rely on what God had told her [which was just what was happening, at the time], she went off by herself and prayed to God, complaining to Him that those she spoke to did not readily believe her," and that was when a voice answered her, "Go! Daughter of God, go!" And a "great joy" filled her, so that "she wished she might always be in that state." And, upon saying this, she totally forgot where she was, and acted as if she were alone in her room or at chapel, caught up and possessed by the Spirit, her heart gone wild.

Anatole France, in our time, applauded her for being an actress capable of turning on such made-to-order ecstasies. I am not sure the four men there were as cynical about it as he. I rather see them fixedly watching Joan get up, panting and bothered: and they were deeply impressed.

Since the Maid was so anxious to get into action, there might still be a way to put her to use profitably, and without danger, provided she were more considerate of the captains than she had been at Orléans.

The English were no longer besieging the city, but they were still nearby, at Jargeau, Meung, and Beaugency. If it were decided—and this plan was still in the *if* stage—to go to Reims for the coronation, the first order of business would be to clear the road, even though from the Berry to Reims it did not go directly through towns strongly garrisoned by the Goddams. Just the same, if the King were to go toward the Champagne country, it would be better not to leave any of the enemy so near his châteaus. Joan was happy. Finally, the kind of work she enjoyed. D'Alençon would be the one in charge of the military end of these minor operations, and Joan got along well with him. The whole thing would be over in about a week, and it would go smoothly, for there was no misunderstanding this time: Joan was authorized to go into battle. Great!

At Jargeau, on June 11, when she saw the captains reluctant to launch the attack—the French were so few, and the English defenses looked so solid—she got angry again: Don't forget that I am here! And you know Who is with me! Don't you remember what happened at Les Augustins and Les Tourelles? You can be sure that I would have stayed home in Domrémy if I were not certain of victory.

That was how they took Jargeau, with Joan in the forward line. As she was climbing a ladder up the rampart, she was hit on the helmet by a rock, knocked over, thrown to the ground, but fortunately not from very high up. Even though she was stunned, she jumped right back into the fray. How could her mercenaries do any less than this heroic little woman? Joan was a tinderbox; she kindled the courage of all about her. And they captured a pretty prize at Jargeau: no less than Suffolk in person. That was more like it!

They spent the twelfth and thirteenth at Orléans, amid

parades, ovations, receptions. Then, for the two down-stream strong points. They took Meung in a walk: the English fled toward Beaugency. And they parleyed there, against Joan's advice, for she wanted to fight it out. The English garrison was allowed to withdraw freely. D'Alençon knew how much the King preferred negotiated settlements to battles. However, this retreat on the part of the English was only a ruse. They knew that Fastolf had left Paris at the head of about fifteen hundred men, and that he was only a couple of days' march from the Loire. The French did not demand their surrender; as long as they abandoned their position, that was all Charles VII wanted. But they were withdrawing only so as to join their relief forces. It was some joke they played on the Armagnacs, who realized it almost as soon as the English were out of sight: their runners announced the impending arrival of Fastolf.

At the same time (June 17) there was another surprise, a ghost out of the past. Not just any ghost, but Richemont, the High Constable, who had gone over to the English in his fury at seeing La Trémoille supplant him at Court. Now he came back without warning, suddenly friendlier than ever, bringing along four hundred horsemen and eight hundred bowmen. D'Alençon was in a quandary. The King detested Richemont. To welcome the Constable openly would be treason to the King; grounds for immediate dismissal, if not worse. And the commanding general could not help but remember certain rumors about leathern wineskins and drownings. This required careful handling! Joan, in her usual innocence, jumped for joy. All those men from Brittany, just when they were needed, in the nick of time, one might say, the very eve of a hard fight. Another sign of divine intervention. Blessed be the good Master of Heaven!

As she radiantly exulted to d'Alençon about the great

stroke of luck this was, she was amazed to hear him reply, "If Richemont is taken back, I shall resign!"

Oh, fine! Just when what they needed most was that extra little push for the next day. And Richemont was being so self-effacing it was touching. He asked for nothing. He knew the King, who had been misinformed, bore him a grudge. But here he was, offering his services anyway, his and those of his twelve hundred soldiers for the imminent set-to with the English. If, afterwards, he were to be sent away again, well, he would not complain; he would go back home to Brittany. But at least let him take part in the action, let him show with his blood that the King's cause was his own. D'Alençon would not hear of it. To have him at his side, never! If, however, Richemont were to take up some isolated position in the rear, independently, that would be his own business. There was some sly machination behind that. Richemont was being scorned, cast aside, yet held in reserve, without his being told so, available for some key role, if needed.

On June 17, Joan made another scene, and it must have been rather extreme, as she was punished for it. Where was she to go into battle? Back in the rear, alongside the outcast. What fireworks, what shouting there must have been until she was finally told to take it or leave it. Boiling on the inside, she champed at the bit. And yet this foray turned out to be the battle of Patay, with its well-known outcome: the English set a trap, but it did not work; exposed, caught short, they mistook a wheeling maneuver of their cavalry for a hasty retreat, broke ranks, and were chopped to bits; it was a real debacle. And now Talbot, after Suffolk, was taken prisoner. The French had "avenged" Agincourt.

This time, it was a great event; by comparison, the skirmish at Orléans the month previous was nothing. Yet Joan, alas, had had no part in this victory, though she had been deliriously convinced of it. How happy and vibrant she had been the day before, until her falling-out with d'Alençon! When the assembled captains expressed doubts about the outcome and put on long faces, she had announced to them, in that volcanic hyperbole so typical of her, "Were those Goddams hanging from the clouds, we would beat them! Beat them we will!"

There was a follow-up to the Richemont episode.

Joan committed a real *faux pas*. She could not get it through her head that politics was not her domain, that she was strictly forbidden from mixing into it. She did mix in. She went straight to the King to plead Richemont's cause. But where did she do this? At Sully, at La Trémoille's, where Charles was staying. A major mistake, a really bad one. The King himself, it seems, let her know it right off. In Perceval de Cagny's account: "Sorely grieved, Joan departed Sully, and took to the fields." Cagny's version of it was that she was sulking because there had as yet been no decision to go to Reims. I rather think she had not been precisely dismissed, but told not to mix into what was none of her business—and therefore she dismissed herself, hurt to the quick.

The King deplored this all too obvious rupture, which was not desirable at this point. The Maid had to be catered to because of her enormous popularity. It would not do to allow rumors to spread about a falling-out between the sovereign and the one who had brought him divine endorsement. Joan's favor at Court, never more than partial, conditional, one of sufferance, and bitterly contested by many other courtiers, had dropped yet another notch. However, at the same time, it was well known that the English thought she was a demon incarnate. They felt the King of Bourges had a secret weapon, a terribly dangerous one, in this girl. The funny part was, they were giving *her* all the credit for their disaster at Patay.

This was obviously no time to let on that Joan had broken with her employer, or even that things were not well between them. Not now, when an anonymous Burgundian clergyman, known in later times only as "The Bourgeois of Paris," was writing in his *Diary* that the Armagnacs for some time had had a strange new aide: "A creature in female form, but what it is exactly, God alone knows!" Not now, when Bedford, in a report to his King (meaning his fellow Council members), would be openly admitting within the month that "all things had prospered [for the English] until the siege of Orléans," that is, until the appearance, beside the so-called Charles VII, of "that disciple and hound-dog of the Evil One, known as the Maid."

So there was a reconciliation with Joan. She was recalled to Sully, and since she appeared to have a penchant for politics, the King kept her happy by asking her assistance in that sphere. He wanted her to write a letter to Philip. Yes, they would be going to Reims, and she could be the one to invite the Duke, in her own hand, to attend the coronation.

To Joan, relations with Burgundy were not something to be settled by diplomacy; rather, armed constraint was what was called for, in her simplistic view. But since the King had finally decided on the great religious gesture which she was there to make possible, and since she was back in Charles' good graces and he was smiling upon her again, well, so be it. She would write the letter to Philip, unseemly though it appeared to her, and make it sweet and polite as His Majesty wished.

But then, Joan would make up for it by sending news in her own fashion to the super-loyal population of Tournai, on June 25, 1429: "The Maid informs you that in a week she drove the English out of all the positions they had held on the River Loire." She did, did she? The Maid, all by herself?

If d'Alençon and his lieutenants saw this missive, they must have smiled wryly and arched their eyebrows. What a girl! Not one to slight herself. She awarded all the laurels to herself alone. But then, they knew that in so stating matters she was really giving all the honors to her God.

V I

Reims: Joan in Decline

The coronation did not mean the same thing at all to Joan as it did to the King and his Council. Joan was a believer. She believed in old ideas about the power of princes, the ones in the minds of simple people, which the VIPs for the most part had long since outgrown. Namely, that no one here on earth, in himself, held any power over others, that God alone was master, He alone had the right to command. The right to give orders was granted to some—heads of kingdoms foremost among them—only for the common good. This was a delegated right they held. Their kingdoms were only "commended" to them (from the Latin *commendare*, to entrust).

God entrusted to each of them the duty of carrying out His will in a given canton of the world. The sole legitimization of the reigning prince resided in the duty he assumed in being "the bailiff" of Heaven, and what Heaven wanted was happiness for all. As long as the heir to a throne had not made his solemn pledge on this account, he could not yet be "the King"—and therefore the coronation was actually a consecration. Which was why (however displeasing, however shocking to those around her) Joan obstinately continued to see Charles VII as only "the Dauphin." To her, he would become Charles VII, King of France in full, only when he had received the holy unction at Reims. And he could only deserve and obtain such unction, such anointment, after he had publicly declared that this was indeed how he saw his function: to be the Lord's *chargé d'affaires* on earth, serving the common good. Joan had used those very words to tell "the Dauphin" that he "had to give his kingdom to the King of the Heavens."[1]

Joan was behind the times. She still believed in Santa Claus. Realists perceived the King's coronation in an entirely different light. Where she saw it as an offering, they saw it as an annexation. She wanted the Dauphin to pledge his heritage to God, swearing that he received this power with the sole aim of doing good, for all, according to the law of Heaven. The realists, on the other hand, felt that through coronation the King was officially adding God's power to his own. The King as a "servant" of God? Just a minute. God was the one the King would be able to put into his own service through the consecration. Certainly the point was "divine right"; the King ruled "by divine right." But where Joan viewed that right as the definition of the reign and of the intentions that limited and justified it, the Royal Chancellery saw it as the authentication of absolutism. Thanks to the consecration, the King became as God; when he commanded, whatever it might be, it was God's command; having received consecration, he was

---

[1]Father Congar (*op. cit.*, pp. 282, 292, 295) recalls the doctrine of the Church concerning the temporal power: "Governments ruled by kings were also meant to lead men to their salvation. . . . Kings had a formal Christian function . . . a veritable ministry. . . . Their power itself was but as a vicarate of the supreme royalty of Christ and the presence of God at the heart of the world. . . ." Consecration, which "confirmed the authority of the [ruling] power," was "the public and liturgical sanction of this condition of kings."

himself consecrated, indeed sacred, sacrosanct, and to be obeyed exactly as God was. Such, in the minds of those sages, were the benefits to be derived from going through the ecclesiastical motions and other prepossessing pretenses. Fortunately, there were still huge multitudes ready to prostrate themselves before the stoles, croziers, and miters. And consecration was a useful business, an eminently profitable operation for achieving the submission of those multitudes, the "people," at whose expense the rulers could be kept in luxury. The priests gave the sovereign celestial warranty, a divine stamp of authenticity, the incontestable and supreme certification of worth.

That was what motivated the actions of the Council, which had never been basically unreceptive to Joan's insistence on the importance of the coronation. Her fixation could be a good idea; her plan could be excellent if revised and updated, naturally, adapted for maximum yield. That would still be the reason why in our own century the atheistic royalist pamphleteer Charles Maurras would shower praise on her. What perception! She had remarkable political acumen, that Maid. She was far from stupid! In fact, she was astonishingly shrewd.

Yet there are tributes that turn out to be insults. In truth, Joan's uncomplicated conception of authority bore a curious similarity to the one Rousseau later would develop and Robespierre try to put into effect. So before some people could praise Joan for her urgent call for the consecration, her image had to be distorted. And if Maurras' forerunners in her day finally urged the King to go to Reims, it was because they believed that it was not a bad idea, all things considered: Henry VI, the baby who was actually King of London and Paris, and who, by the agreement of Charles VI, was "King of France and England," had still not achieved consecration at the hands of his English masters. So it would be a good idea to pull the rug out from under them. After the physical victory at Patay, this could be a meaningful moral victory.

Had Philip of Burgundy objected, none of it would have been possible. In principle, Reims was under Anglo-Burgundian control, and to get from Gien to Reims, one had to cross a zone that was at least theoretically "occupied." Philip could very easily have advised Charles that, should the "Dauphin" presume to go to Reims, the way would be barred by Burgundy's powerful battalions.

But Philip sent no such word to the King of Bourges. The English defeat at Patay had increased his inclination to put more space between himself and Bedford. He did not answer Joan's letter. Attend the coronation? He would not dream of it. That would be an insult to his great ally. But rather, Philip's attitude would be to present no obstacle, affect disdain, as if Charles' little byplay at Reims were of no consequence, a wasted effort unworthy of attention. Be nice to the cousin who seemed to be sailing with the wind for the past two months, but at the same time, do nothing that could turn Bedford against him. At worst, just worry Bedford a little; in a word, make him feel that maybe he ought to be a little more considerate of Philip.

On June 29, 1429, the royal cortege left Gien. Did it include an army? Yes, but Charles VII felt assured he would never have to use it. La Trémoille had warranted to him that Philip would not send any mercenaries out against him, and this assurance was what made the "Dauphin" decide on the expedition. The English had been badly mauled; he would not be venturing close to where they were, so they presented no great threat. There would be time to complete the ceremony in peace before they healed their wounds and raised some new forces. But what if Philip were to change his mind? What if he were to bare his teeth suddenly, because Bedford forced him to through some threat to Flanders? Suppose, without warning, he turned nasty overnight, because it proved to be in his interest?

Auxerre was the first city on Charles' itinerary. Here he might face the first test, judge what power he still held over the local authorities and how people accepted him in his role as true King, though he ruled only at Bourges, as against the false King, who held Paris. He moved toward Auxerre on tiptoe. While Joan was radiant, self-assured, flying her banner high, Charles, though trying to throw his chest out, was really terrified within, taut, sneaking glances to left and right, ready at a moment's notice to look quickly to the rear if need be. He would have liked to give the impression of a victorious sovereign returning home, but the army protecting him was in fact just a precautionary caravan, not a triumphal legion. He prayed to fate that he would not have to commit his men to dubious battle.

Auxerre, July 1. The city was "Burgundian"; it did not open its arms to him as the royal traveler had hoped. But while the city fathers did not proclaim their fealty to him, they did not defy him either. They did not make a stand; in fact, they even allowed that, when the time came . . . With a candid lack of shame, they simply stated that they were waiting to see which way the wind blew, that they would pattern their behavior on the model that would be given them a few days hence by their counterparts at Troyes and Châlons-sur-Marne as they faced this approaching pilgrim. If those towns accepted Charles with open arms, Auxerre would also send pledges of its adherence. Charles VII did not stand on ceremony. Full of understanding, he put himself in their place. He was big about it, a real prince. And besides, while the municipality did not open the gates or countenance the idea of Charles' army entering the city, it did not rudely ask the "King" to vacate the premises, or go to the devil. It would never dream of being so discourteous. It offered no resistance to the quartermaster's acquisition of supplies for his troops; as long as payment was in cash, of course. It was a seller-to-buyer deal, not friend-to-friend. And being a supplier in no way made you an accomplice.

In sum, the stop at Auxerre, without being a success, was not a discouraging failure, either. It was a semi-success, which seemed a pretty good omen.

Now, Troyes. This was the knot that would probably not be easy to unravel; failure to untie it might mean the end. And Charles was determined to "untie" it, not to cut through it. Troyes was a city closely allied to the other side, what with the celebrations that had accompanied the signing there of the awful Franco-English treaty in 1420 under which the Dauphin was repudiated, relegated to outer darkness. That was why the people of Troyes had been so mistrustful and barricaded themselves. Terror filled them with the hostility of the guilty.

Charles, however, was overflowing with good will. Any idea of vengeance would thwart his plans, which prescribed sweetness and persuasion. Once more he turned to Joan for epistolary assistance. He wanted her to write to the city fathers of Troyes. Certainly they would have heard of her. Even though the attempt made with Philip did not seem to have yielded any tangible result, perhaps she would be more successful with these good people who were overcome with terror. The "daughter of God," with her halo, could speak to them without harshness, promising, on His Majesty's behalf, the most generous amnesty, complete pardon for past insults. They need fear nothing. They were quite wrong if they thought he was coming as an executioner, full of rancor and hatred. On the contrary, he was coming as a father, opening his arms to them.

Joan's letter met with silence. That witch! That hussy! A wanton, to be sure! They would not dignify her with a reply. The notables of Troyes had some self-respect. And as for the promises of amnesty, they were not childish enough to fall for that ploy. Obviously, the Maid was a lot less effective than had been expected. She had now taken a double setback, and Charles VII's situation was further complicated by the fact that Troyes would not even sell them the bread and meat the mercenaries needed. The trip from Auxerre to Troyes had taken four days, since they were moving so cautiously, and the soldiers had been forbidden to do any pillaging, because the whole idea was to make a good impression. Beans were all that was left to feed them, and there were more and more signs of imminent mutiny. Regnault was already beginning to talk about dropping the plan, forgetting about the coronation, and going back home. But Joan, as usual, was all for pressing forward. Come on! Push ahead! Let us force the gates of this scandalously reluctant city. They could do it: they had the means. But what about Philip? What would he say? A tacit agreement had been reached between Charles and Philip: no violence. As for turning back, returning to Gien with their tails between their legs, that would give the English a good laugh! Joan said, "Give me three days, and I will deliver the city fathers to you in their nightshirts, with a rope around their necks."

It might be conceivable to stage a mock attack. The mercenaries would be pacified at the prospect of the unbridled license they could have once they were victorious, and the threat alone might be enough to make the city listen to reason. The Maid did wonders, thinking the attack was the real thing. Totally unaware that it was just a bluff, she gave her all. The soldiers under her command piled faggots up in the ditches, displayed their assault ladders, and threaten-

ingly set up their bombards and mortars. I would not put
it past Regnault, that poor man's prefiguration of Talley-
rand, to have maneuvered undercover at the same time to
make the officials of Troyes understand that if they acted
with intelligence (and with liberality toward him personally) he could see to it that their city was not sacked.
Whether or not that occurred, the goal was achieved. The
panic-stricken city of Troyes gave up—on the condition of
amnesty, of course, which had been promised. And it had
been, hadn't it? How could they doubt it? Couldn't they
understand that the King knew his business, that all he
wanted was reconciliation and peace? Everyone kept his
position, at the same pay. In that case, of course. . .

Relief! The city, the key city, was theirs. Plenty to eat
now (for cash, of course), and the King was received with
proper honors. This allowed them to entertain all kinds of
hopes for the future. Auxerre would say, "Fine, since that's
the way it is," and Châlons-sur-Marne, the next stop, would
fall all over itself trying to prove its own loyalty.

Shortly before the surrender of Troyes, Joan was involved in one small incident I find most interesting. A
group of negotiators came out of the city, led by a monk,
Brother Richard, who was a curious body. He had left Paris
some time before, since he had become suspect to the authorities there, seeming of doubtful odor, almost anti-
English. He told the people of Troyes that he wanted to see
for himself what she was like, this Maid who was held to
be a she-devil in Paris. Was she really all that bad? Now he
was approaching the Armagnac camp, and when Joan
walked out to greet him, he raised his aspergillum and
sprinkled holy water before him in the shape of a cross.
Joan thought that rather a joke.

"Enough, enough of your sprinkling," she chaffed

him. *"Nothing to fear, I won't fly away."*

That strikes me as quite a refreshing little flash of our Joan. It is the kind of first-hand account that warms the heart. A pleasant switch from the endless statuettes that show her with hands clasped over her sword, a gown of royal *fleurs-de-lis* hiding the armor on her thighs, as she turns her saintly eyes Heavenward.

Brother Richard was immediately won over, as he was only too willing to be. The witch was truly a saint; he attached himself to her (Brother Pasquerel probably eyeing him furiously). Joan would have been perfectly content to do without this supernumerary monk in whom she felt no confidence whatsoever.

As foreseen, Châlons-sur-Marne gave them the most affectionate welcome. The bishop himself came out to greet His Majesty with all his blessings, bowing and scraping. This affirmed it: Reims would be a scene of real enthusiasm.

At Châlons, Joan found quite a few "countrymen." All kinds of old acquaintances from Domrémy had clustered here to meet her and fête her. The same ones, I am afraid, who had so noisily mourned her when she finally got away at the end of the winter and rushed to console her poor parents. How in Heaven could she ever have done that to you? A girl you brought up so properly—now a "soldiers' girl"! Ungrateful wretch, crazy wench, tramp!

Now their eyes had been opened. What a miracle! Old James' girl had become a lady at Court; she had horses, servants, money. The kind of connection nobody wanted to lose. And they showered her with attention, with tears of joy. Do you remember, Jeannette? But dared one still call her Jeannette? John Moreau, at the rehabilitation trial, would recall: "How good she was! She gave me a red jacket she was wearing" (probably a doublet that she wore over her armor). And Moreau was surely not the only one to ask for and receive favors from her. Even old Girardin had come, Girardin-the-Burgundian, the only one in Domrémy, whom Joan could never stand. He had been converted: now he was an ebullient Armagnac. He, too, would remember, in 1456, something she said that had stuck with him. "There is only one thing I fear," he quoted her, "and that is treason."

Whom did she have in mind? Him, the recent convert? Or more consequential characters, like Brother Richard perhaps, or even an important person like Regnault?

Charles VII made his formal entrance into Reims on Saturday, July 16, 1429.

"*Noël! Noël!*" the exultant crowd shouted. That was how they said "Long live the King!" in those days. It was the phrase that had been shouted deliriously nine years before at Troyes in honor of the future "King of France and England" and would be shouted here in Reims with equal verve if it were the English Henry VI who had come to receive the people's tribute.

The King arrived on the sixteenth, and the next day, Sunday, the seventeenth, it was all over; he was consecrated.

The presence of twelve peers of the realm was required to make it all proper—six Lords of the Church and six lay nobles—and there were some absentees in the group. Small worry; substitutes could stand in for them. The clergy was there, and that was the main thing, with Archbishop Regnault officiating, to guarantee that all was in order and the consecration beyond reproach.

And where was Joan in all this? Why, everyone knows! This was one of the high points of her life, the very highest,

perhaps. The picture of it is famous: Joan beaming alongside the King and the altar, holding on to the staff of her
banner, her presence attesting to the fact that God was
protecting Charles VII, that here indeed was the monarch
blessed by Heaven. Moreover, Yolande's correspondents,
knowing of her interest in the girl and all she had done for
her, tried hard to fill her in on the details. Milady might feel
satisfied, and rejoice. "During all of the mystery [for once,
the word is truly appropriate], Joan remained hard by the
King, her banner in hand."

Unfortunately, Joan herself did not confirm this detail.
Heaven knows she should have been delighted to boast
provocatively of the signal role she played, the preeminent
place she occupied at the consecration, during her interrogation by Cauchon at Rouen. But she clouded up and became sad. She could not remember very clearly. "It seems
to me," she testified (but how could she have had a lapse of
memory about such a special day?), "that my banner was
fairly close to the altar," which could only mean that, first,
she was not carrying it herself, and also, it was not where
she would have wished to see it, right next to the King. It
was not far away, true enough, but it was mixed in with
others and was not awarded any special place of honor. "As
for myself," she added, "I stayed there a bit." Not much,
not long, and not right near, but only "fairly close" (which
doubtless meant fairly far away). After patiently elbowing
her way in inch by inch, she was finally able to get up near
the central "mystery."

Charles VII did not give her any signs of privileged
esteem. He was content merely to tolerate her in his retinue, anxious to see that she did not stand out. When on July
4 he announced his coming to the people of Reims, there
was no mention of Joan in the message. One might have
expected some such alluring addendum as: And just wait
till you see whom I'm bringing along! The ambassador of

Heaven, the miraculous Maid who just saved Orléans. No, not a word about Heaven's handmaiden; she already seemed almost to be getting in the way.

For several weeks, Joan's brothers had been tagging along, and at Châlons, as we saw, a whole flock of people from the Bar country surrounded her. Now, at Reims, her father appeared. Some say that Joan's mother was there, too, but there is no proof positive, one way or the other. Her parents had been "like crazy" (to quote her words from the trial) when they learned she had gone off with six men-at-arms (a fine thing!) heading for Chinon. They got over their upset. Now her father was melting with love. His "forgiveness" was so complete he did not even remember that six months before he had been threatening to drown that bitch of a daughter in the Meuse if ever . . .

That had been just a case of lost temper of which he was now ashamed. Joan? Why, she was a blessing to the whole family, the dear child. How proud the "farmer" was of his daughter! He was staying at the Inn of the Striped Donkey (we might say, the Zebra), and was so comfortable that he was not to move out for quite a long time. The municipal ledgers of Reims show that twenty-four *livres* were paid out for him on September 18, and that the city was getting ready to give him "one horse to get away on" as well (which would seem to indicate his wife was no longer with him, if ever she had been).

The King had been consecrated on July 17, and two months later father James was still there, living it up. He was really having a high old time of it, especially when we consider that in 1440 his widow was given an allowance of only forty-eight *sols* per month, all told, when the city decided to assume responsibility for her support. And on July 31, he had gotten the sovereign to grant a perpetual exemption from taxes not only to himself but also to all of the inhabitants of Greux and Domrémy. She was a real jewel in the village crown, that little Jeannette of his!

In the meantime, his daughter had accomplished all sorts of things far from Rouen.

VII

Paris: Joan Is Threatened

The "three gentlemen of Anjou" who so kindly gratified Madame Yolande with their trumped-up version of the coronation stated at the end of their letter (written on the evening of the seventeenth, right after the ceremony), "Tomorrow needs must the King be off, making his way toward Paris." Toward Paris, indeed! As if that were the simplest thing in the world!

They also informed the illustrious recipient of their report that Duke Philip no sooner heard of the arrival of Charles VII at Reims than he "made embassy toward the King," that is, sent envoys to be accredited. This surely meant peace was coming; a good treaty that would take care of everything. What good news all this was! The gentlemen of Anjou understood the reactions of the mighty: woe betide the bringer of unhappy news. Comforting news, on the other hand, resulted in benefits to those who imparted it.

In the first fortnight of July, Philip of Burgundy had gone to Paris to discuss the general situation with Regent

Bedford. He needed assurances from the English and also wanted personally to see what their morale was like after the Patay disaster. Had he withdrawn his Picards at Orléans? He was now bringing seven hundred of them back to Bedford, who surely must be short of men. But then, you don't get something for nothing, do you? Bedford was short of cash? Well, let him pay in gems. Philip had gone back with twenty thousand *livres* in diamonds, merely as a down payment, for on July 30 Bedford was to pay an equal amount, also in precious stones. The Burgundian's cordial visit to Paris had produced a forty-thousand-*livre* profit. And no doubt he had shown Bedford the letter from that crazy Joan, inviting him to the coronation, so they could have a good laugh over it together. But how had he explained to the Englishman that he had remained neutral through all this?

Just as we have said, I believe: That whole farce at Reims was nothing but hot air. What could the other Charles get out of it, I ask you? And Philip probably outlined what the cost of any military interference on his part would have been. Like Bedford, like everyone else, he, too, had money problems. Bedford was no fool, and he cast a scrutinizing eye on his partner. What was the Grand Duke driving at? He really seemed to be skidding dangerously, right to the edge of their pact. Well, he had better not go beyond that edge! Maybe a way would have to be found to convince him it was not in his interest to switch sides. The Regent was happy to be able to tell his dear ally and brother-in-law that a strong contingent of armed men was about to arrive in Paris: thirty-five hundred mercenaries that Cardinal Winchester, with papal money, had been able to organize on the other side of the Channel for a crusade against the Bohemian heretics, the Hussite rabble. His Holiness had been good enough to recognize that there are orders of priorities, and to sympathize with his English friends over the trials they were undergoing. Colonna had had their support back when he was being elected Martin V. Winchester had sold the thirty-five hundred anti-Hussites to his cousin Bedford for use in the French campaign. After all, was not the Maid, "that hound-dog of the Evil One," a heretic as well? The well-being of religion required that as soon as possible an end be put to the evil works of this dangerous woman.

This news led Philip to the very English conclusion: *Wait and see.* He would see how it worked out and whether the scale which had tilted one way after Patay would now tilt the other way. For the moment, he was smiling at both antagonists. He had proved his devotion to Bedford by furnishing him some reinforcements. But that would not keep him from being courteous and almost friendly toward Charles VII, though within bounds and not to excess. It was true he had sent envoys to Reims, and with their urbanity they might even have been a bit respectful. As for Charles, the tapers had hardly gone out in the cathedral when he made another gesture, once more with Joan as intermediary. He asked her to sign yet a third letter (it almost seemed as if he were making her his secretary). True, the first two missives she wrote for him had had small effect. But since he could not satisfy her persistent and immoderate penchant for military action, this at least would somewhat appease her consuming need to be actively involved. Moreover, Charles had unquestionably humiliated her at the coronation by shunting her to the side. This would be balm to her wound as well as another try at using the persuasive powers that Joan, with her aura, ought to have. Though the people of Troyes had not been moved by them, and Philip had not deigned to answer the Maid's gracious invitation, she might just as well favor him with a second letter, more urgent than the first, in her best religious style.

Docile, perhaps flattered, but above all obedient, Joan complied. She spoke of Christian charity and forgiveness for old hurts. In so doing, at the express instructions of His Majesty (whether or not she fully agreed with them), she was admitting wrongs on the part of the King. She confessed that it was up to Philip to "pardon him"; she used the word in its fullest meaning. In a transparent allusion to the sordid old affair of the bridge at Montereau, she asked them to "pardon each other entirely." Albeit under Joan's signature, Charles VII was really going quite far in offering pledges to his rebellious vassal. This letter was a supplication, imploring peace: "I pray you and beseech you with hands joined," she wrote, "that you wage no battle and engage in no warring against us." It is true that she was warning Philip at the same time: no matter what he tried, if he decided to fight, "however many men" he might put into the line, he could be sure of defeat. That paragraph was necessary so that there might be no misunderstanding. If Charles was sincerely offering peace, it was not out of weakness. On the contrary, he knew he was the stronger, and made no secret of it; but he wanted to spare Philip the blood he might shed in vain. Joan would without doubt have been delighted to refer, as she had once done with the English, to the divine support she represented, which made it impossible for anyone to have any hope of ever triumphing over Charles VII. But the King had not given her permission to be so outspoken in this letter. No allusion here to God-with-me. Those in high places had apparently decided that Joan should remain silent on that point and refrain from stirring up the matter.

Did the King really think that Philip might be moved by Joan's appeal? I doubt it. He knew all about his cousin, that he was more interested in women than in piety ("heavily lubricious" is the way the libertine was described by one of his own Burgundian chroniclers). But for the record, it might be well for the King to have written proof of his complete effort to reach an understanding, his real desire for peace. And since it was just about certain that Philip would not reply to this second letter any more than he did to the first, I tend to think there were those at Court who banked on this third fiasco (including the letter sent to Troyes) to lend weight to their arguments and help in the undercover campaign they had been conducting against Joan the intruder.[1] It would soon be possible for them to wage it with increased vigor.

The gentlemen of Anjou were either naïve or deceitful when they informed Yolande on July 17 that Charles VII would be leaving for Paris the next day. The King did not leave Reims on the eighteenth, but on the twenty-first, and then he did not head for the capital. He went to Soissons, by way of Corbery and Vailly. Laon and Beauvais wanted to see him; they had prepared a sovereign's welcome for him. The municipalities had sent word that they were rallying to his banner, that indeed, secretly, they had never ceased to be faithful. But he refused to listen. He was too fearful that he might offend Philip if he followed in his traces. From Soissons, he went down to Château-Thierry on July 29, and from there to Montmirail (August 1), then to Provins (August 2). It seemed unbelievable! Going home! Returning, falling back quietly, as if nothing had occurred, as if the consecration had never taken place.

But what about Paris? Joan had announced to the English as early as March 22 that, by the will of "God, King

---

[1]Humble folk, writes Rudler in his admirable *Michelet historien de Jeanne d'Arc*, (Presses Universitaires de France, 1925), vol. II, p. 105, never meet with a very warm welcome when they rise from their obscurity and distinguish themselves by some quality or other; "jealousy" and "scorn" surround them. And Bernard Shaw, in the "Preface" to *Saint Joan*, says that to those of importance and position the appearance of a "superior being" is "unbearable" (Penguin ed., 1951, pp. 9–10).

of Heaven," she would "enter Paris," with or without their consent. On June 6, she had confirmed this to young Laval, when she promised that they would soon toast each other there. And on July 17, Yolande's informers stated, "The Maid leaves no doubt that she will bring Paris to obeisance." Yet where did they head after Provins? Ever southward, grotesquely southward. Now the royal cortege was going through Bray-sur-Seine, getting ready to cross the river so as to return to Gien, Sully, and the sleepy banks of the Loire. This was madness; it was nauseating. Joan was furious.

Then all of a sudden orders were countermanded. Charles VII was doubling back. Back to Provins, and then toward Nangis—in a word, toward Paris. They arrived at Nangis on August 6. The day before, August 5, Joan had written to the people of Reims, who had informed her of their concern: The King is letting us down, after we jumped in with him; he is getting out, disappearing. What will we do now if the English, who obviously are furious with us, should come back or if Philip, who pulled in his claws as long as Charles VII was here, should threaten to scratch again? This is not fair! Do not leave us! Help!

I think this call to Joan from Reims is a significant indication that the people there saw her as separate from the Council. Though she had been in Reims only a short time, the city fathers had fully realized that the Council was on one side and Joan on the other, and that there could be no doubt about placing confidence in Joan, which proves that they felt she exercised some authority over the King, or at least some influence. She *was* a miracle worker, after all! A girl who talked with angels every day!

Joan's reply to the people of Reims is an important document. First of all, it explains the change of direction that had just taken place. If Charles was no longer falling back, if he planned to stay in the Île-de-France, it was because he had just concluded a truce with Philip,[2] a "two-week" truce, a short suspension of hostilities. But had not the suspension of hostilities with Burgundy actually been in effect for months already? It would seem that what had taken place was a sudden, strange, and colossal agreement give by Philip; it meant nothing less than his renunciation of the capital. He appeared to have said to Charles VII: Very well, Paris is yours. Enter at will. You have two weeks of official truce to reoccupy your capital.

The news left Joan skeptical, bristling. What was this new machination? It looked all too suspiciously like a trap of some kind. Joan was exceedingly mistrustful of Philip, who had been so rude as to ignore her letters and act as if she did not exist. Fom the very beginning of July, before Troyes, she had been warning the King, without mincing words, to watch out for "false Burgundy," the hypocritical Duke. Joan was convinced that Philip was lying to Charles, and Charles seemed to be walking right into the trap. Truce, indeed! What Philip really wanted was for Charles to think he was safe, and put his sword back into its scabbard. Now he was pushing him toward Paris in this unbelievable turnabout. But what would the English do? Would they withdraw their troops, while Charles VII walked into Paris swinging his arms and looking up at the sky? Be reasonable! Philip could only be setting up an ambush.

Winchester had mustered thirty-five hundred men and the Regent was counting on them to allow him to avenge Patay. They arrived in Paris on July 25. It was now August 5. And the two-week truce had been concluded a day or two before. What could this signify?

Within two weeks, the English would have attacked, and

---

[2]Joan used the plural "truces"; the arrangements must have been purely oral, for what came down to us of the royal archives reveals no trace of them.

Philip meantime would have played the good cousin to Charles, conciliatory as could be. If the King were to win his battle with the English, Philip would find him a grateful victor. But if the English came out on top, he could point out how well he had fixed things for them, misleading Charles VII, and sending him disarmed against them.

Let us listen to Joan. What she had to say on the subject is worthwhile: "Truces so fashioned do not make me happy, nor am I sure I shall observe them."

Well, well! The Maid had taken it on herself to judge the sovereign's policies, and refuse her approval. She said so openly, she wrote it to his subjects. She had gone into opposition. Nor did she hesitate to speak of disobeying. "If I observe them [the truces]," she added, "it will be only to safeguard the honor of the King."

She would not want to see the King accused of breaking his word, of failing to honor a promise he had given, even an idiotic one. Yet Joan was not committing herself: "If I observe them," she said; so, she was still not sure she would. Since Joan dared to go to such lengths, especially in writing, it must certainly have been because she did not care whether anyone else saw her letter before it reached Reims. She was not afraid to admit both her violent opposition to royal policy and her threat of insubordination, in fact she ostentatiously flaunted them.

For a long time before this, things had been going badly between her and the Court. Actually, they had never gone well, but Joan realized this only gradually. Her lightning victory at Orléans had not met with favor. Immediately after it, the King made every effort to send her back into the shadows. He insisted she needed rest, and for a good reason: she was in the way. Then there was the Richemont incident. After that, she had been ill used in the matter of Troyes. And, against her will, perhaps by ruse, she had been persuaded to write dishonoring letters to Philip.

The King had relegated her to a back place during the consecration ceremony, as far from himself as possible, whereas her rightful place was at the sovereign's right, with her banner that bore the seal of God. After all, she, as the direct and visible instrument of Heaven, had been responsible for it all, and that would have been her normal place, dictated, demanded by gratitude. But gratitude to whom? Not to herself, of course, but to the Almighty, to the Saviour.

After that came the shameful retreat: the road to Gien instead of Paris. And now, this specious armistice, this truce accepted in defiance of all good sense. This time, Joan had gone off her hinges. As long as she had only the Bastard, Gaucourt, or the captains as objects of her furies, the matter remained within bounds. But now it was the King she was going after, the King she was defying. It was to be fatal for the little rebel. She had just spelled her own doom, quite literally. She had been barely tolerated by the King's entourage for the past three months. But what she did now, at the beginning of August, 1429, led to her condemnation.

Yet the poor girl was still acting important, telling the people of Reims, "I promise and certify to you that I shall not abandon you, as long as I shall live." They were not to worry, she was there and would fly to their assistance if needed. At any rate, they could relax, for "I will hold and keep together the army of the King so as to be ready at the end of these two weeks."

"I"! The "warrior chief"? The commanding general? Just as if the army were hers to command. As if she had something to say about how it was to be used and held together. In the eyes of the Council, Joan was a gadfly, nothing more. And a fly they were now determined to get rid of, once and for all, for after her intolerable buzzings, now she was threatening to bite, too. They would squash her if necessary, quietly but effectively. Chancelleries everywhere have always known how to set up this kind of delicate operation with finesse.

Joan was precise in dating her letter of August 5: "Somewhere near Provins, in the field, en route to Paris." To Paris. That was a step forward. At last they were on their way to the capital, the natural prime target they should have aimed for the very morning of July 18 in the flush of victory. They were now marching on Paris under terrible conditions, with that tricky "truce" lying in wait for them, but at least they were marching. And Joan swore to herself that she would not allow the army to fall apart on the way.

However, on the sixth, they were no longer going to Paris. Charles VII had changed his mind again. Perhaps, after all, he had recognized Philip's insincerity, the duplicity of his offer. Perhaps, also, he had just heard that Winchester's thirty-five hundred men were in Paris. The King's road now veered away from the west toward the north. At any rate, they were staying in France, they were not resuming that pitiful retreat toward the south. Which meant that they were not backing away, and maybe even that they would stand and fight.

On August 7, the column was at Coulommiers; August 10, at La Ferté-Milon, and there (or perhaps the day before at Château-Thierry), Charles VII received Bedford's "cartel." On August 7, Bedford had sent Charles VII a grandiloquent ultimatum: "We, John of Lancaster, Regent of France and Duke of Bedford, do hereby advise you, Charles of Valois, who . . . without cause, call yourself King because you did unwarrantedly take arms against the crown . . . of Henry, by the grace of God true and rightful King of France and England. . . ." The Regent was "advising" the false King that he "called upon" him to "appear in person" on the field of battle for a man-to-man showdown, just as he, Bedford, was ready to do "in person." Charles was called upon to designate "some convenient and reasonable place in the field," as well as the day that would suit him, so they might conduct this ultimate test of strength.

Let us take a good look at this challenge, this cartel, for it is enlightening, if not entertaining. The bandit beating his victim because the latter dares defend himself will lecture him at the same time, If you did not fight back, but willingly and immediately gave me what I am trying to take from you, I would not have to hurt you. Those words of wisdom, couched in high-flown sentiments, were the very ones that the Regent "of France and England" used in his touching appeal to Charles: "Take pity and compassion on the poor Christian people." If you persist in denying us this kingdom which should be ours, "through your fault [*sic*] the pillaging, ransoming, dispatching, and depopulating will continue." It would be so much less painful, and in accordance with your beliefs, if you let yourself be robbed without resisting. Be a good fellow! Think of your responsibility, of all that you are criminally inflicting on so many poor people! A piece of fancy footwork from Bedford the moralist.

But there was something else worthy of note in this missive. Bedford cannot refrain from mentioning the Maid here, he refers to her twice. He shames his adversary for "taking help" from such a horrible source: this "shameless and nameless female, dressed in men's clothing, and of dissolute behavior." It was English dogma, as we see, that Joan was a prostitute. And at the end of the letter she reappeared again, in the Regent's sarcastic tone: For the great battle to which I invite you, Charles, this battle loyally to be fought between the two of us (through the clash of interposed mercenaries, naturally; people of breeding were not ragpickers), you may, if you wish, bring along "the above-mentioned nameless and apostate woman"; we are not afraid of her. Proving that they were, indeed, very much afraid of the "witch," and were protesting just a little too loudly about it. What sad comedy it was that at the very moment when the King and his Court had had their fill of Joan and were thinking only of appropriate ways to get rid of her, her prestige was greater and more terrifying than ever it had been among their enemies.[3]

The English and French forces confronted each other at Montepilloy, between Crépy-en-Valois and Senlis, on August 14–15, 1429, but nothing happened. It was to be a sort of foreshadowing of Valmy, but at least at Valmy some cannons were fired, whereas there was not a shot at Montepilloy. Neither Charles nor Bedford (despite his saber-rattling of the seventh) was willing to launch an attack. Each was scared of the other.

We already know that Charles VII had a really visceral revulsion for cold steel. Whispered exchanges between negotiators always seemed to him a thousand times preferable to any armed encounter. As for Bedford, he was surely overcome with terror at the witchcraft that Charles' demonic auxiliary would be able to unleash against him. Even though it was Assumption Day, Joan herself rushed excitedly near the English positions to taunt the Goddams, but all in vain.

"Are you coming out or not? Come on, you bunch of cowards!"

The English refused to come out. They stood behind their pikes, waiting for the Armagnacs to attack, hoping for a repeat performance of Agincourt. But the French were not crazy; they remembered 1415. So nothing happened, a

---

[3]Both of Bedford's writings about Joan, this one and that of the preceding month (the report that called the Maid a creature of the Evil One), show how seriously the English took her.

big fat ridiculous nothing. And in the evening, the two dispirited sides turned their backs on each other and returned to camp. If the other side would not start, good night to them! Charles went back to Crépy. Bedford went back to Senlis. A real burlesque blackout!

Nonetheless, in Charles' mind, the road to Paris was closed. The King must certainly have known that Bedford had turned the military government of Paris over to Philip on the twelfth, before leaving for this (aborted) showdown. If the Duke of Burgundy had ever intended (though, by all evidence, he never had) to deliver Paris to Charles, now he would not dare. Moreover, Philip, although grateful to Bedford, had chosen not to go and take command in person. He had merely sent Louis of Luxembourg to represent him in the capital. And Charles, trying to show that he would not let himself be intimidated, went to Compiègne, where he made a resounding entrance on the seventeenth. Thank goodness, anyway, that he had not turned back toward Provins and Bray-sur-Seine. That would have been just too much for Joan, after that odious August 15 when Charles had shown himself as much of a coward as Bedford. Better if he went on, right away, to Saint-Quentin, Corbie, Amiens, Abbeville, all of which had been clamoring for him. He had a whole string of these "good cities" right at hand. But no! That was too dangerous. It would mean skirting Flanders, and Philip might take umbrage.

With the least bit of nerve, virility, or honor, the road to Paris would have been opened by now. The English? If the French had marched on them as they ought to have done, on August 15, their army would be gone by now. It would no longer be worth mentioning, and they might even have captured Bedford, as they had taken Suffolk at Jargeau and Talbot at Patay. And then you would have seen how insignificant Philip would have made himself, how he would have lain down after this ultimate victory—and it was abso-

lutely certain to end that way, guaranteed, since we were
there with you, God and I. That was what heavy-hearted
Joan was thinking, biting her lips.

It may have been at this time or a little earlier that Joan
pronounced these words, attributed to her by Dunois:
"Would that it pleased God, my Creator, that I might now
withdraw, forsake arms, and return home to serve my father and mother in herding their sheep, with my sister and
brothers who would so rejoice to have me back!"

Dunois' account was given in 1456, and Joan's words, as
he recounted them, are unacceptable. She could not have
spoken of her sister Catherine being so happy to have her
back for the simple reason that Catherine was no longer of
this world; she had died before Joan left home. Her brothers waiting for her? Another good one! They were riding
with her, two out of the three at least, John and Peter,
sticking as close to her as possible—as long as there was a
profit in it. Father? He was not at Domrémy either. He was
having the time of his life at the Zebra Inn in Reims. As
for the "sheep," they seem tailored to fit the bucolic imagery rife in the 1456 campaign, "Operation Catholic Virtue," all sweetness and sentimentality. But as the testimony
at Rouen would confirm, Joan never pictured herself as
having just come from tending cows back home; the image
rather irritated her. Livestock? Yes, in her turn, when she
had to, she did go to the fields to watch over it. That happened occasionally, but it was in no way her regular work.
Yet, though Dunois may have been transposing, arranging,
decorating, adding foolish trivia, as was expected of him in
1456, I nevertheless believe the tone was essentially correct.
Joan did want to leave in August, 1429, and drop the whole
thing. She had had more than enough of the royal entourage, of Regnault, La Trémoille, and the King himself. She

felt in the way when she was with them. She knew they had had their fill of her, and I believe she now had contempt for them. Why should God put himself out as He did for the sake of creatures like that?

But let us pay careful attention to the beginning of her sentence: "Would that it pleased God . . . that I might. . . ." Which means that she could not, for two reasons. First, the Court would never allow her to retire; the King wanted to keep her right where she was, under his thumb, on his payroll. While insiders might feel that her halo was becoming tarnished, the radiation it shed, like the light of extinct stars, continued to shine far and wide, to the wonderment of some and the terror of others. So Maid, step up and fall in! Second, a personal reason: Joan's work was not yet completed. She wanted Paris; she had to take Paris. As a result, even under these awful conditions, she had to hold on, stay where she was. Physically, she simply could not leave. Morally, she certainly could not desert. So she was captive twice over, to King and Duty. Hers was not a happy lot, not at all! Where was the bridge at Orléans now? And where the light-heartedness she had known, such a short while ago, on the road from Vaucouleurs to Chinon?

Joan was now experiencing some changes. She was becoming bitter, and finding it hard to keep control of herself. This was the time of the incident, repeated so often, of her flareup of temper, cursing the trollops who followed the army from stop to stop. One day in August, 1429, Joan raised her weapon against one of these strumpets and chased her, sword in hand, in a totally inglorious display. According to Michelet and many others, the Maid broke her miracle sword, the one from Fierbois, on the poor girl's back. And this inspired another of Michelet's flights of theatrical rhetoric: "The virginal blade could not abide such contact. It broke, and never suffered to be forged anew." Michelet, as we know, never went to sources. If he had, he might have read the deposition of her page Louis of Coutes that Joan never struck the girl. Having chased and caught her (an embarrassing sequence for an adulatory *Life of Joan*), the witness said she "spoke kindly to her," ending, " 'We'll let it go this time, but don't let me catch you at it again! . . .' "

It was true about her sword, but she broke it before she ever caught the poor girl, on some stone or other hard object as she waved it threateningly through the air. Joan was never to be proud of this incident. When questioned about it by Cauchon, she steadfastly refused to explain why in 1430 she no longer had her "sword of Fierbois." She said she "lost" it, that was all. Before she got to Paris? Yes. But where? She did not want to be bothered any more with this irrelevant detail, unrelated to the "trial."

What happened next is cloaked in so dense a fog that the historian can only indicate what he is able to discern.

No later than August 16, with the truce coming to an end, Philip received the visit of Archbishop Regnault, bringing a most attractive proposal. Charles VII did not stint on humility. He apologized to Philip. How remorseful he now was over the sad event at Montereau, ten years back! Could it not be forgotten and forgiven?

Charles was ready to concede almost anything. He was even ready to tell his well-loved cousin that he no longer considered him a vassal, and that he would release him from any kind of oath. He would give him back Compiègne as well as all other cities having bridges across the Oise River. Burgundy would thus control the river's entire course, which would render Flanders absolutely secure. This exorbitant document was signed at Arras on August 21. The main thing, for Charles, was to get the truce prolonged, and Philip agreed to extend it till Christmas, with the possibility of further extension after that. The Burgundian felt cocky; the way he had Charles crawling was vastly entertaining. For a "consecrated" King, he was really acting unexpectedly—like a little boy. What price would the "Grand Duke of the West" not be able to exact from now on, not for his friendship, but simply for neutrality?

Yet there was one strange clause in that treaty. While a general armistice was declared between Burgundians and Armagnacs, there was one exception: Paris was "outside the truce." How could that be? Philip was no longer saying, as he was alleged to have said at the beginning of the month, "You want Paris? Go ahead; it is yours." Now he only agreed that Charles might try to take it from him. Incomprehensible. So unheard of and disconcerting that one has to ask what was behind it.

It recalls, in more recent times, a comparable provision, in the agreement signed in January, 1871, between the intriguing French politician Jules Favre and Bismarck. They winked at each other as the Franco-Prussian War drew to a close and they, too, concluded a general armistice—with the exception of the Army of the East, left "outside the truce." Today we know what that meant. The idea was to crush the last army of French resistance, the final trump in the hand of Léon Gambetta, the Minister of Defense, who wanted to fight on. The clause was put in to dispose of Gambetta himself, hated as much by Favre and the other two reactionary ruling Juleses (Ferry and Simon) as by Bismarck. That little clause in the Versailles understanding was supposed to break his back.

And I, for one, am ready to believe that the clause concerning Paris, that unlikely provision of the Treaty of Arras, had a very similar goal, for in 1429, too, there was someone to dispose of: Joan.

Taking Paris was the last thing that Charles VII had in mind. He was giving the Burgundian everything he could want, so he would certainly not try to take away the prize possession which had belonged to Philip ever since 1418. But still he could pretend to, in order to keep Joan happy, since she never stopped talking about *her* Paris. It was a nice gesture toward her, a concession. And, at the same time, things might be arranged so she would fail in the attempt, and come a cropper. Remember: the tree is judged by its fruits. Now this would be demonstrated. The "daughter of God," tool of the Lord, who with His help succeeded in everything—see how successful she was at Paris, and judge for yourselves!

What was that divine protection of hers at Orléans—a dream, a magic trick? It was the captains who freed the city! Jargeau, Meung, Beaugency? Ditto. At Patay, she was not even present. And now there would be a full-scale test of her talents. Now at her request she was being given a specific responsibility, charge of an entire action. The result should be illuminating!

And it was. But I, for one, doubt that the King and his councillors stopped at this in their campaign to discredit the Maid. They hoped for more. Thierry Maulnier suggests that perhaps "Joan's setback at Paris" might well have been "desired, prepared, by her own side."[4] And Bernard Shaw goes a step further in his play, correctly, I believe, when he has Dunois addressing Joan on the eve of battle, "I am not so sure they will let you take Paris. . . . Some of them would rather Paris took you, I think. . . ."[5]

I would alter just one detail here: Joan was not to be taken prisoner by the Anglo-Burgundians, which might create some problems. She was to die; that would really have been infinitely better. Gloriously killed in action, fallen on the field of honor—what could be more perfect?

---

[4] Thierry Maulnier, *Jeanne et les juges* (Joan and the Judges), 1951, preface, p. 36.
[5] *Op. cit.*, p. 124.

They would have saved face. They could all go into mourn-
ing, sob over their great loss—and silently bless the Burgundians of Paris. For they gave the Court the quiet opportunity, so long sought, to do away in style with the
escaped-lunatic girl, the pretender, the flibbertigibbet, the
stubborn wench who had seemed useful for a while, until
she turned into an unendurable pest.

King Charles strikes me as being rather ill at ease, worried, uncomfortable, unsure of himself. This plot was being
worked out around him, involving him directly as little as
possible.

He let Joan leave for Saint-Denis on August 25, accompanied by d'Alençon, who was not in on the scheme and
really wanted to take Paris. They had just one detachment
with them. It was only a reconnaissance mission. That was
why, they were told, they could go right up to the outskirts
of the capital. Saint-Denis had become a deserted hamlet.
At the approach of the Armagnacs, the inhabitants took
refuge within the Paris walls, where work went ahead feverishly to make the city impregnable. The King had promised to follow, but he settled in at Senlis and was not stirring. On September 1, d'Alençon returned to Senlis to
entreat His Majesty to come to Saint-Denis himself with
the main body of troops to launch the attack. The King
stalled: Tomorrow; I'll leave tomorrow.

What was Joan doing during this time? She was "skir-
mishing," morning, noon, and night, looking for contact,
exposing herself. Fine. Good girl! September 2, 3, 4 went by
in this way. On the fifth, d'Alençon, anxious for action,
reappeared before Charles VII. Sire, what about your
promise? Oh, certainly, tomorrow—this time, without fail.

On the evening of September 6, Charles VII finally
reached Saint-Denis. September 7 was the birthday of the

Blessed Virgin, but there was no choice—Joan attacked anyway. Attacked with what? A few battalions. The Burgundians had a crushing superiority in men and masses of matériel. They rained iron and fire on their weak assailants, who kept coming on as best they could, and were repeatedly repulsed. Joan's main page, young Louis, had been taken from her; she had only his substitute, Raymond, who was killed before her eyes. She herself took an arrow through the thigh. She fell, but she continued to call, "It is nothing! Nothing! Have at them, lads! Go!"

It was useless. Night was falling. "The men-at-arms were wearied of the long attack they had made," hours on end, losing dozens of their comrades. Joan herself was out of action; this had been reported to the King. "The Sire of Gaucourt [her old enemy] and others," wrote Perceval de Cagny, "came [at whose orders?] to get the Maid and, against her will, took her away. . . . She was filled with regret at thus leaving, saying, '*Par mon martin*, the position would have been taken!'" Still having her visions.

Though she was wounded, limping, and racked with fever, Joan was up at dawn on the eighth, urging d'Alençon, "Back at them! Call the men!"

As the bugles blew, the Count of Montmorency, until then one of Philip's men, came riding out of Paris to switch sides, rallying to the King "with fifty or sixty gentlemen."

But, at the same time, two other lords, of infinitely higher rank, René of Anjou and the Count of Clermont, came from the opposite direction. They brought an order from the sovereign, an imperative command for Joan to cease and desist immediately. They were even empowered to add the following, if required: Whosoever might resist the royal injunction "would be constrained by force, if need be, to obey." The two emissaries of the Prince had a cohort of dissuaders with them.

The Maid had not been removed from her command by

death, but Charles thought it better not to go any further. They had tried to get him to do a very serious thing, and for a while he had let himself be carried along. The girl was a strange one, not bad, definitely not; now, if she would just come back. Her presence could be tolerated, as long as she was kept in check. Providence sometimes smiled on you, if you knew how to wait.

VIII

Winter, 1429-1430:
Joan in Eclipse

Let us take stock. How long did Joan's "public life," her active life, from the beginning to the end of her work in the service of the King, actually last? Fifteen months. After that, the year in prison, and then, the stake. But these fifteen months of service had two distinct periods: from Chinon to Paris, something over six months; then from Gien (after the return from Paris) to Compiègne, where she was captured, eight months plus. Now, this latter period of a little more than eight months, prior to the brief final campaign, is summed up in one paragraph in Michelet's standard history—only a few lines for this final stage, even though it lasted longer than the first. This should not surprise us: there were almost no battle actions in the second period.

And to think that we are still repeatedly told about the unusually abundant supply of information we have on the Maid's career! We have already pointed out and circled a few of the shadowy gaps in her story, from March to September, 1429. Now we come to the real zone of darkness: for concerning Joan's existence during the fall of 1429 and the winter of 1429–1430, in truth, we know virtually nothing.

After the Parisian machination, Charles VII, thinking only that he had nothing more to fear from Burgundy, at least until Christmas, went off to his peaceful châteaus. On September 15, it was back to where they had been on August 6, Nangis, this time having crossed the Seine at Bray. As agreed, on September 17, Paris was included within the truce; then they went on to Gien, by way of Montargis. At Gien, before Joan's eyes on September 21–22, her "Consecration Army" was disbanded, having been involved in not a single engagement except for the minimal incidents we noted on September 7. After that? Total darkness.

We have nothing to go by from then until November 9, a day when Joan wrote a letter from Moulins. All that we can assume to have happened is that Joan spent several weeks in October at Bourges, but not as a guest of the King at the château, rather, this time, with the lady known as La Touroulde, whom she had met in March at Poitiers.

Quicherat (in his *Aperçus*, 1850) depicted Joan here as being disheartened, "full of unhappiness and disgust," and I believe he is right. And Péguy, who in his *Jeanne d'Arc* had drawn some fancy arabesques around the Maid, came back to the subject in 1914, and on the last occasion he had to write about her (in the *Note conjointe* just before he was killed in World War I), he made some meaningful and relevant observations about her and the King. Péguy saw a Joan fallen from her high horse, a Joan who had come looking for "a king of Christendom" and found instead "a businessman-king, a king in brokerage." She had imagined she would find "a knightly king" and instead got "a tradesman king." She thought she would meet "a mystic" but found before her "a politician." Péguy read in Charles VII's attitude "the profound and prideful ingratitude, the unatonable resentment, of the rich man toward the poor person to whom he owes much, in this case all." He was perhaps exaggerating only a little in saying Joan's disillusionment with the King was "the greatest secret sorrow of her life, her extreme point of pain and catastrophe."

Joan, demobilized in the fall of 1429, was idle, at loose ends, with no idea what to do next. La Touroulde, her landlady, was to testify in 1456 that they went together to the "bath and sweatbaths." Joan at the bathhouse is not quite how tradition has taught us to picture our heroine. Yet why should she not have gone for daily hot baths at Bourges? Why should she not have enjoyed the ministrations of masseuses? The sordid mid-fifteenth century, for all its horrors and baseness, had at least one big advantage over the seventeenth, no less replete in atrocity and foulness: in Charles VII's time people washed and were devoted to bodily cleanliness, whereas in that "great century" known as the Age of Louis XIV they were allergic to hydrotherapy and at Versailles the scents of frangipani and benzoin were hard put to overcome the asphyxiating stenches.

At Rouen, the theologians who were after Joan heaped cartloads of accusations on her, including Article 13, that charged her with having displayed herself "many times attired in precious stuffs, gold and furs"; and Article 55 described her as an artificer who "transformed" her so-called divine mission "into temporal luxury and profit, for she did acquire riches in great number, great equipage and great estate." But Joan, who protested, revolted, shouted "No!" at the end of other articles, remained silent when taxed with "luxury" and elaborate wardrobe. For she had no answer to this; monstrous though it was to depict her as a greedy schemer, the fact is she enjoyed jewels, "precious stuffs," and minks. Joan knew what a delight it was to be well dressed, she enjoyed luxury. She had a passion for horses; her personal stable included "five steeds" (for warfare) and "six trotters" (for travel). The King, knowing her tastes, had made her a gift, as the royal account books attest, of one horse worth 38 *livres*, and another costing 137, the latter price implying, beyond the cost of the animal, that of a sumptuous harness. During the months of August and September, 1429, His Majesty gave Joan no less than 234 *livres* and 13 golden ducats—to say nothing of the 60 *livres* her father had been able to get from the Prince. At Rouen, Joan made no reference to her father at all; she simply pointed out that if her brothers had received any presents from the sovereign, it was they who had asked for them, not she.

Joan, since her admission to Court, was no longer the penniless peasant she had been at the beginning of the year. She was somebody. She was the recipient of the master's largesse and special compensations. When interrogated at Rouen about her wealth, she said that when captured she must have had "ten to twelve thousand *livres*" (managed by her brothers; these money matters took up all of their time). Ten to twelve thousand *livres* was a tidy little sum. The annual salary of the Chancellor of France, the King's closest aide, under Louis XI, was four thousand *livres*. The sum in question, Joan added, was her war chest and was intended for her military undertakings. It was not much, all told, she went on, if you considered it had to cover the subsistence and pay of an army of mercenaries. It would not go very far, would it?

I am sure she was sincere in this, and equally sure we would be fooling ourselves to imagine that after Chinon she never departed from her little pageboy outfit, that she would later again wear exclusively, but not voluntarily, in prison. At Bourges, living with La Touroulde, she was a lady of fashion.

A lady of fashion, but suffocating in the role. Throughout all of her meaningless amusements and compensations, she was miserable and desperately trying to get away. She understood perfectly that she was under house arrest; she was in eclipse, a princely eclipse, to be sure, but to all intents and purposes rejected, canceled out.

What could she do about it? Even Yolande had dropped her. The King's mother-in-law now was mainly concerned with having her son, René of Anjou, become Duke of Lorraine, and thought the best way to raise him to that high position would be to show repeated and increasing kindnesses to Philip. And everyone knew Joan had no soft spot in her heart for Philip, and he in return had little use for her. The Maid could be an embarrassment to those who now had nothing but smiles for Burgundy.

But now she was being offered a job. The only meaningful place to do anything, she felt, would be up toward Paris, "in France," as she put it. But she was being asked to go and fight along the Loire, far upstream from Orléans, and even from Gien. Not against Philip—there was that good truce! —nor even against the English. No, some kind of police action against a petty tyrant of the neighborhood, a bandit called Perrinet Gressart, who had set up his own territory between Saint-Pierre-le-Moutier and La Charité-sur-Loire, and occasionally left it to go raiding. Once he had even ventured as far as Bourges, while Charles VII was there, and trapped him for several days, like a rat in a hole.

La Trémoille had a score to settle with him. In 1425, the fat man (La Trémoille was big as a vat) had been on his way (this seemed to be a habit of his) as an emissary to Philip, when Gressart grabbed him on the road and did not release him until a fourteen-thousand-ducat ransom had been paid. Since Joan was ridiculous enough to be bored, rather than take advantage of the comfortable idleness in which she was privileged to live, it was thought she might enjoy a little martial sideshow. But she just kept repeating, "Paris! Paris!"—unaware, as usual, of what she was saying.

They spoke kindly to her; no one wanted to rub her the wrong way. They used the kind of tolerant understanding with her that people exhibit toward those who have fixations. They explained: Go to the Île-de-France? Surely, but only later, later. Perrinet Gressart was the one to be beaten "first." And who knew whether the Court's fond desire, unfulfilled the last time at Paris, might not be accomplished this time? The Maid could be so fiery when she went into action! She was always ready to run risks, any kind of risks. I am quite tempted to endorse this version of the mysterious episode, especially in view of the circumstances in which it took place. The King was so parsimonious both with money and with men that it would really seem this affair scarcely interested him. It was as if he had said to La Trémoille, Go ahead, but it is your own business. But if La Trémoille had really been trying to get rid of Gressart, he would have gone about it quite differently. As I see it, it was not Perrinet Gressart they were after. He was only a pretext, a means to an end.

The expeditionary corps assigned to the job, commanded by d'Albret, La Trémoille's half-brother, was so wretched and ill equipped that Joan and the commander-in-chief were reduced to begging for help with munitions and money wherever they could, at Riom, Clermont, Bourges, and Orléans. Saint-Pierre-le-Moutier was taken easily, but before La Charité-sur-Loire they stalled. Could the King accept being brought to heel by a tenth-rate rebel who decided to defy him? He could and did. He gave up, despite the humiliation involved. Here again, I wonder whether the King, well aware of what was afoot, having allowed La Trémoille to move ahead while he turned his back, did not feel the chance had passed for the anticipated accident. Did he not give an order (as he had at Paris), by way of conscience-salve, to call it quits, drop the sordid plot, and forget it, so far as Joan was concerned? Charles VII wanted to believe—as in fact it would turn out—that there must be a nice simple solution to the problem of the Maid, that everything would straighten itself out without his having to get involved and later have to run to his father confessor in search of absolution.

Nor was it a bad way to "sink" Joan a bit more and further show up that "gift of gab" Gerson had mentioned. It could be quite an effective confirmation of what had already become evident at Paris: Say, the Divine Messenger really had us going there for a while with her God of Hosts sitting faithfully behind her as she rode into battle, didn't she? Well, I guess He must have hopped off somewhere on the way!

Charles VII wanted to be above suspicion. He wanted no idle tongues implying he had any ill will toward the Maid or even that, instead of favoring her, he was letting her down, turning her away, unappreciative of what he owed her. A sure proof of the royal gratitude and esteem for his admirable supporter was what he did for her after the snag at La Charité. The King was magnanimous, and ignored that mishap, especially since the undertaking itself was of so little importance. Charles VII conferred upon Joan and all of her family (what was the clod's family name? No one really knew. Let's say, "Day") the signal privilege of nobility. And in what terms! In order "to recognize the very pure and abundant graces which the Divine Majesty visited upon him through the ministry of our dear and well-beloved Maid." What more could be said? It was dated "Mehun-sur-Yèvre, December 29, 1429." The "Day" clan would now be allowed to call themselves "du Lys." *Jeanne du Lys!* Joan of the Lily!

How could it happen that history failed to pick up so honorable and official a designation instead of the purely fictional "Joan of Arc"? This new name raised our farm girl–inn maid out of the mire. She was now socially acceptable; she smelled sweet. Pending the odor of sanctity, she had the scent of lilies; and not just those ordinary "lilies of the field" that are mentioned some place or other, but courtly lilies, the royal *fleurs-de-lis*, which have another kind of elegance altogether and raise one's standing in the eyes of proper people. Charles VII conferring nobility on Joan set a precedent for Napoleon III to have one of his prefects, in his Imperial name, pin a cross of the Legion of Honor on the cassock of that holy man, the *curé d'Ars*,[1] the only "cross" to carry any weight in the eyes of realists.

Joan-the-saint becoming Joan-the-noble brought things back into perspective. Her aura, which had been upsetting because it set her apart excessively, was now replaced by a title of nobility that reclassified her on a more normal scale. She had called herself the liege of God; from now on she was obligated to the King. With the help of God, Joan, the "humble shepherdess," had climbed the steps to the throne until she was able to throw her arms around His Majesty's knees. That was her Ascension. Now her Assumption. For it was no longer she who was raising herself; the King was calling her to him, sweeping her up into his sphere, making her a part of that aristocracy whose social peak rested in the royal residence.

Was Joan gratified by this elevation? I would not swear to it. The act of nobility was made public on January 14. On January 19, we find her at Orléans for a magnificent reception at which were consumed " six capons, nine partridges, thirteen hares, and fifty-two pints of wine," all of which cost six *livres* and twelve *sols*, plus the price of a doublet her brother John was able to procure for himself. Yet at Rouen, during the identification interrogatory for her trial, though entitled to it, Joan never once used the name "du Lys."

---

[1] Saint Jean-Baptiste-Marie Vianney, for forty-one years parish priest of the tiny village of Ars-sur-Formans, a French folk saint, in many ways the modern counterpart of Saint Joan. (*Translator's note*)

"Jeannette," yes, and "Joan," those names she gave. But no mention at all of "du Lys."

Perhaps that trip to Orléans, in mid-January, was a welcome one to Joan, wiping from her mind, for the time being at least, a painful and irritating run-in she had had at the end of the year with the monk Richard. He will be remembered as the character who came on the scene at Troyes at the beginning of July, sprinkling holy water in the path of the putative "witch" in order to exorcise her. Eighteenth-century readers of Voltaire's *Philosophical Dictionary* would learn that Joan was "long directed, along with a few other devout women of the populace [*sic*] by a crook named Richard, who performed miracles, and taught these girls to do likewise." Which was the way Voltaire enjoyed rewriting history.

Brother Richard did have a protégée, it is true, but she was another and different "daughter of God," called Catherine of La Rochelle, whom he intended to set up at Court as a substitute "seeress," since Joan was not in the highest favor. The supernatural communications that Catherine received outranked Joan's, inasmuch as she purported to deal only with the Blessed Virgin herself. Catherine said that each night she was visited by a "lady in white," who gave her revelations. And excellent revelations they were, right in line with what His Majesty and the Council wanted to hear: that the one thing needed, for the good of the kingdom, was a reconciliation, a permanent "good peace" between Charles VII and Philip. Catherine had nothing against Joan; far from it. True, she had urged her not to go to La Charité-sur-Loire, because the weather was bad and it was really "too cold." True, she also deplored the fact that Joan had so little confidence in Philip of Burgundy and kept hammering away that the only "good peace" to be gotten out of him was "at the end of a lance." But Catherine nonetheless said that Heaven had commissioned her to travel through the kingdom, taking collections for His Majesty and his devoted Servant.

But Joan did not believe in Catherine's apparitions, so she asked to be allowed to share them, and spent two nights with her. The first time, sleep was stronger than she, and the Blessed Virgin came while she was slumbering. The second, though she succeeded in keeping her eyes open all night, no "lady in white" appeared. But it seemed that Brother Richard had gotten the King's ear, so Joan firmly warned His Majesty that all of Catherine's accounts were "but madness and naught." It was dirty pool, and was to bring the characteristic ironic smile to the lips of Anatole France as he later described this contest between rival "illuminates," with the girl from Bar trying to defend her exclusive rights against her competitor from the Atlantic seaboard. But it is worth looking into what later happened to Catherine, and how we know about it. This Catherine, edged out by Joan, later went to Paris (but how did she get in among the Anglo-Burgundians?), appeared before the competent tribunal and was acquitted. Since Joan was a prisoner at that time, she recommended to the judges that they see to it the Maid be kept vigilantly under watch, for it she were not, this good friend of the English told them, Joan would surely succeed in escaping: "The devil will help her."

As for Brother Richard, Joan did not hesitate to tell Cauchon that he had been "very unhappy" with her. It is clear that in unmasking Catherine, Joan had made herself another enemy in the royal entourage, and a virulent one.

She was aware of that fact, but what she did not know was what was being planned against her in even more dangerous quarters. One of the Venetian traders whose correspondence has been preserved and furnishes us with

substantial details about Joan and her times heard from
several religious in November that the University of Paris
—which had been "English" since 1418—was intensely interested in Joan. We already know that Bedford saw "that
woman" as an "apostate." But however devout a Christian
Bedford might be, and however devoted to the defense of
orthodoxy, the repression of heresy was not one of his
functions. That job belonged to the clergy. The University
of Paris was alerted. Joan's case, touching on religion as it
did, concerned the University and indicated that it must
take action. It had to intervene, since it was the guardian
of Catholic truth. And it seemed to be common knowledge
within the orders that the University of Paris had gone to
work on it: it had "denounced" Joan to the Pope. The
Church could not help being moved to action by the out-
rages committed by a "dissolute woman," scandalously
dressed as a man in defiance of Holy Writ, and bringing
trouble and "sedition" everywhere. This was flagrant heresy.

The University of Paris at this time was unquestionably
the brightest light in the Western Christian world. But the
flame of a light could also act as a torch. It illuminated, but
could burn if need be. The stake at which Jan Hus perished
in 1415 was only a short time gone. And while Joan was
going to the baths with La Touroulde, the whole ecclesiastical apparatus was being put into motion against her. The
theologians at Paris were beginning to gather the faggots
on which they would burn her, two years hence.[2]

---

[2]Rome was concerned with Joan, as well. Surely, Charles VII had at least sent
word to His Holiness of his coronation. In a letter of May, 1429, Jacques Gélu
noted that the Cardinal of Foix, coming through Embrun in April on his way
back from Rome, spoke to him at length of the Maid. So Martin V was well aware
of the activities of this girl who, cutting in on his functions, claimed to have
special celestial attention. And we must not forget the Inquisitor Turelure among
the investigators at Poitiers in March. An inquisitor was an agent of Rome; it was
his duty to keep his superiors informed and seek their advice.

Will anyone ever get to see the "Joan file" that must exist somewhere in the
Vatican archives? On some subjects, there are no caves deeper, no dungeons more
secret, than those.

What was happening, politically, in this winter of 1429–1430, and in foreign affairs?

Philip had been perfect. He had made no difficulty whatsoever in December about the extension of the truce. It was now to run to April 16, and Charles lulled himself with the idea that in April everything would work out. Philip was at the moment very preoccupied with his new marriage, his third. In January, he was to marry Isabel of Portugal, and Bruges was to be the scene of dazzling festivities. But the situation was deteriorating, and Charles was beginning to worry. He could tolerate the fact that cousin Philip had been promoted "lieutenant general" for France by Bedford in October. That did not affect the King; it was just tinsel, a gaudy title and nothing more. Just another proof of how worried the English were. The Goddams—thank God!—had not dared fight at Montepilloy. They were unsure of themselves and wished above all not to lose the support of Burgundy. But despite his "lieutenantcy," Philip had had no qualms about confirming the truce in December, and the Royal Chancellery was still congratulating itself on the way things were going. Unfortunately, on February 13, 1430, Bedford made another, more disturbing, move in Philip's direction. He "gave" him Brie and Champagne: in other words, those territories that the English theoretically controlled, where Charles had made a disagreeable foray the summer before, Bedford now decreed as part of the Duchy of Burgundy. This was on condition, of course, that Philip occupy them by force, when he saw fit. It was a sizable annexation, which made Philip's eyes light up. And Charles wondered whether the troubles were not about to start again.

The people of Reims were aware of this maneuver, and once more they turned to Joan. Afraid of being attacked, they called on her for help. On March 16, Joan replied. She was unchanged. The fall and winter months, during which we know so little about what she did except for the Gressart episode,[3] had not spoiled her. Full of vim and vigor again, she even displayed her old swashbuckling style: should the "Burgundian traitors" ever dare lay siege to Reims, Joan would strike the attackers like a whirlwind and, she proclaimed, "I will make them go for their spurs [to run away] so fast that they will not know where to find them." On March 28, Joan wrote a second letter. The first had not been enough to calm apprehensions in Reims, and Joan tried to buck up the people's courage. In all likelihood, they would have preferred her to talk not only about giving them the help they needed herself, but also about some from the King.

Joan answered, "Why, of course! That goes without saying; should you have the need, the King would succor you."

And to revive the flagging hopes of the frightened populace, Joan imparted an important piece of news to them: "All of Brittany now is French, and the Duke is to send the King a thousand soldiers, paid for two months."

Where did she ever pick that one up? Neither contemporary documents nor events that followed give any confirmation of this amazing report.

By all evidence, Joan's morale was high again at the end of March, 1430. One senses she was warm with joyous excitement. She was thrilled at the prospect. She was going to fight. And the fact was, in a few days, she would be on her way again, standard aloft, going off to war, toward her rendezvous with fate.

---

[3]The only solid facts: on December 25, she was at Jargeau (what for, remains a mystery), and on January 19, at Orléans. No light whatever on what happened to her during February, 1430, nor where she spent that month. After March 3, she was at Sully-sur-Loire, La Trémoille's château (a curious place for her to turn up).

I X

The Capture

Why and how did Joan go off to war the last time?

Why? Because the truce with Burgundy was just about to end, and this time—Alas! said the King in consternation; Hurrah! shouted Joan—the dark machinations were over, they were back to reality. This time, the hateful armistice that should never have been signed would not be renewed.

According to word coming in from the north, John of Luxembourg, one of Philip's henchmen, had already started the campaign. He appeared to be heading for Compiègne, which had never accepted the terms of the August 21 agreement. Charles VII had been stupid enough to award Philip a right to occupy this entirely "French" city, but its people had refused to knuckle under to Burgundy. Archbishop-Chancellor Regnault, always ready for dirty work, had gone there and tried in vain to get them to listen to his infamous urgings: Be nice! Give in! and so on. This had been a pure waste of time, happily, and Compiègne had held out. The war was about to start again. So going to the assistance of that faithful city was of the first priority. Joan would approach it, roam about in the neighborhood, be ready and close at hand—that was what she had in mind. And perhaps a few side ideas, which I think we have proof of (as will be seen), about Paris itself.

On the other hand, we must not lose sight of Joan's own conviction, born of the warning she had received: Joan knew that she did not have much longer. She said it clearly back at Chinon: "I will last but a year, scarcely more."[1] Now the twelve months that had been allotted for her task were over, finished; all that was left was the "scarcely more," the meager supplement. That, too, was a reason why Joan had to go back into action as April began in 1430.

Under what conditions did she go? Perceval de Cagny (an Armagnac in the service of the Duke d'Alençon) asserted that Joan departed Sully "unbeknownst to the King and without begging his leave." That seems doubtful to me. It must have been more involved than that. D'Aulon remained alongside her, and d'Aulon was one of the King's men: it was the King who a year before had assigned him to her, as a sort of steward, or equerry, or majordomo. He was well organized; all spit and polish; not the least bit given to impulse. It would surprise me very much if he had ventured to go with Joan on some clandestine undertaking. Her brother Peter was with her,[2] and he was not one to join in an enterprise that was dangerous and might meet with the disapproval of His Bountiful Majesty. To my mind, Joan left with permission, although not on His Majesty's orders. Did she want to fight? Was that her aim? Then go to it, girl, the King said, at your own risk.

Charles VII was not taking up arms. He was not going

---

[1]The previously mentioned Giustiniani correspondence shows her predictions were known throughout the kingdom in the spring of 1429: "said damsel is to accomplish two great feats, and then die."
[2]And brother John? Perhaps he was also along, but lucky or shrewd enough to avoid being taken, as his younger brother was, before Compiègne.

to appear before Philip on the march, like a gladiator confronting a wild beast. On the contrary, as ever, he still desperately clung to the hope that nothing was lost for his grand design, even now and under these circumstances. The friendly understanding between himself and cousin Burgundy had to come, and he would do everything to bring it about. Charles would not give Joan a *sou* for her guerrilla warfare. He did not oppose it; by ignoring it, he was not required to forbid it.

Twice, in September and again in November, he had looked the other way and had allowed his Council to plan to rid him of Joan incidentally, in the Paris trap and the one at La Charité, where the Maid was to come to a glorious end fighting the enemies of her King. Both times Charles had thought better of it, and called it off. But now the chance he had been awaiting for months, a method of doing away with Joan which would not compromise his salvation, was at hand. It was suggested, indeed demanded, by Joan herself. What a relief! It was she who insisted on going out and courting death. He could not stop her. But he would not encourage her. No one around him encouraged her (unless that unfounded report about Brittany was fed to Joan by someone like La Trémoille, with that very specific aim in mind). If the Maid were to free him forever of her importunate presence at long last, Charles would in no way be to blame. He would be pure as the driven snow, and on all counts delighted.

For this, her last campaign, Joan would have no commander over her. This had never happened before. No Dunois, no d'Alençon, no d'Albret. The little "warrior chief," leading her soldiers entirely on her own, as she saw fit, and with divine inspiration. What soldiers? The ones she got with her own money, since the King had given her no mandate, and hers was to be a band of true "free-lances." Joan had been able to buy two hundred Piedmontese mercenaries whom their leader, Beretta, had put on the market. That was how things really stood in April, 1430: Joan was a gang chieftain. With these mercenaries on her payroll, she was off to adventure—just exactly, Regnault must have been thinking, as befitted an adventuress.[3]

We do not know the date of her departure, and once again, trying to follow her day by day would be difficult—indeed, impossible. What solid facts do we have?

Joan first went toward Melun. By what route? No indication. She was beneath Melun "in the week of Easter," as she would specify at her trial. Easter, in 1430, was on April 22. Therefore, she was before Melun between April 17 and April 22.[4] And that was where, she would say later, she *knew* through internal warning, that "before Saint John's day of the summer" she would be in enemy hands. Saint John of the summer was June 24. And she was to be taken "before." So, she had only a few weeks left.

At Rouen, Cauchon would press the point: "Did not your 'voices,' as you call them, tell you the very day when you would be taken prisoner?"

"No."

"What if, on the morning of May 23, you had been told: it will happen tonight. Would you still have gone to skirmish?"

"I would have been afraid," Joan said hesitantly. Then, after a silence, "Yes, I think I would have gone out anyway."

The following year, she was to give her judges one addi-

---

[3]It cannot hurt to stop and smile in the course of so depressing an account. If we refer to the great French *Encyclopedia* of 1776, we find, under the "Joan of Arc" entry: "The Prince [that is, Charles VII], all too well aware of the value of her services, had the Count de Dunois approach her and invite her to go with him to the siege of Compiègne."

[4]She mentioned the "moats" of the city. Did that mean she attacked it with so few men? No; rather that she came close to the walls, to show herself, to see what would happen.

tional detail, namely, that as soon as she knew her capture was imminent, she "left all matters of making war up to them" without revealing it to her "captains" (in the plural, Beretta having a second in command, no doubt). In other words, as for the conduct of operations, routes to be followed, engagements to avoid or provoke, she ceased giving orders but relied on her lieutenants. This, no doubt, so that her men would not be precipitated into any kind of critical situation if she should suddenly be taken from them. So Joan would not in fact retain her command very long on the only occasion when she actually held it; just the few days it took from Sully to Melun, in April, 1430.

We next find her at Lagny, where there were two events, two things she did that would be deemed incriminating at her trial. One, she was alleged to have played the faithhealer at Lagny and "brought a child back to life." A lie! Never, anywhere, before anyone, had Joan claimed any magical powers. While she was at Lagny, it had just happened that she was told of a newborn infant, three days old, who seemed doomed not to live. He had stopped breathing and was all "black." The parish priest dared not baptize him under these conditions. And yet, the heart must have been beating, for the little body remained warm. And several "maids" had begun praying before the picture of Our Lady.

"I went there," Joan testified, "with the other maids, and I prayed. And finally some life appeared in this child. He yawned three times, and was immediately baptized. He died shortly thereafter and was buried in consecrated ground."

That was what was important to the child's mother: that the poor little thing be spared the horrors of limbo, that he not be excluded from the cemetery, and a Christian burial open the doors of Paradise to him. That, point by point, was how it had all occurred. Where, in any of that, could one find anything wrong done by Joan? The court dropped it.

The other matter was more serious. Joan's mercenaries had taken a bandit known by the name of Franquet of Arras. Why? How? The Maid had not gone to war for police purposes. But the man was a "Burgundian," and perhaps he had attacked them. At Rouen, Joan, was to be accused of having violated the laws of honor by turning this Franquet over to the authorities at Senlis, who wanted him for a variety of crimes and put him to death. A prisoner "taken for ransom" could not be sent to his death. And though Joan made a poor case for herself, what she said makes us raise an eyebrow today. She wanted to exchange this Franquet for a prisoner she was interested in, an innkeeper, who had the Inn of the Bear in Paris. Well, in that case, she must have had some contacts in the capital: she would appear to have been in touch with what we would call a "network." And perhaps the soldiers that she had gotten together had not been intended merely to stand by in case Compiègne needed them.

It has been clearly established that there was a plan for an Armagnac uprising in Paris. The plot, however, was betrayed by a monk, a Carmelite friar, and on April 8, 1430, seven people were executed. When Joan took to the road with her battalion, marching in the direction of Paris, or at least of its approaches, had she not already nurtured a plan of going to the aid of these insurgents once their attempt was launched? She remembered September 8 and the horsemen who had come unexpectedly out of Paris in the wake of the Count of Montmorency to forsake the Anglo-Burgundians and rally to the King. She was convinced that there were people in Paris who were for Charles VII. What a magnificent operation it would be if the coordination of a Parisian uprising and her own arrival were to bring about that thunderbolt: the liberation of Paris!

At Court, she was being shunted aside; she got on everybody's nerves there. They had sent her out to be beaten by one Perrinet Gressart—and instead, in a fantastic turnabout, she would be turning his Big City back to her King. But the whole thing fell through because of an informer.

The theory I have just outlined does not seem inconceivable. We do know that Joan knew the name of one of these Parisian "Resistance" men (the innkeeper of The Bear) and knew he was in prison. She had anticipated having this friendly prisoner turned over to her in exchange for Franquet, whom she had taken.[5]

But then, "When I learned that the man from Paris was dead," she would say in Rouen, ". . . I said to the bailiff [of Senlis], 'Do with that one [Franquet] what justice demanded you do with him.' "

The criminal Burgundians had killed her Parisian contact, so it was too bad about Franquet! He could be killed, too. It is doubtful whether this actually corresponded to the (theoretical) code of medieval warfare. But Joan had a violent nature, as we have so often seen. And particularly at this time, when she felt that at any moment she might be falling into the trap, her nerves were strained to the breaking point. The happy face (*hilarem gerit vultum*) that Perceval de Boulainvilliers saw on her in June, 1429, was, I daresay, no longer the same: a dark ridge between the eyebrows had replaced the light and joy. Drawing and quartering, that was what she was threatening for Bournel, the governor of Soissons, about this same time: "If I take him, I will have him sliced in four." The warrior reaching the end of her line was not soft-hearted. Bournel had wel-

---

[5] And why can we not imagine that, with that exchange in mind, she had deliberately sent her men against Franquet and his gang in order to take him alive? Do we not read that in her words: "I had asked to have this Franquet so as to get in exchange a man from Paris."

comed her graciously, but no sooner had she turned away than he surrendered his city, sold it out to John of Luxembourg. Joan could not contain her rage against this scoundrel, and I would imagine her encounter before Soissons at Compiègne, on May 13, had done nothing to reassure her; for there she had bumped into Regnault, up to God only knew what underhanded dealings. He had never been able to stand her from the beginning. And the archbishop was inside Compiègne on the twenty-third, that fateful May 23, 1430, when Joan was unable to make it back in.

On May 6, 1430, Charles VII had made his disappointment known publicly. He sent a circular letter to all his subjects telling them that Philip of Burgundy was resuming his aggression after having "diverted and misled [him] through truces and otherwise." (At which, Joan must have shouted, although without glee, At last! At last! Didn't I tell you so?) Charles' letter was certainly no war cry. It was a groan. He donned gloves—not armored gauntlets—to delineate the situation. He did not thunder; he deplored. He did not even want to come right out and say Philip was a bad Frenchman who was an ally of the invader. Such rude terms were out. England was referred to only as a "certain power" that Philip had only "sided with." Charles was not issuing a call to arms. He was shaking his head, and lamenting. He wanted to make out that this new twist of events was but a minor setback to his cousin on the road which, come what might, led to better days.

While Charles VII was shedding tears, Philip had gotten into the saddle without leaving his château. He recaptured Choisy-au-Bac on May 16, and on the twenty-second he set up his headquarters at Coudun, a stone's-throw from Compiègne. Joan heard of this the very same day. From Crépy-en-Valois, where she was, she was able to get to Compiègne

before dawn. By afternoon, she was leading her troops out
to "skirmish." She went too far forward. The enemy saw
her mistake and cut her off. Her mercenaries panicked and
yelled, Every man for himself!

Perceval de Cagny, writing of these events, attributes the
conveniently retouched words to Joan: "Be quiet! It is
within your power to undo them [the enemy]. Think only
of striking them!" We can translate this into something
closer to what the Maid must have shouted at her panicky
men: "Cowards! Cowards! Just stick in there and keep
punching! Forward!" But they were running for their
lives.

The Piedmontese scrambled madly toward the bridge,
the river, the boats. Joan followed. She was about to reach
the drawbridge when it was raised. She was surrounded,
with only a few of her companions around her. A Burgundian grabbed the skirts of that "cloth-of-gold surcoat" that,
ever elegant, she wore over her armor, yanked with all his
might, and pulled her from the saddle. Joan fell and remained "all flat on the ground," as Georges Chastellain
would chronicle it. The armor weighed some forty-five
pounds. The Maid was captured.

Had William de Flavy, the military governor of Compiègne, deliberately intended that Joan be taken? Perceval
de Cagny, despite being a faithful Armagnac, did not so
accuse him; on the contrary, he excused him: "When the
Governor saw the English and Burgundians near to entering the bridge, lest this mean loss of the position he ordered
the bridge raised and the gate closed."

I would, however, call attention to three points. Has
there ever been an example of a city being captured
through an open gate? It falls only if the walls are overrun
by a multitude of assailants. A gate can always be blocked.
Restricted to a front of twenty to thirty feet at most, however heavy an assault, it cannot be powerful. I find it hard

to believe that Flavy really thought his city was imperiled by such a struggle, even at its very gate. Secondly, it was indeed Flavy himself who ordered the bridge raised; it was not some decision made in desperation by the detail guarding the bridge. The governor was watching the skirmish from the top of the watchtowers. He could see Joan in danger, and nonetheless ordered the shelter toward which she was galloping closed against her. Finally, we must note that Flavy, a minor figure but not without some protection (in 1427, as governor of Beaumont-en-Argonne, he had surrendered his city, but was not cashiered as a result), was not alone inside Compiègne. He was under the eyes and control of Chancellor Regnault of Chartres in person. I am not attempting to determine the governor's guilt (able advocates have defended his memory); I just say that, by all evidence, the question is moot.

The capture of the Maid was quite an event for both Bedford and Philip. Monstrelet the Burgundian does not hide the fact in his *Chronicle:* "Those who belonged to the Burgundian party, as well as the English, were very joyful over it, more than if they had captured five hundred fighting men, for they feared and dreaded no captain nor other warrior chief as much as this Maid until this day."

The same evening, May 23, Philip dictated a letter announcing the news to those in his states. He had the prisoner brought before him. We know nothing about their interview. The Duchess, his third wife, may also have asked to see the soldier girl who was in contact with either Heaven or Hell and whom everybody in Europe had been talking about for a year now. But we know nothing of how Joan may have fared before her.

John of Luxembourg's mercenaries had captured Joan. Philip knew what the custom was. He let his impecunious relative have the enticing chance for ransom, and that gentleman's mouth was already watering over it. Surely the English would make an offer for the purchase of the prisoner, but surely Charles VII would do likewise. John would put Joan up at auction. But he waited in vain for any proposal from Charles VII. There was absolute silence. Charles had no interest. The Burgundians had done him too perfect a favor in ridding him of Joan for him to ruin it by getting her back. This, despite the fact that Jacques Gélu, the respectable and respected Bishop of Embrun, had written him rather daringly, "I would recommend to you that, for the recovery of this girl and the redemption of her life, you spare neither means nor money, lest you be ready to assume indelible blame for a very reprehensible ingratitude."

The King's indifference seemed so ugly and so repellent that people everywhere refused to believe it. There were many naïve enough throughout the kingdom to keep spreading the rumor that, of course, naturally, His Majesty was trying to save Joan, and was intervening, maneuvering, threatening. Even recently, the Duke de Lévis-Mirepoix tried in vain, after so many others, to convince us that Charles VII organized armed raids to free the Maid.[6] For his part, Thierry Maulnier, with the detachment of a sage, has demonstrated for us once more that Charles VII was right in his determined standoffishness. Raised as he was at the knee of the royalist Charles Maurras, and therefore an unerring parroter of that party's slogan about the "forty kings who, in a thousand years, made France," Thierry Maulnier learned his lesson well: our kings always had an exemplary understanding of what was in the national interest; and the national interest, in 1430, ordained

---

[6]See *Mémorial* (1956). The Duke also adds that Charles VII "did pay the ransom of [her brother] Peter." He is misinformed.

that the King leave Joan where she was.

"Trying to free her by a military operation," he writes, "or by offering a huge ransom, would have been to continue identifying his side with a person who was henceforth controversial, and no longer of any use. . . . The royal cause could not afford to remain tied to a lost cause."[7]

Nothing could be more reasonable, as one can readily see. I do not think that Joan in prison had any illusions whatsoever about what she might expect from her onetime "sweet Dauphin."

As for Regnault, he would write to those in his diocese that the inconvenience that had befallen Joan was all too predictable, in view of the Maid "heeding no counsel and doing ever as she pleased." He made a point of informing them that the King had been visited by a little shepherd of the Gévaudan "who said neither more nor less than the Maid, and had commandment from God." Regnault then hastened to add an explicit opinion voiced by this child of Heaven about Joan's fall. This was an inevitable result, the boy said, because "she had set herself up in pride" and "because of the luxurious attire" (remember that golden surcoat!) which she enjoyed wearing. Only one possible conclusion: she got what was coming to her.

John of Luxembourg first locked Joan up at the château of Beaulieu, not far from Compiègne. She was well treated there; d'Aulon, who was with her, showered her with all the attentions he could. Nonetheless, she tried to escape. No shrinking violet, the Maid: she had drive, initiative, and ingenuity. She darted out of her room and locked her warders inside (perhaps as they brought her a meal); she picked up two planks, in the corridor, and loaded one on each

---

[7]Thierry Maulnier, *Jeanne et les juges*, preface, pp. 37–38.

shoulder, in such a way that her face could not be seen from the side. She hoped that, with her stocky build and rather masculine walk, dressed in men's clothes, she might be taken for one of the carpenters who were working at the château at the time. Unfortunately, the gate tender came along and recognized her (the ones she had locked up, above, doubtless assisting in the discovery with the racket they must have been making). Joan ran; she was chased; she was caught and subdued. It had not worked.

Her captor then had her transferred to his own fortress, at Beaurevoir, where there were two other Joans, his wife and his old aunt, both of whom were very kind to her. They offered her a beautiful gown or, if she preferred, "some fabric" so they could have one made to suit her tastes. Joan answered that she "had not permission therefor from God," and that "the time is not yet." At Bourges or elsewhere, yes, when she was resting and temporarily relieved of duties, she could afford adornments; but here, as a prisoner, she remained a soldier. It was not over yet. She smiled, and the ladies understood that she fully intended to escape. Just not to be turned over to the English! That was what terrified her. The aunt promised Joan that she would make such a request of her nephew. But it was no use. The nephew cared only about the money.

A young lord of the neighborhood, Aymon de Macy, came to visit her sometimes. They had some good times together; but when he got a bit too intimate, Joan gave him a tongue-lashing. And after that, he minded his manners.

Tournai was only thirty leagues away and Joan wrote to its people, in a brief letter that was allowed to go through, that she could use a few gold pieces "for her necessities." What "necessities"? She had everything she needed at Beaurevoir. What was behind her request seems clear enough to me: those gold pieces might be enough to buy off her guards. Was Tournai ungenerous, or were the guards above corruption?

Then Bishop Cauchon, that hateful "renegade French-man," came to Beaurevoir to demand control of her in the name of the English, and Joan saw red. She jumped. Her "voices" had forbidden her to try it, but she "could abide no longer." She would quite frankly state at the trial, "I preferred to die rather than fall into the hands of the English."

Was she really trying to kill herself? She remembered Les Tourelles, on April 30 of the year before, and what the Goddams had yelled to her on that day: "We will burn you, you witch!" Better to smash her skull than that horrible death by fire. Yet at the same time she was hoping that she would not die. She hoped the angels might perhaps carry her, so she could go to the aid of Compiègne. The city was still resisting, but there was word that if they won, the besiegers would kill all the inhabitants, down to and including seven-year-old children. It has never been clearly established what height Joan jumped from. She broke no limbs. I wonder whether she did not land in the water of the moat or a ditch. She got off easy, with only a slight concussion that left her "two or three days without being able to eat or drink."

She had already been a captive for five months. Fall was turning into winter, and nothing was happening; there was no help. The English were about to lay hands on her; she could see there was no way out of that. Joan, at Beaurevoir, was a little trapped animal, and she was frantic.

X

Thrown to the Wolves

❖ ❖ ❖

And good Joan of Lorraine
Burned by the English at Rouen

as Villon would write. These two well-known lines greatly
contributed to perpetuating the wrong impression. For the
English did not burn Joan. The Inquisition did.

On May 25, 1430, news of Joan's capture reached Paris;
the ledger of Parliament proves it. The very next day, the
twenty-sixth, the University of Paris sprang into action.
Or, rather, back into action—if, indeed, it had "denounced" Joan to Rome eighteen months earlier. The
eulogy by Bishop Bossuet, a couple of centuries later, for
one Nicholas Cornet, provides the best idea of what the
University of Paris was: "Nowhere else is the treasure of
truth so inviolable. The very fountains of Jacob flow no
more incorruptible. Its mouth is ever open, to speak only
the truth. Nothing which infringes the rule can escape its
censure."

In the fifteenth century, this impeccable University of

Paris was the great breeding ground of theologians, the gathering place of doctors, the sacred mountain, the temple, the light, the honor and conscience of Catholicism. And, since 1418, this University of Paris had been English —though Roman at the same time, because of the benefices, and it would be understatement to say the University welcomed these. Many of the benefices in the "English" half of the country were distributed by the "King of France and England," in other words, the Royal Council of His Majesty Henry VI; but there were all those other prebendaries that were directly dependent on Rome, and the University had always been gratified with a goodly assortment of these from the Holy See. If the designation of "successor to Peter" was slow in coming to Martin V at Constance, a touch-and-go affair at best, it was because the matter of the benefices was so closely tied in to it, and that layman promoted a priest in a bare forty-eight hours was never allowed to forget how much his election owed to the theologians of Paris.

They kept an eye on him, insisting he keep the promise he had been forced to make about convening periodic councils. That whole idea had been odious to Martin V, and so far he had succeeded in getting around it, but now he was being threatened. He was forced to resign himself to it, and a council was scheduled to be held the following year at Basel. So this was no time to cross the illustrious and dangerous "corporate body" in Paris.[1]

The University of Paris, guardian of Catholic truth, meant to make short shrift of the "apostate" whom the Regent Bedford had indicted. Joan was hardly in the hands of John of Luxembourg (meaning in those of his master Philip), when the University demanded imperatively that

---

[1] We might also note that Martin V held Cauchon in great esteem. In 1426, he had written him, "By reason of your faithful services and other virtues, you will find Us ever favorably disposed toward you, and full of benevolence."

the Duke of Burgundy hand over his prisoner. The letter was signed Brother Martin Billorin.

And who was he? The vicar-general of John Graverent who, for the moment, just happened to be in Rome, where his functions suggested that he had a close connection with the Holy See. John Graverent was none other than "Inquisitor-General of the Faith and of heretical perversity, delegated by the apostolic authority for the Kingdom of France."

So Brother Billorin stated as follows: "In the name of his office and the power vested in him by the Holy See," he required that Philip of Burgundy immediately turn over to his jurisdiction "the said woman who calls herself the Maid, by means of whom the honor of God [*sic*] has been offended beyond measure, the faith exceedingly hurt, and the Church sorely dishonored." This dread heretic had been captured and put where she could do no further harm, Heaven be blessed for that. "But little would such capture mean if there were not to follow what behooves in order to satisfy the offense perpetrated against our merciful Maker, the faith, and the Holy Church." Consequently, the Duke was requested graciously, and without delay, in accordance with his Christian duty, to have his captive brought to Paris so that a tribunal of the Church, convoked for the occasion, might judge the criminal.

One can only admire the disregard for caution with which Father Jean-Baptiste-Joseph Ayroles dared entitle one chapter of his five-volume *La Vraie Jeanne d'Arc* (The Real Joan of Arc) (1894–1903), "The Pseudo-Theologian Enemies of Joan and of the Papacy." "Pseudo-theologians," indeed! There was nothing counterfeit, nothing at all surreptitious about them. They were as qualified as anyone within the brotherhood; they were authentic masters. "Enemies of Joan"? That, to be sure. But "of the Papacy" at the same time? One of them was the "delegate of the apostolic authority," and far from being against the Pope in any way, they were acting in his name and in full concert with him.

Let's stop playing with words and record this one historical fact, this undeniable truth: Joan was following Jan Hus and Jerome of Prague to the stake, as she herself would be followed by Savonarola. She was deemed heretical and "seditious." The latter term would appear in the specifications against her, though only subtly slipped in—it would have been maladroit to give it the first place it truly warranted, the first and capital place. For it was the major, decisive charge. If the Maid had come out on the right side, if her visions and voices had served the cause of Henry VI, there would have been no grounds for objection by the Paris theologians that Joan had taken the name of Heaven and claimed to have received a divine mission. The tragedy for Joan was that she was on the other side, for Charles of Valois, not the English King. Her wrong political option thus became a religious crime. Because she was "seditious" and in rebellion against the Anglo-Burgundians, the doctors deemed her an "apostate." If Jan Hus and Savonarola had not been politically bothersome, and a menace to the profiteers, they would not have been subjected either to the "religious" trials that cost them their lives. It was an old ruse to hide behind "the honor of God" and the needs of wholesome theology, where the matter was in reality purely political. It was more convenient not to admit that, but to disguise as a defense of the faith what in fact was mere protection of material interests.

That was how they would move against Fénelon in the seventeenth century when he dared criticize Louis XIV's absolutism; Bossuet would immediately declare him theologically in the wrong, culpable in religion, and liable to the censure of Rome. The Reformed Christians would do the same, a century later, with Jean-Jacques Rousseau. At

that time, the civil authorities of Geneva—the Petty Council which had become the private den of the bankers—were
concerned over Rousseau's political ideas: the man of the
"lower streets," to whom the masses were listening, was
growing dangerous to the "order" set up by the affluent,
and the "venerable class" of pastors, totally devoted to
those in high places, issued appropriate maledictions
against Rousseau. He became an enemy of the "true religion," and the Protestant ministers of Geneva, comrades of
the bankers, condemned him in pious indignation.

It took the English some time, however, to grasp the
favor the theologians were so anxious to do them. They
kept insisting it was they who should have Joan; they
wanted possession so as to confine her within their own
prisons. So they in turn demanded her of Philip.

Weeks went by. June came to an end. John of Luxembourg was not planning to deliver his prisoner to anyone
except for money. He was still hoping that a munificent
ransom offer would come from the Armagnacs. But they
sent no emissary. Deathly silence. The University of Paris
and the English, meanwhile, were both growing impatient.
On July 14, an important personage, both political and religious, came to visit the Burgundian camp before Compiègne. It was Bishop Cauchon, whose ardor for the occupying power had always been so great that, as we said, the
English had made him a member of their Royal Council.
He was therefore both a representative of the Church and
an important politician. Actually, he was not too well liked
at the University, precisely because he was a bishop, and
an endless quarrel over the benefices had been going on for
ages between the bishopric and the doctors. They had resigned themselves to using him because of his standing
with Bedford, and the University entrusted him with an

entreaty to Philip, which this time was virtually a summons. An arrangement was suggested: Let the English take
the "witch," since they felt so strongly they should have
her, but on the express understanding that if Joan was
being "sent" to Henry VI—the King, "our Sire"—it was so
that he might immediately turn her over "to the Church."
This truly vital specification was categorically stated, and
the doctors continued to pride themselves that it was
through the University and its works that Joan would be
tried for her multiple "crimes" of "witchcraft," "idolatry,"
diabolical "invocations, . . . and several other cases," as well,
"affecting our faith."

Cauchon convinced the English that the only sure way
to get John of Luxembourg to give up his little treasure was
not to be miserly, and he arrived with a fitting proposal:
Bedford was ready to pay "ten thousand *livres*" for the
Maid—truly a king's ransom. And to try to get Philip to
urge his vassal John to accept, the English government
applied pressure on July 17: it temporarily forbade all English tradesmen to make any purchases whatever at Ant-
werp.

John of Luxembourg was a realist, and realists believe
only in hard facts and cold cash. Before letting go of the
Maid, he wanted the money there, on his table. The doctors
of the Church could hardly contain their irritation; the itch
for their good deed was devouring them, while days and
weeks went by without Joan being delivered to them. It
was all the fault of the English, those knaves, who were
willing to agree to ten thousand *livres*, but were not willing
to pay the sum, or even advance it. The "occupied" French
would have to foot the bill: Bedford had just decreed a new
tax of eighty thousand *livres* for the states of Normandy,
ten thousand of which would go for the purchase of the
apostate. But collecting it took time.

Here it was November, and the theologians were still

awaiting their prey. Finally, after the fifteenth, around the twentieth, the sum was counted out to the girl's owner, and the English took possession of her. On November 21, the University of Paris sent two simultaneous letters, one to the King of England and the other to Cauchon. One reminded the sovereign respectfully, but with a bit of asperity, that "on several occasions" (so apparently not all the documents have come down to us) the person in question had been honorably requested of him, unfortunately in vain, and the letter deplored this "great delay of justice which must displease any good Christian." Fortunately, the theologians added, "we have recently heard that this woman called the Maid has now been delivered into your power, a fact for which we are greatly joyful," and now they were "confident that, through your good offices," it would finally become possible to "repair the evils and scandals brought about" through her fault "to the great prejudice of divine honor." And therefore, Joan was to be "brought" without delay "into the City of Paris," there to be tried and judged.

The other letter was to Cauchon himself, and it has an unusual tone. The doctors of the University on Saint Genevieve's hill were most displeased with him, and they did not politely beat around the bush in telling him so. True, they addressed him by all of his religious titles and the salutation was worded as coming from the University of Paris to "the Reverend Father in God, our very honored Lord Bishop and Count of Beauvais," but that was merely a polite formality preceding criticism of his inefficacy: "We note with astonishment the great delay incurred in the sending of this woman. . . . If Your Fatherhood had devoted more active diligence" to pursuing the matter, the maleficent, demoniacal Maid would already have paid for her crimes. A bit more energy there, if you please, Lord Cauchon. Your conduct is surprising and one might be tempted to say suspicious, at any rate, unworthy of a servant of Heaven and distinguished son of the Church. The University jumped at the chance to cast blame on a member of the episcopacy it so disliked. It was cruelly unjust in doing so, for the Bishop of Beauvais had not been idle, as is attested by the compensation of 765 *livres*, due him and paid by the English Treasury. This sum was for the "one hundred and fifty-three days" during which he "performed the service of the King," especially "in several voyages toward Milord the Duke of Burgundy or toward Messer John of Luxembourg . . . in Flanders" first, and then "at the siege of Compiègne," then "at Beaurevoir . . . in the matter of Joan, who is called the Maid." And he could really not be held responsible for Bedford's stubbornness in refusing to pay Joan's ransom so long as the taxpayers of Normandy had not made it possible for him to do so without using his own funds.

So it was agreed that the Maid should be tried by the Church, but not in Paris. Bedford wanted the trial at Rouen, and nowhere else. Not that he questioned the devotion of the University's theologians, but Paris was not secure enough a city. Bedford had been keeping an eye on Philip, whose behavior for quite some time now had concerned him, as he had not even found it possible to take Compiègne—or not found it convenient, to state it more accurately. By fall, he became discouraged, and on October 23, he withdrew his soldiers and lifted the siege of the city. A strange way for him to behave. Philip certainly did not seem to be waging war against the counterfeit King Charles either as a serious fighter or as a loyal ally. It was out of the question to let Joan be tried in Paris. Rouen was the right place for that, Rouen, second largest city of the kingdom, the true English capital, since that was where the

young King resided with his governor, the Earl of Warwick. But let the University of Paris have no fear: it was not
to be kept from participating in the trial, quite the contrary. Not only would it be invited to send a whole delegation, but nothing would be decided without consulting it,
and the University's opinion would in all instances prevail.

Joan was transferred in November and December, by
easy stages. The English took possession of her at Arras,
and then circled her through a wide arc outside the reach
—as if the King of Bourges were interested!—of any Armagnac attack. She was held for a short time (for reasons
we cannot explain) at the fortress of Le Crotoy; then went
through Saint-Valery-sur-Somme, Eu, Dieppe, and on the
afternoon of December 23, 1430, she arrived at Rouen,
where she was incarcerated at the château of Bouvreuil.

On January 3, 1431, the "King of France and England"
(now nine years old) *lent* Joan to the ecclesiastical authorities. On December 28, Cauchon had had no difficulty in
getting the Rouen chapter to recognize the requisite "territorial concession" that would allow him to officiate outside his diocese as Bishop of Beauvais. And, according to
canon law, he associated himself with the local representative of the Holy Inquisition. In this way, the sentence that
was already virtually pronounced and needed only to be
substantiated with the appropriate whereases would have
the supreme sanction by which Rome itself and the Church
entire, acting through the Pope (here represented by the
"apostolic delegate"), would become a full party to the
condemnation and punishment of the Maid. The English
letter of January 3, as I said, *lent* Joan to the Church; it did
not *turn her over*. It further specified that the accused was
to be "taken" to the Reverend Father in God "as many
times as he shall deem necessary . . . it nevertheless being
our intention," said the English, "to recover and take back
this woman if it should happen that she were not convicted

and attainted of the above-stated cases." For the English did not hesitate to remind the tribunal that was about to convene what they wanted Joan formally "convicted" of. First, the unspeakable outrage to morals and to divine law constituted by "that woman's" adoption of male garb, then the "homicides" which she instigated or of which she was personally guilty, and finally, the "dogmatizations" she was said to have espoused, "scandalous and most perilous to our holy Faith."

Did the English fear some disloyal action by Cauchon, or think that the University of Paris would turn out to be timid? Surely not where the theologians of Lutetia were concerned, for they had given ample proof of their exemplary vehemence. Cauchon? He was their man, and they trusted him, even though at times he perhaps acted less enthusiastic than they might wish and was occasionally seen to hesitate when he should not. No, the English were not worried about the churchmen of Beauvais, Rouen, or Paris. It was Rome they mistrusted. Why the devil had those priests insisted on bringing the Inquisition into their business? Well, that was the way it had to be. Otherwise the procedure would have been valueless, for the trial of a heretic came under the jurisdiction of the Inquisition, period. But Rome was a bureaucracy. And who could say what deplorable influences, bolstered by hard arguments, might not affect it in a way against which they had to be on guard? The English still could not believe Charles would not intervene. For he was the one they were really getting at, through Joan. What they wanted was to destroy the effect that his consecration at Reims might have on so many people. Once the Church had pronounced the dishonor of the Maid, he might go and whistle with his consecration, since it had been carried out under the auspices of a witch so declared in the very name of the Vicar of Christ.

Obviously, Charles had to move, to act, to bring pressure

to bear on Rome so that such a trick could not be played on him. Which was why Bedford was being so cautious. If it happened that the Church shirked its duty in the end and did not bring in the verdict he demanded, he could take back the captive whom he was only conditionally entrusting to it.

But these were superfluous worries, as it turned out. Rome was most dependable. If Charles did make a move (something we will probably never know for certain), the Holy See disregarded it. The "apostolic authority" made no objection to the doings at Rouen; it was too concerned at the time with keeping a low profile before the "Fathers" of the coming—and now all too imminent—Council of Basel.

I want a "fine trial," Cauchon said. This meant a canonically unassailable trial, which, through its absolute observance of all the rules, would disguise what it really was as much as possible. Nothing was to be neglected. Everything was to be handled with the most exacting thoroughness, typical of any Inquisition trial seeking nothing but the truth. There were just two small problems, two bits of law that needed to be stretched. One, an accused to be tried by the Church was supposed to be kept in a Church prison. But Joan remained in her lay prison, guarded by soldiers. The other concerned who was paying the costs of this Church trial. It was not the Church, but the English. They allocated a *livre* per day for the assessors; or that, at least, was what would be paid to the delegates of the University, who were granted an additional twenty-five *livres* each for the Paris-Rouen round trip. One of the more important delegates, Beaupère, also received a supplement of thirty *livres*, in view of the impending Council and the preparatory meetings for it that he would have to attend.

Now everything was ready. There were to be only two actual judges: the Reverend Father in God Peter Cauchon and "very religious person" Brother John Lemaître, Vicar of the Inquisition at Rouen, holding delegation of powers from his superior John Graverent, Inquisitor-General for France, who was Rome's eagle eye. It will be noted, however, that Brother Lemaître stayed in the background during the trial: the transcript does not reveal a single word of his, not one question he put to Joan. Was he under instructions or did he remain silent of his own accord? The latter hypothesis seems more likely, to judge by what he told Cauchon on February 20: that "the scruple of his conscience" induced him not to wish "to involve himself in the matter." He was there on assignment and could not do. otherwise. Inquisitor Lemaître was "covering" this event for his superiors because he had to; he obeyed his orders, but his heart was not in it. To me, he seems a most unhappy man who would have liked to be elsewhere at the time.

The six representatives of the University of Paris were of an entirely different stripe, however, and right in their element: they were incandescent and "most joyful," as they themselves wrote. Two of them were stars of the illustrious institution: young Thomas de Courcelles, who was on the rise, and the famous John Beaupère, dripping with benefices, the champion in amassing cumulative canonries. He had no less than seven at the moment, being at once canon of Autun, Beauvais, Besançon, Laon, Lisieux, Rouen, and Paris. All of them were "assessors," as would be the whole cohort of ordained characters who attended intermittently. On some days there were only twenty of them, but often forty, and at the most important sessions there were up to sixty canons, abbots, bishops, and even the Cardinal of Winchester who deigned to attend. The "promoter"—as they called the prosecutor—was John d'Estivet, a tool of Cauchon's. Cauchon was not the worst of the lot, but his reputation has grown inordinately, largely because of his unfortunate name.[2] It was not true that hatred dripped from his words. Claudel was to speak of the horrible clerics at Rouen "foaming at the fangs," tearing into Joan, taking whole mouthfuls "of that innocent flesh, with the appetite of cannibals." Thomas de Courcelles, certainly, and some of the others, were several lengths ahead of the Bishop of Beauvais in their ferocity. Cauchon was just doing his hideous job with detachment. Flanked by the silent Lemaître, he loquaciously presided over the convicting bee.

A preliminary inquiry was made in Joan's home region. It was the second time this was done; but as the monks sent by the clerics of Poitiers to Domrémy two years before had known they would be welcome if they brought back a harvest of favorable testimony, so now Cauchon's agents were anxious to come back from the Bar country with a barrel of filth to please their employers. Nothing could be easier.

Joan was tarnished at the moment, since her setback before Paris and her capture; and since it always pays to be in step with the powerful, everyone was ready to follow Baudricourt's example. Modeling himself after his superiors (René of Anjou, Yolande, and the King), he was, to put it mildly, acting extremely reserved. The hirelings sent on this mission must have worked uninhibitedly over the information they got, adding to it, embellishing it, dressing it up in all kinds of finery, yet I would not dare suggest that they made up out of whole cloth the precious arsenal of gossip that they brought back.

There were some lively tales here, transferred into the

[2] A homonym of *cochon*, or "pig." "One of fate's great comic gags," Joseph Delteil would call it in his prize-winning *Jeanne d'Arc* (1925), while Paul Claudel felt it to be "this proper name which it is hard not to consider the proper noun."

dossier and echoed clearly for us in the seventy articles, or
charges and specifications, drawn up by the "promoter,"
Canon d'Estivet, to indict Joan. Judge for yourself.

"Joan's early years were not given to education or instruction in the belief in the principles of our faith, but
instead accustomed and trained by certain old women in
the uses of wizardry, divination [and so on]. . . . Toward her
fifteenth year, of her own accord, and without the leave of
her father and mother, Joan betook herself to the city of
Neufchâteau and, there, for a certain time was in the service of a certain woman known as the Redhead, keeper of
an hotel, where there lived continuously several young
women of no decorum [translate that: whorehouse]; and
where there also lodged, for the most part, men of the
military [implying: and everyone knows what soldiers are
like]."

Now, Joan was a virgin, and Cauchon knew this, for he
had had her examined. Just as Yolande herself at Chinon
had carried out the bodily inspection, this time it was the
French wife of Bedford, the English Regent, who effected
on Joan's person the verification that she was indeed a "girl
intact."[3] But the assessors were never to be informed of
this. The Inquisitor knew it, but he kept still. What followed was even better:

"Joan filed suit against a certain young man who, knowing she had lived among the said women [the Redhead's
whores], refused to marry her. He died, while the case was
still pending [no mention of his losing his case!] and Joan,
out of despite, left her service at the hostelry."

As for Baudricourt, according to these investigators, he

---

[3]Naturally, propounders of the theory that Joan was of "royal lineage" believe
this strengthens their view. See who troubles to examine her each time—prin-
cesses! For Yolande, we saw how it happened. With the Englishwoman (by
marriage), this seems to be just another case of the burning curiosity about Joan
at the royal courts. By 1431, it had waned at Bourges, but it persisted in London.

repeatedly told how Joan had regaled him with a racy boast: "that she would have three sons, the first of whom would be Pope, the second Emperor, and the third King." To which, the Sire, in proper Gallic fashion, had replied, "I would gladly sire one upon you!" and laughed good-naturedly.

The tribunal's informants, it is true, did not assert that Baudricourt himself had related this scene to them, but the terms of the dialogue had been repeated to them by "notable personages, prelates and grand masters," to whom the captain of Vaucouleurs had been delighted to recount them.

What ensues, therefore, from the information gathered at Domrémy, Neufchâteau, and Vaucouleurs, on the early history of Joan as the tribunal was to hear it, was summed up as follows:

"From the time of her young years, Joan has said, done, and perpetrated many shameful, cruel [sic], scandalous, and dishonorable misdeeds and crimes, sins and offenses."

So behold our nineteen-year-old Maid, thrown to the wolves, sitting on a stool, in the center of this half-circle of churchmen. Stocky, well built, in gray and black and upright in the pageboy costume that clung to her thighs, all these connoisseurs' eyes were upon her.

And now—did all those "historic sayings" come bubbling from her lips, the ones everyone knows "by heart," the ones, as Claudel wrote, today's "listener expects to go parading by"?

On the "state of grace":

"If I am in it, may God keep me in it; if I am not, may God put me in it."

On her banner, at Reims:

"It had been through danger; it was only fair that it be shown honor." And so on.

Of course, everyone knows that throughout her long

trial Joan was at all times the incarnation of nobility, proud, poignant, sharp, quick, giving her questioners tit for tat, and at every turn nailing them to the mast. We possess the double version of the transcript, both French and Latin. At her later (rehabilitation) trial, it would be alleged that the document was undependable, being incomplete, partial, and defective, but that was pointless. The "notary," William Manchon, assisted by William Colles and Nicholas Taquel, performed properly. Of course, what he left us was not taken down stenographically and it has nothing like the accuracy achieved today with magnetic tape. But there can be no question that Manchon did as conscientious a job as he could, and one might even be surprised[4] to find him recording some of the exchanges in which Joan clearly came out ahead. A careful line-by-line reading of the text (now available to us in its original form) makes it more difficult to fall in with the tradition and repeat as everyone else does that Joan was constantly "sublime" (the word that seems generally to be considered appropriate) before her judges at Rouen. A serious assessment of the transcript somewhat modifies the legendary picture.

First of all, quite understandably, Joan was not the same at the beginning of the trial as she was at the end. There were things she had to realize; and these realizations, in a series of shocks, had a profound effect on her state of mind. In the first days, the Maid never really believed she faced the supreme penalty. If she had been before an English tribunal, a court-martial, she would not have had the illusions she still retained when arguments began on February 21, 1431. The English wanted to "burn" her and had told her

---

[4]As was the former head of the French bar, Jacques Charpentier (*"À propos du procès de Jeanne d'Arc"* [On the Trial of Joan of Arc]), *Revue de Paris*, November, 1963. I would add only that the notaries surely *translated* Joan, for she spoke a very countrified French. So what the transcript gives us is not literally the words she pronounced, but rather those words as transposed into proper French.

so themselves; but the judges facing her were priests and
not soldiers, they spoke her language and were men of God,
members of the Church she venerated and considered holy.
It was not conceivable to her that they might want to take
her life. They were mean to her because they had sided
with the English King, whereas she, as was fitting, supported the King of France. She felt herself strong, stronger
than they, ready to shame them with their wretched conduct, and she did not hesitate to threaten them, since she
was so sure of herself, and Heaven had spoken to her. They
were truly putting themselves in grievous peril by going
after her. They were very wicked people, who had betrayed
their "rightful lord," Charles VII, and had the effrontery,
the mindlessness, to disobey Him Whose messenger she
was. Let them beware!

"Were you well informed about me, you would rather I
were outside your hands. . . . Consider well whether you
hold yourselves to be my judges, for you undertake an
awesome charge and place yourselves in grave danger."
She would cease talking this way once there was no more
question of exactly what she might expect from them.

Before she fully realized the horror of her situation, she
was still capable of smiles, sarcasms, and taunting insolence. With a smile and teasing defiance, she told the scribe
who had not properly written down what she said and
whom she caught out in his mistake, "Next time, I will
tweak your ears." When Cauchon asked her whether Saint
Michael came naked to her in her visions, she ignored the
implications and with sarcasm, retorted, all wide-eyed and
deliberately naïve, "Do you think God could not afford to
dress him?" Cauchon realized he had put his foot in it, and
to try to recoup by pursuing innocent detail, he put in a
silly question: "Did he have hair?" At which Joan laughed,
"Why would he have cut it off?"

And there was admirable insolence and raillery when the

Joan of Arc

Charles VII, King of France *(From an old engraving.)*

Joan's arrival at Chinon *(From a fifteenth-century tapestry. Reproduced by kind permission of the Musée Historique of Orléans.)*

Philip, Duke of Burgundy
urtesy of Bettmann Archive.)

The Duke d'Alençon (*From a drawing in the Bibliothèque Nationale, Paris. Courtesy of Bettmann Archive.*)

Charles VII, King of France *(By Jean Fouquet. Reproduced by kind permission of the Librairie Larousse, Paris.)*

Miniatures from "Vigiles de Charles VII" *(By Martial de Paris,*
Bibliothèque Nationale. Reproduced by kind permission of the
Editions d'Art Lucien Mazenod, Paris.)

The Cathedral of Reims *(Courtesy of Bettmann Archive.)*

learned Doctor Beaupère questioned her about the lights
that surrounded her when Charles received her at Chinon.
Oh, yes, Joan replied, there were lots of lights, a wealth of
light, for "all light does not emanate from you, Monsignor." A "subtle" girl, Beaupère would term her in 1452,
still bitter and not yet recovered from his pain twenty-one
years later, "subtle, with the subtlety of woman"—which
is the worst kind, as everybody knew.

Was Joan quick, precise, direct, and of "infallible memory" during the interrogations, as Régine Pernoud depicts
her? That was not exactly the case. There were her many
refusals to reply and her increasingly numerous answers of
"Let it go!" And especially we find in Joan a perpetual
system of ducking and evading, which is normal behavior
when the accused feels he or she is foredoomed and the
accusers are setting trap after trap. Rudler was well aware
of this, noting that at her trial Joan "evades, breaks off,
beats the bushes, . . . takes tangents, dodges, twists questions, misunderstands them, answers at cross-purposes."[5]
Nor was that all the poor girl did. She also lied. And that
was why she had to shy away and look for ways out when
they insisted that she swear to God that everything she
answered would be the truth. She firmly declared at the
start that she would not tell all, that certain subjects were
untouchable, and this applied in particular to what she had
"revealed" to her King. She also implied (hoping that
Heaven would forgive her) that she would present things
in the way that struck her as best. She told the whole truth
about what in her eyes was the most important part (that
she belonged to God, that she loved Him, worked for Him,
and was His child and His servant). Here there was no need
to cheat, and that was the sense and extent to which, after

---

[5]Gustave Rudler, *Michelet historien de Jeanne d'Arc* (Presses Universitaires de
France, 1925), vol. I, p. 83; vol. II, p. 90.

all, she did swear an oath. Yes, I will tell the truth, the truth you do not wish to hear, which is that you are bad men who are persecuting a witness of that Master who is also your Master. Joan, covered by the distinction she privately made to herself between the absolute and the relative, allowed herself plenty of room to accommodate whatever she chose!

Of course, she came "from God," and the real King understood this immediately: the proof was that he received her, welcomed her, recognized her, almost the minute she got to Chinon. And why would he not have seen it at once, since she appeared before him led by an angel, if you please, who preceded her, bearing a splendid crown for the King, a crown made to last "a thousand years" and so rich and fine that none other so magnificent would ever be seen? And the angel greeted the King with a bow, and said to him, "This is Joan, sent you by Heaven!"[6]

Could any witness corroborate this tale? she was asked. And she enumerated them imperturbably: the Archbishop of Reims, Charles of Bourbon, the Sire of La Trémoille, the Duke d'Alençon—a pretty fair list. This statement was made after having said, "I think there was no one else there," when asked the day before, "Was your king alone when the angel-with-the-crown brought you in to him?" However, she had quickly corrected herself: ". . . although, close by, there were a lot of people." She was in quite deep,

---

[6]This story proves a great embarrassment to Joan's true and rightful admirers. But to Michelet it was another chance to reveal the depths of his unperceptiveness; he suggested it was some practical joke, a fake "mystery" organized at Court with Joan as its butt—and that she fell for it, believing it a true angel with real wings and that the cardboard crown he carried in his hands was made of solid gold. When Michelet was not glorifying Joan in his overblown rhetoric, he wanted us instead to take her for the village idiot!

It is much simpler, and closer to the truth, to admit unabashedly that Joan had a lively imagination. She made up, invented, and spouted whatever came to mind to try to convince her judges of her divine mission; and what did come to her mind was quite naïve and gives us a fair idea of what her mental imagery must have been like. But, apparently, to admit that "Saint Joan of Arc" might lie would be a sacrilege!

on March 13, with all those names she reeled off, and when the insidious Cauchon suggested to her on May 2 that he would request depositions from those she had named, she quickly took another tack, with, Fine, you give me a courier, "and I will write them all about this trial"—which, of course, was something else again.[7]

Another time, Joan was caught red-handed in a deception. She was asked, "Which Pope do you consider the true one?" and she answered, "Are there two?" But they confronted her with her letter to the Count d'Armagnac who had asked her opinion on that very subject. She had not answered him by saying, "The real one is in Rome," but only, "Wait a bit. For the moment, I am busy. When I get to Paris, we will see about it."

Sometimes she would also contradict herself inadvertently. She was asked if, when her "angels" appeared, she saw them in full. No, she said then, faces only: "I do not remember whether they had arms, or any other members." But then this answer collapsed when she reported that she "kissed the ground where they had lain," and Saint Michael was dressed like "a true wise man of law," and she had been able to put her arms around both Saint Catherine and Saint Margaret.

There was another fateful contradiction, concerning her departure. Had her angels advised her to disobey her parents by running away without telling them? And Joan replied, "My voices would have been satisfied had I told my parents," but on another day, "My voices left it to me whether to tell them or not."

---

[7]On May 9, Cauchon asked Joan whether she would abide by the testimony of Regnault, which might be procured, and she dared him, "Bring him here! He would not dare say other than what I have told you!" But that was only bravado, for she knew Regnault would never come to Rouen. Besides, she had twisted the matter, for Cauchon never meant to bring the Archbishop there, but only to seek his deposition on a specific point: the question of whether the angel appeared before her at the King's.

Her voices! What a permanent role she assigned them! To believe her, they continually joined in her actions, even in things where their assistance was hardly appropriate. If she recognized Baudricourt the minute he finally consented to see her (after three fruitless attempts, but no matter: "The voices had told me this was the way it would be"), it was the voices that pointed him out to her. The same at Chinon: Charles granted her an audience, and the voices said, "That one is the King." On the afternoon of May 4 at Orléans, when the whole town was astir and she woke with a start, it was her voices once again, saying in her dream, "Get up! Get up! The fight is on!"

And if in the fall of 1429 she had seen through Catherine, the impostor, the fake illuminate from La Rochelle, it was because her voices had warned her. She said so categorically. "Everything I did, I did on commandment of the Lord," and beyond that, "Nothing I did was other than on commandment." Ha, ha! the judges chuckled; so it was the Lord Who sent you on that fruitless attack against La Charité-sur-Loire? And she took a breath, and dodged it with, "Who said I had been commanded to enter it?"

As for her voices, her dear voices, she was not even the only one to hear them; the King heard them with her. And since these awful "English" judges wanted to know the whole truth, well, she had seen not only Saint Michael, Saint Gabriel, Saint Catherine, and Saint Margaret, but also Saint Louis in person, and even Charlemagne. And when the questions got tricky, and she wanted time to think because she feared a trap, she said she had "not yet permission" to explain; she had to consult her "counsel," and the court would have to wait. I thought, Cauchon had retorted, that your voices came to you every day? Of course, of course, but she had not "quite caught" their commandments; there was so much noise in the prison, what with the guards always at each other! And besides, she added, when she asked her angels something, they had to go and find out from Our Lord, then come back with the answer, and all the coming and going obviously required some time.

On one point, and a serious one, there is still darkness; we must be honest enough to admit it. Joan was accused of "homicide." She maintained, "I never killed anyone," even adding this detail: "If I charged the enemy with banner in hand, it was in order to shed no blood." This was something that would be emphatically underlined, later, at her rehabilitation.

But then, why did Joan herself at the trial make so much of that new sword she had taken from a Burgundian and carried with her since Paris? Why did she so imprudently boast of it as an excellent "sword of war" that she had come by, so easy to handle, and so well suited for *"bonnes buffes et bons torchons,"* which, if our modern interpretation is not mistaken, means to thrust and smite, hip and thigh? And especially why did d'Aulon not see how damaging his 1456 testimony was to Joan, when he told of what happened outside Orléans on May 6, how, as she was in retreat, she turned about, intoxicated with joy because the English had come out of their fortifications. She then charged them with La Hire, the two of them, d'Aulon said, being "the very first to begin to strike"? The wording is clear: "To strike." One does not strike with a banner.

There is also the matter of the soldier girl watching without protest—*c'est la guerre*, that was how things were done—as her men slit the throats of the English who had surrendered at the battle of Saint-Loup, just as she wildly sent her men to the attack, so they might bloody their hands by killing, but not she. What of this sending others to perform what for her would have been a sin? Such cunning does not seem like her. She was not afraid of blood, we have ample evidence of that. Nor of lies. One is justified in lying to people who want to take one's life, and more. Joan conceded to herself a right to lie to these judges who denied her voices, who called her a witch, who imputed every type of crime to her, and were ready to describe the fact that in war she acted like a warrior as transgression, outrage, and defilement.

The seventy articles (or specifications) had been boiled down to twelve by the Parisian doctor, Nicholas Midy. D'Estivet did not know how to do this. He was a provincial who got bogged down, scattered his shots, lost his nerve; Midy had to show him how to go about it when you wanted to hit the mark. This dozen was the catalogue of the mortal sins Joan had committed, through which the shameless woman had wrought upon the Christian universe unspeakable scandal. To begin with, there was the capital accusation that Bedford set such great store by: with poisonous inversion, she had dared to "wear that which pertaineth to a man . . . an abomination unto the Lord thy God" (Deuteronomy, 22:5). She had ordered and practiced "the shedding of human blood," a "horrible and abominable" thing (suddenly all these ecclesiastics, among them the bellicose Cardinal of Winchester, had become advocates of nonviolence, 100 percent pacifists). Joan had turned the illegitimate pretender Charles from the ways of peace, "dissuading him with all her strength from making any treaty" and incessantly "inciting [him] to murder." (In vain, the Maid demanded, what about my letters to Philip of Burgundy, especially the one of July 17, 1429?)

Another mortal sin, obviously, was her attempted suicide at Beaurevoir, and the evilness of this rebellion against divine law was exacerbated by a statement Joan had made, without realizing how damaging it was: It was a temptation, she had said, that she had been unable to resist. So did she prove that she had "fallen into the error of those who maintain that man is impelled by ineluctable dispositions" and thus held with the "negation of free will" (the judges, already Tolstoyans, now became Pelagians, too). Nor should we forget that other infamy: she had dared to attack Paris on the day of the Nativity of the Virgin, and stolen "the hackney of Monsignor the Bishop of Senlis." Joan protested. "Stolen" what? She had paid the bishop for his horse! But just a minute. Not so fast, missy! Whether she paid or not, at Senlis, she had taken over something that belonged to the Church—an unforgivable crime. And what about Franquet of Arras? And all the rest, including, alas, that she "had not feared to lie to the court, in violation of her own oath, at different times affirming contradictory things"?

All of which was just fine, but the trial was beginning to drag out, and the University of Paris found that offensive. Cauchon submitted the matter to the University through the six delegates who were making a trip to Paris especially for this, so that it might make known its sentiments, and confirm, if that seemed just, the severe intentions of the tribunal. All the sections of the Holy House gathered together and were of one mind: Charles' Maid had piled deviltry on deviltry; all known perversities were to be found in her, she was the total incarnation of Evil. The Church needs must act, must punish. The University was indeed perplexed that so many weeks had been taken to reach a conclusion, when the tribunal was faced with such evidence. And, on May 14, 1431, it sent to the King of England the following solemn entreaty: "We humbly implore Your Highness that this matter be brought most diligently and soonest to end, for delays are very perilous and a great reparation is required . . . for the exaltation and integrity of our Faith and for the praise of the Lord, may [He] in His grace keep Your Excellency in prosperity unto eternal glory."

Amen.

XI

The Heretic Must Die

Now, let us get a clear picture of what was happening to Joan. She was dumbfounded when she realized what the judges really wanted to do, when, so to speak, she located the heart of the question.She was not really being accused of any specific thing. All the charges being piled up against her amounted to only one very simple thing: they wanted to prove that she was *against God.*

This seemed so unimaginable to her, so mad, that it drove her to distraction. She had anticipated antagonism toward her political actions, since she had fought the protectors of these false judges, these "renegade Frenchmen," the henchmen of the invaders. But then she realized little by little what the priests were out to prove: that it was she who was the bad Christian, the traitor to Heaven, in revolt against Heaven, as much a heretic as the Hussites she had heard about and was horrified by.[1]

---

[1]Could she really have written them the letter found in Vienna in the chancellery of Sigismund of Luxembourg? The date, "Sully, March 23, 1430," seems to make it authentic, for she was at the château of Sully on that day. But it is the style

But that she, of all people, should be looked on as an enemy of the Faith, a hypocritical foe of Our Lord Jesus, whose image she had put on her standard, this was beyond her. So that was why, right from the start, they had asked her whether she frequently took communion. And she had answered, "Let that be. That is not part of this trial." Not part of the trial? Why, to her judges, it was the very heart of the trial. Their point was to prove that she was outside the fold, that she did not belong in it, and must be driven out completely. She was worse than just a sinner, she was contagious, a carrier who might spread infection anywhere. She passed herself off as a Catholic, and nothing could be more dangerous, for she was the very opposite of a Christian; she was the sham and opprobrium of Catholicism. That was what the judges were out to prove.

Now, Joan knew who she was, and what passionate good will she had always had. She had always prayed, and loved to pray. She went to confession often. She respected her curé in Domrémy. Wherever she might be, she often went to church, preferring the children's mass when possible, as we have seen. Since being in prison, she had begged to be allowed to attend services, at least on Sundays. But she was forbidden to.

When she was led to the interrogation room, the chapel was on the way. Could they not let her go in for a moment, kneel and look at the altar, the cross, the unreachable tabernacle? Absolutely not.

---

of the letter and its rhetoric that bothers me: "What mad fury possesses you? . . . I should long ago have visited you with my avenging arm had not the war with the English kept me here. But should I not soon hear of your mending your ways . . . I may leave the English [so as to come and] exterminate [your] awful superstition with the blade of my sword and put an end to your heresy or your life."

By all evidence, some pedantic bookman must have written those sentences, someone like Pasquerel perhaps. We know of Joan's own style; her letter to the English had none of that convoluted elegance. Yet it is possible that she agreed to sign such tirades. Heresy, to her, was evil per se.

That was it: they were rejecting her, saying she did not
love God, that she worked against Him, that she belonged
among the impious, the miscreants, the religious malefac-
tors. But where could they get such mad ideas? She cried
out, "If, without knowing it, I did something against the
Faith, tell me so and I will ask for pardon," I will repent,
I will never do it again. But, tell me!

How, in what, had she been at fault? What could she have
done that warranted her being called a bad Catholic, being
kept away from communion, denounced by the Church as
an infidel? She believed in everything the priests taught,
subscribed to all of it. Their Credo was her Credo; she
recited it in her daily prayers, with the Our Father and the
Hail Mary. Did they deny her apparitions and what those
visitors come down from the Kingdom had said to her? All
right, suppose that were not true, and she had just imagined it all. She was nonetheless a good Christian, a little
Christian girl like the others, a daughter of Holy Mother
Church, obedient to all her commandments.

Obedient? Submissive to the institution? But Joan, each
day you give us further incontrovertible proof of your insubordination, your indiscipline. Most unambiguously,
you place yourself outside the Church. All we are doing is
noting the facts, with regret. You are a rebel. You do not
heed the Church. You get deeper into your disobedience.
Look, isn't it clear? Anyone who claims to be a Catholic
must first of all, obviously, obey the Church. And you do
not obey the Church. So, you are not a Catholic, and we can
really not avoid making note of it, with the sad conse-
quences that that entails for you. The syllogism cannot be
refuted.

I do not obey the Church? Joan asked.

No, you do not obey, since you will not repeat after us,
as we urge you to do, as it is our duty to command you to
do, the condemnation of your "voices." Let us admit that

you *did* hear such voices; we are not trying to accuse you
of lying on that score. We are, on the contrary, quite ready
to concede that you did receive communications from the
invisible. But what we do know, we being the Church, and
having authority to recognize this, is that those "spirits"
did not come from Heaven; they came from Hell. Our
expert doctors of the University of Paris precisely iden-
tified those diabolical spirits. You—scandalously—call
them Saint Michael, Saint Catherine, Saint Margaret. We
know, by unquestionable knowledge, what their names
really are: "Belial, Laban, Behemoth." And as long as you
refuse to agree with us on this, you are, as is only too
evident, in rebellion against the Church, "apostate, schismatic, and heretic."

But this was something Joan could not admit. To make
demons of the angels who had never counseled her anything but good? When she was thirteen, they said to her,
little one, just stay as you are, a good girl; hold on to what
is so precious, your purity of heart. And what they instructed her to do later was along the same line, the special
vocation she had been put on earth for: You who cherish
the will of God and have no other joy than to see it done,
listen to us; this is what Our Father wants of you. You
think you can't do it? Well, don't worry, we'll help you.
And she had answered, Yes, yes, yes, I will do it! Of course,
I will do it!

And now, here were these priests in Rouen, leering at
her with eyes like burning embers, trying to force her to
say, All that came from the devil, and I was but an instrument of the demon!

It was unbelievable. Monstrous.

In her simplicity, Joan imagined she had found the way
to escape from the pincers the judges were closing on her.

She could tell them two things. First, you, Monsignor Bishop of Beauvais, "you are not the Church; you are only my enemy." And second, since I have but one wish, one thought: to serve God, to work for Him, since I am His servant, His Maid, since Our Lord is my Master, you have no right to read me out of the Church, that makes no sense, for "it's all one thing, Our Lord and the Church; why are you trying to make out it is not one thing?"

How unreasonable she could be! Her own words were turning back against her. Who was "trying to make out" that the Church and God were not "one thing"? Why, she was. We are the Church, said the judges, and a bishop acting as a bishop and in full exercise of his mission as a bishop, speaks for the Church and represents her. (And I am a little surprised that at this point Cauchon did not turn to Brother Lemaître and, pointing him out to Joan, say, What about him? Would you cast doubt on him, the "delegate of apostolic authority," the Inquisitor, for such is his title, "of the faith and of heretical perversity"? But Cauchon was aware that his quiet, and somewhat embarrassed, colleague wanted to figure in this as little as possible.) And we are so far from deserving your reproaches that we reject as blasphemy the distinction that you, and you alone, Joan, are making. For you are the one who is refusing to admit the equivalence or, actually, the identity between, the will of God and the will of the Church, which is the basis of our faith, of *the* Faith. In resisting us, how can you not see you are resisting God Himself?

But Joan hung on desperately, restating that she was with Jesus Christ and all the powers above. And they had to explain to her, to overcome her ignorance, that there was the Church Triumphant and the Church Militant and that the two were bound together: triumphant in Heaven, militant on earth. And that the Church Militant, *Una, Sancta, Catholica,* was the hierarchy which "could neither be wrong nor fail" by the dogma itself. Yet, "I believe that the Church Militant can neither be wrong nor fail," the stubborn little mule replied, "but as for my sayings and doings, they are all up to God, Who made me do everything I did." Decidedly, she had a closed mind. God, always God! And her obtuse mind refused to see what they were exhausting themselves repeating to her: The Church and God were one and the same. Understand? There could be no difference in the order of the required submissiveness.

Joan then tried to go over their heads: "I appeal to the Pope, His Holiness the Pope!" He would be able to settle it. He, the Good Shepherd, the Vicar of Christ, would know that she was not a heretic, but with all her soul a true Christian, a Catholic. The Pope, indeed! The clerics smiled, inwardly (what they had on their minds was not for publication), without even having to exchange glances. None of them had any doubt where His Holiness stood, least of all the six doctors from the University of Paris. Pierre Champion points out in his introduction to the *Procès de Condamnation* (Trial of Condemnation) that "messengers were constantly going from the University to Rome." This was the eve of the Council of Basel, which quite understandably struck terror into Eugenius IV, who had succeeded Martin V on March 3. The Holy See was not about to risk making things any harder for him than he could see they would be by some vexatious ill-advised gesture. But Joan was suggesting to the theologians one more, final, way to get at her. She called on the Pope? Very well, then. Let us suppose, said Cauchon, that "the Church Council and our Holy Father and the cardinals were here, would you abide by their decision?" Joan could tell that her life depended on how she answered; so she withheld the "no" that would mean her doom, but she could not pronounce the "yes" that would have implied a future renunciation. "I abide by what I have said; I will say nothing further; you will get nothing more out of me," she answered.

But they pressed her to reply: Would she, yes or no, accept the judgment of the Pope? Once more, she dodged, sparring for time: "Take me there [to Rome], and I will answer him."

One last time, they tried to force it out of her: "Yes or no, do you recognize that you are subject to the Church here on earth?" And Joan, overwhelmed, torn, but ever faithful, shouted, yes, its subject, yes with all her heart, all her being, she was subject to the Church, but "God must be served first"; in other words, provided that, on condition that, the Church did not oblige her to betray her Lord and her God.

That was the fatal restriction. Joan had just pronounced her own sentence of death. On condition? But no conditions were tolerated. It would be madness, criminal insanity, to admit, even to let it be supposed, that the word of the Church, the Holy Church personified in its own hierarchy, might not always coincide with the Word of God. Did Joan refuse to say she had conversed with Behemoth? Then she was rebelling against the Church, and against God. Let her be anathema! Article 62 of d'Estivet's bill of particulars was quite correct: the accused "sets herself above all ecclesiastical power," and her behavior, were it not to be immediately punished with all the severity of the law, would lead to nothing less than "the total subversion of the authority of the Church."

"Have no fear about your martyrdom," her voices had told her. So Joan must have known, as soon as she set out on her way, that she was following her "sisters in Heaven" toward martyrdom. She was radiant at the idea—from afar. But now the time was near. There is always such a gap between what one has envisioned in glory and what one is subjected to in the night. So much accumulated suffering! Being locked up was painful for a girl who liked nothing so much as the open air, the wind, the sunshine. The chains riveted to her legs, connected to a beam sticking out beneath her pallet; the men, the English soldiers, not even outside the door of her cell, but with her, inside the cell, day and night; the cold, the vermin, the plague; and the animal terror of death approaching, atrocious death, death by fire.

Michelet accurately described Joan's distress in her cell, on Easter Day, 1431—April 1—as the five hundred bells of Rouen rang out all together, proclaiming the Resurrection, while her judges forbade her to take communion. On Easter Day! O God! There was good reason to bury her face in her hands, sitting on her bed, and to sob until her heart might break. Those judges! The horrible judges in their long gowns, watching her. What could be worse than eyes that look at you and do not see you, refuse to see you, resolutely insist on seeing in you another being, one they invented? How could Cauchon and the others empty such cartloads of accusations upon her? To say that she had been initiated into the rites of witchcraft as a child, that she served as a whore at the Redhead's, that her near-marriage was called off by her fiancé, when actually he had even tried to force her into it, that since entering the service of the King "she has always refused the company and care of women, wanting only men for the private functions of her bedchamber and intimate matters," that at Beaurevoir her first words on regaining consciousness, after her fall, had been to curse Providence, to insult the deity! And worst of all, she never guessed that the priest, Canon Loiseleur, who acted as her confessor in prison, only heard her so that he could inform on what she had told him, confident of the secrecy of his confessional vow.

What she did know, on the other hand, was her total

abandonment. Why had the clergymen of Poitiers forsaken her? They were priests, just like these, and bishops and doctors; there was even an Inquisitor among them. They had investigated her thoroughly! Had they not bothered her mercilessly with questions about her orthodoxy? And yet they had ended up finding her above reproach. So why were they silent now? Were they not the Church, too? Why did they not do the least thing, make the smallest gesture to defend her? Did their "Book of Poitiers" count for nothing? Whenever she referred to it, she was ignored. It was as if it had never existed. Were there two different weights, two different measures in the Church, judged according to the way the political wind was blowing?

The doctors at Poitiers were "French," so they had found her a good Christian; but the doctors of Rouen and Paris were "English," and they declared her schismatic, apostate, and an enemy of Heaven. Joan understood; it slowly dawned on her that the clerics of Poitiers were in complicity with those of Rouen. She now saw what Cauchon had meant when, closing his eyelids in a half-smile, he had asked her whether she really imagined that "the ones on her side truly believed in her divine mission." Of course, she knew they did not; to her chagrin she had seen it all too well, dozens of times. And now she dared not lie, because she felt that Cauchon had been told. "I don't know," she answered, but then added, violently, defying Cauchon and all the others, the ones who were present and the ones who were not, that if, indeed, they did not believe she had been sent by Our Lord, well, they were just wrong, that was all!

Now Cauchon, feeling sure of himself, went further still. He offered in a hypocritically ingratiating manner to arrange for safe-conducts for "three or four clerics from her side" (Regnault first of all, no doubt), if she wished, so they could come to the trial and give their opinions about her voices and her visions. And Joan, letting down her guard and at last revealing she had lost confidence in everyone at Poitiers, answered, "Do you expect to catch me in that way?"

Oh, yes, the King! Well, no use even mentioning him. That was the tragedy: it was because of him she would die. Yet however he might act toward her, he still was King "by the grace of God." She would never betray him, since that would mean going against God. But Saint Michael, Saint Gabriel, and her Saints Catherine and Margaret? They had absolutely promised to free her. On March 14, she was boasting, "Saint Catherine told me I would receive help, and I do not know whether that will be in being freed from prison, or whether having been judged [that is, at the last moment, on the scaffold], there might be some commotion [a people's uprising] by means of which I might be delivered; I think it will be one or the other," and added, "On several occasions, my voices told me that I will be freed by a great victory."

A few days later, on March 17, when Cauchon had clearly informed her that she would be sent to the stake, she was beginning to sound less sure of herself: "I firmly believe," she said, "that God will not let it happen that I should be laid so low. I think I shall receive help very soon, and by miracle." But the miracle did not come; Joan started to doubt that it ever would. She was abandoned, even from on high. Joan asked her voices whether she would be burned. "They answered that I should put my trust in Our Lord Jesus Christ and he would help me." No further promise now, except that God would "help" her. Help her to die?

The pontiffs, the six doctors of the University, returned from Paris to Rouen on May 21, bringing the peremptory and patently short-tempered opinion of that august body. After close examination of the dossier, the University of Paris (the judges of its "venerable Faculty of the Decree" concurring) felt Joan had to recognized as a "prevaricatress of the law of God, . . . traitress, cruel, bloodthirsty, seditious," and moreover as having evidenced a "pusillanimity leading to despair and implicitly to suicide," with, by her own admission, a "condemnable opinion concerning free will." It was therefore necessary that she be solemnly declared "schismatic and apostate," and, "if this woman refuses publicly to recant her error," she must be "left to the discretion of the secular judge and receive punishment fitted to the seriousness of her crime." How did the "secular judge" get into this Church matter? What a question! The Church shed no blood. She merely pointed out the victim to the arm that would kill. She herself would never so soil her hands.

While the Church foreswore inflicting death (she did no killing, just caused it), she did not foreswear torture. So Joan was led to the place provided for this. She was shown the boots that would be fitted on her feet and limbs, with the screws to be tightened until her bones burst, the funnel through which quarts of water would be forced down her gullet, the irons that would be heated to press into her flesh and melt her eyes. All she said was, "Go ahead! Do your worst! The words you extract from me under suffering I will retract immediately afterward."

They thought this over. Cauchon felt torture would be pointless in the case of this maniac. Young Thomas de Courcelles, on the other hand, was all for trying it. The majority refused him the pleasure.

Cauchon who, as will be recalled, was trying meticulously to make this a "fine" trial, supervised the drawing up of a report that set things out properly:

> A certain woman named Joan, and commonly called the Maid, was taken and held by illustrious warriors . . . upon the territory of our diocese, . . . notoriety

having previously proclaimed that this woman, completely forgetful of the decency which is becoming to her sex, exceeding all brakes of shame, repudiating all modesty, amazingly and monstrously dissolute, did wear scandalous attire . . . and did dare to say and spread a thousand things alien and contrary to Catholic faith.

The venerable University of Paris and Brother Martin Billorin, vicar-general of the Inquisitor of heretical perversity, called upon . . . the very illustrious prince Duke of Burgundy and noble Lord John of Luxembourg . . . to turn over to us said Joan as to her ordinary judge.

We, bishop, as is incumbent upon our pastoral charge, and desirous of working with all our strength for the exaltation and triumph of Christian faith [as well as] the Most Serene and Most Christian prince, our Lord King of France and England, made the same request toward the same end.

The Duke of Burgundy and John of Luxembourg acquiesced willingly [*sic*] in these requests and, wishful of contributing with a Catholic heart to the reparation and increase of the faith, [did deliver the said woman to King Henry VI].

Finally, His Royal Wisdom, ardent to serve the orthodox faith, did turn over to us, bishop [etc.]. . . .

The ritual prescribed solemn entreaties and monitions, for the Church must untiringly attempt everything, even kindness, so that stray sheep might perceive the errors of their ways. If Joan showed repentance and confessed she had been misled by the devil, all would be well. The desired end would have been achieved: Charles VII dishonored, his consecration invalidated.

On March 27, Cauchon, filled with self-righteous goodness, had suggested that Joan select a "counselor" to guide her in the right path. "All persons here present," he had said to her, "are men of the Church, men of consummate knowledge, who wish and intend to act toward you in all piety and mercy, seeking only your instruction and your sojourn in the path of truth and salvation."

But despite all the goodness shown her, the generous offers made to rescue her from evil and perdition, she remained unyielding, refusing to listen, to go along, to lend a hand. On May 23, a new and pathetic effort was made to help her redeem herself and admit her mistakes. That day, the theologian Peter Maurice, of the University of Paris, made the attempt, with the persuasive, tender tone he felt was called for: "Joan, my very dear friend . . ." In a didactic turn, he tried a demonstrative comparison which should have weighed decisively with Joan since, in spite of all good sense, she continued to call herself a Catholic while acting as a rebel.

"Just suppose, Joan," he explained to her, "that your King had left you in charge of some position, forbidding that anyone else be allowed in there without his authorization. And then someone arrived, saying the King had sent him, but without royal safe-conduct to prove it. Would you let him in? No; obviously not. Well, in the same way, when Our Lord ascended to Heaven, He left Peter and his successors in charge of His Church, and forbade them to welcome anyone arriving in His name, without having proofs or guarantees." That, alas, was her case. She should be able to see they could not accept her as the Christian she claimed to be, unless she had that safe-conduct, in this case an act of obedience to the Church, Our Lord's representative.

Of course, there were some things askew in the doctor's reasoning, since, while the terrestrial king did issue permits for entry into his city, it was not the King of Heaven but the very people in charge of what they called His house, their house, who took it on themselves to determine whom to accept and whom to reject. Yet this stubborn, fixated, hardened, and opinionated Joan was not willing to give up, and persisted in maintaining that she loved God, that she was "from God," that angels visited her. She did not want to be withdrawn from the community of believers, for she was a believer, believing in the Trinity, the Incarnation, the Redemption, and the holiness of the Church. Believing, in a word, in everything—except what they were trying to make her admit: that her Saint Catherine was really Behemoth, her Saint Michael, Leviathan. She clung to her position; she resisted with savage energy. "Even before the fire, even in the fire," she said, I will never disown my angels; "that, you will never make me do."

Peter Maurice raised his eyes to the sky, and Manchon, the clerk, curate of Saint-Nicholas and a canon of the collegiate church, entered a comment in his transcript: *Superba responsio*, an answer fraught with "superbity," all arrogance and pride.

Thursday, May 24, 1431. This was the day the University of Paris and the Inquisition were to have their satisfaction. This was the day that sentence on Joan was to be handed down. The setting chosen for this was a cemetery, the old cemetery of Saint-Ouen.

During the previous night, the head theologian, Beaupère, had not felt it beneath his dignity to come into Joan's cell to exhort her once more in person, explaining what the next day would bring. There were only a few hours left, and if she did not recant her error, her body would be delivered to the tongues of fire, the fire of death.

At the Saint-Ouen cemetery, the preacher William Érard called upon her formally once more to submit. And now for the second time, she said the five words that sealed her fate: she would submit, submit completely, *but* "God must be served first." Perhaps in the grip of terror, she was still trying to change the outcome, or at least delay it, for she not only said, "I leave it to God," but added, "and to Our Holy Father the Pope." Now she was ready to leave it to the Pope; she no longer demanded to be taken to him. It would seem that she was implying, I will say to him alone, if he so demands, what I cannot bring to cross my lips. Cauchon pretended to think she was asking that the Pope be brought there. With indulgence, he patiently explained to her that "he could not be brought from so far." But, anyway, why the Pope? Why disturb His Holiness? "The ordinaries [that is, the bishops] each represent him in their dioceses," he said; or the Pope and I are one and the same, as with the Church and Jesus Christ. His Holiness and my own Fatherhood should mean nothing other to you, Joan, than "our Holy Mother Church," to whom you owe obedience.

And then, as Joan stood mute, her heart pounding, her breast beating, the bishop began to read the death sentence: "We, having before our eyes Jesus Christ and the honor of the faith, . . . have stated and decreed that you have been a liar, blasphemer, seeress, seditious, cruel, apostate, that expressly and on various occasions you refused to submit to Our Holy Father the Pope. . . ." The words seemed out of place now, but the text he read had been prepared earlier. What Joan had just said, which looked like an acceptance, was not to be considered since it all too obviously constituted nothing but a delaying tactic the girl had devised. And as he went on, Joan suddenly started to scream.

Canon Loiseleur was right next to her up on the small platform, and kept repeating in her ear, "This is the last second, Joan! You are going to be killed, Joan! Recant! Recant! You know you don't want to die! Recant, Joan! Save your life!" She looked wild-eyed now, as she interrupted the bishop: "Stop! Stop! I recant!"

She had broken. Now she was ready to do whatever they wanted, if they just did not kill her, did not send her up on to the cart where the executioner was already waiting. It depended only on her, whether she was to live or die. Just those three syllables to say, and she would live, and the imminent, awful ending would be nothing more than a nightmare.

Just those three syllables, and she would save herself, since there had been no "great victory" to free her, since no angel had come into her cell to put the guards to sleep, knock her chains off, and open the doors, and since the people were doing nothing, the people whom she had hoped to see rise up in her defense. The people were there; hundreds of them were staring at her, waiting, and enjoying it in advance.

Joan had broken. She repudiated everything. It was a terrible thing to do, perhaps, but how much more terrible for her flesh to be in the fire. She pronounced the required words, asserting that she "recanted and repudiated" all her anti-Christian lies and acts, and in particular the commerce she had had with demons; she "swore and promised" before God "to Milord Peter, Prince of Apostles, Our Holy Father the Pope, Monsignor Bishop of Beauvais, and religious person Brother John Lemaître she would never more return to her errors."

Loiseleur had won; Beaupère had won; the tribunal had won. And they were not surprised. The recantation formula was all ready. They had overcome her with terror, as she had once overcome the people of Troyes. Cauchon had no desire to see her burn, and certainly Brother Lemaître did not either (as for de Courcelles, it was another matter). I feel that Cauchon breathed easier. We have no way of knowing exactly what text Joan was called upon to repeat aloud, word for word, for the tirade that appears in Latin in the official transcript seems too long to have fitted on the parchment, which the witnesses, twenty-five years later, were to describe as being short. But three of the witnesses agreed that during this word-for-word recantation Joan "laughed," or at least "smiled" *(subridebat)*. The interpretation of this simple detail, which seems quite incontestable, has inspired a thousand different hypotheses. It reminded Régine Pernoud that Joan in battle (during her last campaign, it is to be presumed) put a cross on fake messages. She sent these expressly to mislead the enemy in case they were intercepted (but if the detachment for which they were apparently intended actually received them, its men would understand seeing the small agreed-upon mark). She concluded from this that Joan did laugh, or smile, when signing—with a cross, as it happens—a recantation which she was thus, within herself, canceling at the same time. It is true that Joan did not sign this with her name, as she did so many other documents. Here, I believe, we find some evidence of mental reservation on her part. She thus avoided authenticating an absurd document by endowing it with a complete signature which might be binding on her. But the witnesses left no doubt: it was not *as she signed* that she laughed, but *as she spoke*, repeating the words she was being forced to echo.

Anyway, now that she was saved from the stake, why would she not involuntarily smile, as would anyone reviving after such awful moments? She had thought she was going to die, and now she was not going to; it was a visceral feeling of relief. But it may also be that, now that she was out of danger, she could only laugh at the things they were demanding that she own up to—they were funny, farcical, ludicrous: that she had "pretended to have revelations," that she had "invoked and adored evil spirits," that on many occasions she had uttered "blasphemies"; and, especially, that unexpected adjective that Cauchon or one of the scribes had come up with, describing her male dress as not only "disreputable," but "misshapen." Well, all these fine Lords of the Church who had been ogling her for the past three months with more than passing interest certainly did not seem to be saying that she was "misshapen" in her tight-fitting little jacket or the black leggings, which always seemed to her rather to make the most of her female architecture.

The popular excitement that Joan had naïvely counted upon did occur, but exactly in the opposite sense of what she had expected. Testimony would show in 1456 that "the English" were incensed because Cauchon was willing to accept her recantation and not turn Joan over for execution; that Cardinal Winchester's "secretary" (?) had insulted the bishop, calling him a "traitor," and the cardinal had had to intervene to shut up his employee. And stones had been thrown at Cauchon, who apparently just missed serious injury.

By the English? Must we blame the English? Even though probably a certain number of them were there, the crowd that had gathered was far from being all English, the excited, curious crowd, awaiting that choice spectacle: a beautiful young girl to be roasted. I can very well see how irritated that crowd was at the show being called off. Disgusting! Unfair! Give us our money back! Hell, this is what we paid for! For the English had squeezed the ten thousand *livres* needed for the purchase of the Maid from the pockets of the people of Rouen. They were looking forward to the fun they would have when her dress went up in flames. And now the curtain came down before the finale. Everybody out! Show's over! Over, with the "star attraction," the spectacle they had come to see, the one they had paid for with their hard-earned *sous*, canceled, called off. It was a shell game, a swindle! They wanted revenge! And the stones began to fly.

A crowd is a funny kind of animal. When Voltaire saw the people of Paris deliriously acclaiming him a few days before his death, he grumbled under his breath that they would show the same kind of excitement if he was on his way to be executed. Did not the crowd, wrote Victor Hugo, "laugh when Jesus went by, and before the stakes for Savonarola and Bruno and Jan Hus and Joan of Arc? Did they not spit into the shattered countenance of Robespierre?"[2]

Cauchon allowed Joan to live, but condemned her to life imprisonment, on the "bread of pain" forever. She was taken back to her cell. It will be recalled that the English retained a formal right (by the letter of January 3, 1431) to "recover and take back" the Maid. And this was a severe blow to Joan, for she had truly believed, no doubt on the word of Beaupère and Loiseleur, that by recanting she would be spared the prison of Bouvreuil as well as death, and that at least—if, indeed, they had not let her believe she might be freed—she would no longer go back to a soldiers' prison, but into a Church prison, with women warders, and no awful chains on her feet.

Now she was lifeless, depressed, vacant. On the afternoon of the twenty-fourth, she was forced to take off her masculine clothes and put on a dress. She obeyed. Now she appeared as demanded by decency, not in the vermilion gown the Duke of Orléans had given her, nor the furs of Bourges, nor the cloth-of-gold surcoat she had worn at Compiègne. She probably wore some hideous dress, some

---

[2]See manuscript of item XX in the satirical book, *Quatre Vents de l'Esprit* (Four Winds of the Mind).

prisoner's sack. Then they shaved her head, in a punishment that would become traditional for dishonored women; but what was most important here was that they do away at once with that impious hairdo that she wore. Snip! All gone! Her skull was bald.

On the evening of Sunday, May 27, Cauchon, Warwick, and all the authorities were informed that Joan had just committed a new crime. She had kicked over the traces. She was no longer cooperating. She had resumed her men's clothes.

Cauchon, with a whole crew of the doctors, naturally including Thomas de Courcelles, waited on Joan early in the morning of the twenty-eighth. What was this? What had gotten into her? The reason was that she had been lied to, and she was saying so right to Cauchon's face and all the others'. She had been given (by Beaupère, perhaps, and by Loiseleur, too?) two promises which had not been kept: that she "would no longer be in irons," and that she might "go to mass and take communion." She had waited three days. But on Sunday, May 27, she had been refused mass. The ban had not been lifted. That was too much, too unfair! If that was the case, what good had her recantation been? Besides, she was angry with herself for having recanted; that was wrong. Yes, that was a big mistake she had made, her only one, but immeasurable. Everything that she had said four days before at the Saint-Ouen cemetery was said only "out of fear of the fire. . . . It was treason [committed] to save my life; and I was damning myself in saving my life." In her terror, she had dared to say "that God had not sent me," and that was when she lied, "because it is true," do you hear? The real truth was that "He sent me."

Although the men's clothes she had put back on greatly upset the doctors, they were of no concern to her, in them-

selves. It was only her mark, her uniform as servant, warrior, little soldier of Heaven. Of course, it was "more appropriate" in the position in which they had placed her,
certainly more appropriate than a skirt, among all those
males whose proximity they had forced upon her; but if
they insisted, she would give in, all right, "I will go back
to women's clothing," in order to show her obedience. But
for the rest, she withdrew, she retracted, she erased, she
canceled everything she had said, all of it!

"Never did I a thing against God, nor against the Faith,"
and it was shameful of her ever to have agreed to such an
avowal. Fear was no excuse. She could not lie against God.
For she belonged to Him, she had never ceased belonging
to Him. Do with her what they would!

And there was one more thing she did not hide. Life in
prison? Life like this, between these walls, in this suffocation and solitude, for years, for decades—she was not yet
twenty—until she grew to be an old woman, hidden away
from the sun (for even if the English were driven out and
forced back home, they would take her with them, that was
self-evident; they would never let her go). No, that was too
much to bear! And Joan came right out and said it: Better
to kill me right away. I would prefer it that way. "I prefer
to make my penance [as you put it] all at once, which is,
namely: to die, rather than to suffer the penalty of prison
any longer." Here she was again, in the same mind as at
Beaurevoir, preferring death, deliberately looking for suicide, but this time with nobility: she would not kill herself.
These fine gentlemen-priests would have to accommodate
her.

The law is the law. Even if, as I suspect, Cauchon was not
anxious for Joan's death, even if on May 24 he felt a secret
relief that her recantation spared him, as bishop, the re-

sponsibility for this murder, the rule of the Inquisition was
inflexible. The relapsed heretic had to be turned over "to
the discretion of the secular judge." Just a paraphrase for:
to be burned alive.

Tuesday the twenty-ninth, a bill was drawn up, following general consultation. The theologians unanimously
stated that all they could do was record the fact: Joan had
rebelled; she had repeated her crime, claiming her authority from God beyond the Church and despite the Church.
She must therefore go to the stake. The orders were exped-
ited so that everything might be in readiness the next
morning, Wednesday, May 30, 1431, around eight o'clock.

Wednesday, May 30, around seven o'clock, Cauchon
came to visit Joan. He was accompanied by Thomas de
Courcelles (who was always along; there was no more in-
trepid herald of the Faith, the "honor of the Church" was
his life's passion), as well as Peter Maurice, that other emi-
nent doctor; and Nicholas of Venderès, Archdeacon of Eu;
John Le Camus, Canon of Rouen; Nicholas Loiseleur,
Canon of Rouen and Chartres; and two preaching brothers,
John Toutmouillé and Martin Ladvenu.[3] The reason for
this was the final interrogation, required by law. The condemned person, knowing that he or, in this case, she was
to die in a few moments, might agree to a confession she
previously refused. Her fate was settled; one way or the
other, she would die. Even if she retracted her retraction,
it would be too late. But if she repented, the law would
allow her to receive communion. And all the members of
the tribunal that had condemned Joan knew how she
longed for that.

She was going to appear before God; she had to cleanse
her soul of anything impure that might remain in it. And

---

[3]It is notable that Brother Lemaître was not there; until the very end, he did all
he could to avoid being personally involved in this dirty work.

she did admit that she had made up the story of the angel coming to bring Charles his priceless crown: "I was" the angel, she said. Then they wanted her to admit that all the rest of her supernatural communications were nothing but fabrications. She stood firm. Absolutely not! She had not deceived them, nor had she been deceived. In this final hour, she now repeated what she had said to Cauchon, looking him right in the eye. As for the angels, "I saw them as I am seeing you." It was true; she swore to it; and God could hear her, and they could be sure that at this point she was not about to commit a sin. She swore that she had seen them, that "they appeared to me"; they came "specially when the bells tolled, at the hour of nightsong, and in the morning." They wanted her to agree that they were "evil spirits," but she said that that was only their opinion, and anyway, "good or evil, they appeared to me," so there! There was nothing more she could say.

At least, perhaps she would admit that her voices had cruelly "misled" her by promising her that she would be freed. But she just bowed her head and wept (according to Brother Toutmouillé, testifying in 1456, she was kneeling and sobbing). All right, she had been "deceived"; she admitted, "I see they deceived me." And the clerics took this up feverishly, to get her to see that these then could not be God's angels; the Lord's angels never lie! But Joan was never willing to come to that crucial conclusion. She did not want to go against the priests, for that surely would be a sin, nor deny what they said. They asserted that they knew, were well informed, sure of what they were saying . . .

But there was no way she could accuse her dear Saint Michael, her sweet Saints Margaret and Catherine, and call them demons. Not that; never. Nicholas Loiseleur was still trying to get the edge on her. He asked Joan, urgently demanded of her, that shortly, before the crowd, from the top of the stake, she repeat out loud that her voices had tricked her. She dodged, as she had done so often during the trial. "Remind me of it" later, she answered. She twisted her hands, humbled herself, beat her breast. Very well, so be it, let her take communion. And the host was brought to her.

The cart. The trip through the crowded streets. The Old Marketplace. Joan, head shorn, in a long shirt (perhaps dipped in sulphur to make it catch better), wearing a sort of miter on her head inscribed with the list of her crimes: "Heretic, idolater, apostate, relapse." And when she got before the stake, she saw another sign, at the top of the post, again with an enumeration stating that this punishment was being meted out to a "lying, pernicious, miscreant, blaspheming, cruel, dissolute" woman.

The Bishop of Beauvais proclaimed, in his own name as well as in that of the Inquisitor, from a paper he held in his hand:

In the name of the Lord, Amen!
Whenever the pestilential virus of heresy effectively impregnates one of the members of the Church and transforms him into a member of Satan, it is necessary to take measures, with attentive care, that the detestable contagion may not find its way into the other parts of the mystical body of Christ. . . .
Now, then, do we, Peter, by divine mercy Bishop of Beauvais, and we, Brother John Lemaître, vicar of the illustrious Doctor John Graverent, Inquisitor of heretical perversity for the Kingdom of France, since . . . —as we recall with great pain—after having perjured the holy and divine Name . . . Joan, incorrigible heretic, did relapse into error as a dog returns to

its vomit . . . pronounce and decree that, as a rotten
limb . . . you must be rejected by the Church, cut off
from her body, and left to the secular power.

And we therefore reject you and so leave you, begging the said secular power to be merciful in its sentence toward you, and to treat you kindly, this side of
loss of life or of any limb.

For such was the remarkable formula that the Inquisition
used against those it was sending to the stake.

The "secular arm" was the bailiff, Raoul de Bouteiller.
He knew the meaning of words, and what "merciful in its
sentence" meant: conventional hypocrisy, absolutely nothing. He did not even bother to say a word. What for? It was
all settled. A flick of his chin toward the executioner, no
more: "Your move." And the Pontius Pilate of Rouen
washed his hands.

Joan came down from her cart. The scaffold before her
was made of a thick and high clump of plaster, covered
with faggots and cordwood. That way, everyone would be
able to see the show; the crowd, unruly as we have seen,
would get its money's worth. Often, when the smoke got
thick, during executions by burning, the executioner
would go in and strangle the already half-suffocated victim,
thus sparing him the horrors of slow combustion. But this
time, none of that. The height was too great. Once the fire
had caught, the hangman would not be able to go back up,
to get anywhere near the woman to perform the merciful
deed on her. And even should he be able to, everyone
would see him doing it. They would boo him, mob him
perhaps. No, this one would crackle to the end.

After the reading of the sentence, a terrified Joan made
her act of contrition, displaying, as the witness John Massieu would later say, "great mark of her repentance and
fervor of faith." She no longer knew what it was all about.

The priests who doomed her were the priests of her own God. They were the ones who had taught her her prayers. So why were they killing her? They must be right to kill her. Were not the priests of Jesus Christ always right?

Well, she was not rebellious. It was by listening to the priests that you got into Heaven. They held the keys. She had always believed they held the keys, and she believed it still. She was not a heretic, not a wicked woman! They knew that, since they had let her take communion. So then, why, why? It was all just an awful misunderstanding. She had tried only to do good, but she must have done some evil, too. Those killings, that bloodshed; she had waded in blood. But it was all for the Lord; and Saint Michael and Saint Catherine and Saint Margaret had ordered her to do it. She did not repudiate them; she did not accuse them of anything; she even kept from saying her voices had deceived her. She did not curse anyone, neither her voices nor the judges. She just begged pardon of everyone,[4] on earth as in Heaven, pardon, and pray for her! And she blamed herself. For what, exactly? Still, she blamed herself. She did her *mea culpa*. Convulsively, she looked out at the crowd and called for help: Prayers! Prayers for her salvation! Her cardboard miter slipped down on her nose, as she sniffled through her gasps, talking, talking, as if she would never stop.[5] She was taking up precious minutes, and Cauchon did not dare interrupt her, but the head of the English detachment surrounding the stake and keeping the crowd back was beginning to feel enough was enough: Did they expect him to stay here through dinner, or what?

The executioner put his hand on Joan's shoulder. Time

---

[4] ". . . begging pardon of all manners of people, whether of her side or the other, very humbly, and that they might be good enough to pray for her" (testimony of John Massieu).

[5] In her "repentance and continual confession" (Ladvenu testimony), she "persevered a long stretch of time, like half an hour" (Massieu testimony).

to get going, little one. She asked for a cross. An English soldier broke a twig that had fallen from the faggots and crossed the two pieces, tying them together with a bit of string. Through the top of her shirt, Joan slipped this wooden symbol against her chest. The executioner, having shoved her up the ladder—she was now standing on top of the faggots, with the whole scene stretched out at her feet —tied her arms, behind her, to the post. She could no longer touch the little cross, so she called for another that she might have before her eyes to the end. Preaching Brother Isambart ran to the nearby chapel and came back waving a processional cross. The executioner had come back down. He lighted his tinderbox; the fire crackled. Joan coughed, choked; the heavy smoke partially masked her. Through the creaking of the flames, she could be heard shouting, at the top of her lungs, "*JE–SUS!!*"

"The Bourgeois of Paris" related: When "her dress was fully burned, the fire was pulled back so that the people should have no doubt; they saw her stark naked, revealing all the secrets of a woman; and when this vision had lasted long enough, the executioner rekindled the fire high around the poor carcass."

What was left of her body, a little bloody pile, was put into a sack and thrown into the River Seine.

One day, at the beginning of the trial, when she was still self-assured and full of daring, Joan had said to her judges, "What am I doing here? Send me back to God, whence I have come."

They had taken her at her word.

XII

Recertification

This matter once fittingly settled, the University of Paris dispatched word to the Holy Father, unfortunately without being able to inform His Holiness that the Maid, that abominable heretic, had at last admitted it was Behemoth and Leviathan that had masqueraded as Saints Catherine and Margaret. But it could at least be said that Joan, at death's door, had confessed being "misled and mocked" by her "voices." "Mocked" was an unwarranted embellishment: Joan had never used that word, as the "posthumous investigation" shows. It was just a slight ornamental flourish the theologians tacked on.

The University was triumphant. On July 4, in Paris, a Dominican father, speaking to a huge crowd, depicted the details of the witch's shameful career and her life "full of murders and blood," mercifully cut short. Then, on September 3, they burned a woman named Perrinaïc in the capital; one more madwoman, or she-devil, who dared publicly and scandalously to come out for the relapsed apostate, whom she held to be some kind of saint.

We have no idea what the Holy See, in the person of Eugenius IV, the new Pope since March 3, may have answered the illustrious and very redoubtable University.[1] But we can well imagine how Rome must have felt about a troublemaker who had forced Cardinal Winchester to divert to France the mercenaries meant to be used against the Hussites. And this was a girl who, besides, had been disobedient, stubborn, and guilty of the worst kind of insubordination, considering that, as the King of England (speaking through Bedford) stated in his circular to all the princes, this odious schismatic claimed "not to recognize any who might judge her on earth, and spewed [*sic*]" particular venom upon "Our Holy Father the Pope, the Council, and all of the Church militant."

Truth to tell, Cauchon did not feel so secure. The Council of Basel was about to open: the city was already teeming with ecclesiastics. Cauchon was concerned lest Charles VII, probably feeling somewhat encouraged, might have his delegates act up. In fact, they might even try to do something in Rome to counter the Rouen verdict, which did tend to tarnish his anointment. And on June 12, 1431, in the name of Henry VI, Bedford sent the Bishop of Beauvais the "letter patent" he had requested, promising him "on the word of a King" that if ever any of the clan of the counterfeit King of Bourges were to get an "appeal . . . interjected before the Pope, the General Council, or elsewhere [?]" against the "sentence" of May 30, "the King of England will act and cause his ambassadors and messengers to act at the Roman Curia and the Council." If there were French political pressure on the religious authorities, then there would be immediate English political counterpressure. Rome and the Councils were used to this kind of

---

[1] We have already noted how impenetrable the archives of the Vatican can be on such "restricted subjects."

intervention by "ambassadors." It rarely failed to work, and Cauchon, more aware of this than anyone, took every precaution. A stickler for detail, he had even secured the written assurance that these diplomatic *démarches*, if required, should be charged to the government ("at our own cost and expense," Bedford confirmed). That was something one might have taken for granted, but Cauchon was one who felt there could never be too many assurances.

Needless to say, we know nothing of the hidden moves and countermoves that may have been executed in the Roman Curia or behind the scenes at Basel on Joan's account. Perhaps Charles VII preferred to do nothing, either because he felt that an affectation of disdain was a better tactic (Joan was no longer his concern), or because he knew it was a lost cause. Perhaps, however, he did try something; here we are in total darkness.

What is clear and interesting, on the other hand, is the behavior at Basel of the same theologians who in Paris in 1431 appeared ready to rend their clothing because Joan was reluctant to leave matters to the judgment of the Supreme Pastor. Said Supreme Pastor, the ill-starred Eugenius IV, was later unceremoniously "deposed" by them in 1439. On June 15 of that year, the Council of Basel declared Eugenius IV a "heretic" and named in his stead Amadeus of Savoy —a very upstanding widower and father of nine—to be Felix V. (Thomas de Courcelles got a cardinal's hat out of the deal.) Eugenius, as might be imagined, could not simply let this happen. Even though the Basel cabal said he was "deposed," he clung to his throne, remaining real Pope of Rome as against the shortweight impostor, and they exchanged the usual anathemas. Rome officially declared Felix V a "son of Satan" and "a new Antichrist" and, even as Charles VII had been, a "plaything of wizards and witches."

Years went by. The name of the Maid seemed to sink into oblivion, the passing fad of a moment. Only the people of Orléans honored her faithfully in their memory. On May 8 of each year, their city was the scene of a procession of great pomp and circumstance, accompanied by a "mystery" that played on for hours, and in which Joan's social station had been considerably upgraded. She now came from a "good family." "As for my father's estate [sic]," the actress portraying her would declaim, "it is in the country of Bar" (not in Lorraine, as Villon would later say).

Outside of Orléans, though, none would venture to refer to the crucial role she had played in the royal fortunes. Yet diplomacy had not been asleep and at last through devious ways the "Peace of Arras" had been signed with Philip in 1435. Burgundy finally split away from the Goddams. Paris was Armagnac once more the very next year. The first impetus of that happy chain of events had come from Joan. Better not to remember. His Majesty preferred not to and would be displeased by any explanation that did not give him full and exclusive credit for the favorable turn of events.

Yet one untoward episode must be mentioned. It was in two parts: 1436 and 1439. It is untoward in that it sheds further light on Joan's brothers and their moral character. We already know they were not bad at wheedling, any more than their father was.

Jacquin, the eldest, seems to be no longer there, nor does the father; we have no clues as to their whereabouts. The other two connivers, John and Peter, in the month of May, 1436 (the twentieth, to be exact), at La Grange-aux-Ormes, near Metz, got hold of a short, stocky girl with more gall than was good for her and a more than passing resemblance to the late Maid in build as well as looks. It was easy to change her name from Claude to Joan, and then they were ready to present her as their sister Joan herself. We do not know whether she was supposed to have come back by miraculous resuscitation or whether a substitution in Rouen was alleged to have saved her from the stake.

At the end of July, John du Lys (or "Dallie") made a trip to Orléans to look the place over. Claude-Joan, still held in reserve at some distant place, furnished John with letters she had written, or at least dictated. This still-unseen reappearing Joan was guaranteed to be the real thing by her own brother. Who would know better? Orléans, however, was but one step in this shady business: its real goal was the King. So John went to see His Majesty, who was then at Loches. John returned to Orléans somewhat crestfallen, but putting on a good front. He told the city fathers that Charles VII had promised him a hundred *livres* but the Royal Treasurer, either misinformed or dishonest, had given him only twenty; so he was requesting the balance of eighty from the municipality. He got only twelve, and went off with his tail between his legs. The two thieves and their thievess left it at that for the time being.

But Claude-Joan was not one to waste her time. After a prolonged intimacy with the young Count of Württemberg, in November, 1436, she married Sire Robert des Armoises, to whom she later bore two children. Yet she was not ready to abandon the idea of making something of her resemblance to the recently famous Maid. And in the summer of 1439 (what did her husband think? where was he?), Madame des Armoises decided to play for top stakes and appeared in Orléans, saying to its inhabitants, "Here I am again, dear friends!" Almost ten years had elapsed since the real Joan had left Orléans for the last time in January, 1430. Naturally, in ten years, her looks had changed somewhat, especially after the terrible ordeals she had been through; but the brothers, her accomplices, had trained her well. She knew all the right gestures, the words to use, the people she ought to "recognize."

The trick worked like a charm. On July 18, 1439, the city authorities gave a banquet in her honor, and on August 1 she was paid—that was what she came for—the neat little sum of 210 *livres*. Being cautious, and doubtless aware of how the King felt about the Maid, she sedulously avoided making any move toward the Court.

Then suddenly, on September 4, with a new reception arranged by the city fathers awaiting her, she slipped out, disappeared. Perhaps the reason was that word had come of the King's imminent arrival in the city; perhaps the Royal Chancellery, which must have been investigating her, was about to unmask her. The next year, Milady des Armoises was convicted of impersonation by the Parliament of Paris, and finally confessed.

The only reasons for recounting this pitiful anecdote here are to put an end to the absurd legend of the substitution of another victim for Joan at Rouen—which so many writers have perpetuated[2]—and to give one more clear portrayal of what Joan's family background was really like.

Ten more years went by. 1449: Charles VII, his star on the rise, was in the process of reconquering Normandy. On December 10, he took Rouen.

Once there, it was hard to ignore Joan, and we may quite well believe that the city fathers—several of whom, perhaps, applauded Joan's death eighteen years before—felt it would sit well with the new sovereign if they made

[2]The Diderot *Encyclopedia* of 1776 considered this a moot question. "One cannot overlook the force [*sic*] of evidence indicating Joan reappeared," wrote its contributor, who obviously relished the idea that Joan had been saved from the fire, got married, and lived happily ever after. Jean Bancal makes no definitive judgment on this, but suggests the woman might have been Joan's sister Catherine, of whom we do in fact know so little.

amends. Why not put the brand on the memory of Cauchon (dead seven years, since December 14, 1442)? That would wipe their city clean of the crime perpetrated there by the English. And, at the same time, the legitimacy of the consecration would be straightened out. The royal lily, its whiteness tarnished by a venal tribunal, could again be as clean as snow. All that was needed was to destroy, to abolish as quickly as possible, the hideous sentence that tended to associate His Majesty with impiety by making Joan, our wonderful Joan, a witch. Time to do away with that abomination!

Eighteen years do represent a lengthy penance. But until now Charles VII had not seemed aware of it. Unless there were secret maneuvers that we have found no trace of, he and his French government had not raised the question in Rome during all this time. For the Holy See alone could reverse the 1431 judgment, a Church judgment pronounced by a Church tribunal, to which the presence of an Inquisitor had given the stamp of Rome's approval. But during those years, Franco-Roman relations had not been the most cordial. In 1438, Charles VII had dealt Eugenius IV a really vicious blow with his Pragmatic Sanction of Bourges. That instrument brutally stripped the Pope of the advantages he enjoyed in France through the naming of bishops and the conferring of the great benefices, just when Eugenius was under such pressure at Basel. Moreover, Charles VII had cut off the first-fruits that the Pope received by way of "annates," so named because they were the annual tributes Roman law exacted from anyone who had received a benefice from the Holy See. He had done it by fiat. Charles VII had really acted with the utmost disregard for His Holiness, since the time was right for it. So from that date on, there could be no expectation of Roman atonement for the "apostate" burned by the Church in 1431.

Things had just taken a new turn, however, in 1449. First,

Eugenius IV had been dead since 1447, and Nicholas V was on his throne. The anti-Pope, Felix V, the Savoyard, had finally been gotten rid of after ten years of dogging Rome with his presence. And Charles VII could take some of the credit, for Dunois was the one who had conducted the final negotiations and brought the thing off. Now Rome was under obligation to France. One "good turn" deserved another; simple maxim. There was, of course, still that Pragmatic Sanction which the Pope found difficult to swallow. But now at least it would be easier—or so Nicholas hoped —to talk about everything in a more relaxed manner.

All evidence tended to show, and increasingly would show, that Charles VII was most deeply interested in a review of Joan's trial. So if he did nothing about it any earlier—as far as we know—it was not because he did not hope to see the Roman sponge wash away the odious verdict of Rouen. He must have realized the almost insurmountable difficulties he would have to face. A decision of the Inquisition could not be appealed, but apparently this was only in principle; for we do know that in June, 1431, Cauchon was worried about the possibility that some appeal would be interjected. All principles, when one knew how to get around them, could be twisted a bit. What Charles VII was now asking of Rome was no less than that it go back on its own word, retract, admit its error.

From a strictly legal viewpoint, this was an impossible request. It was well known that the Church Militant was "incapable of error," especially in matters of faith. And the Joan affair was one of faith, without any doubt. She was burned as a "heretic," and only the highest religious considerations had prompted her condemnation in 1431. The Church, acting as such, never concerned herself with anything except the integrity of the doctrine she had been given to guard. Let no one whisper that considerations other than those of faith weighed in her decisions; the

insinuation would be sacrilege. Yet Charles VII audaciously summoned Bouillé on February 15, 1450, and instructed him to put the operation in motion.

Who was this Bouillé? An important churchman, a former Rector of the University of Paris. And as soon as Paris
was back under Valois authority, the University brilliantly
made up for its previous position. It was magnificent,
aflame with passion, running over with enthusiasm to hail
Charles VII, true King of France, after that sad interlude
of the English King, whom only so recently it had been
calling "Most Christian." But the University had no trouble wiping yesterday's misguided raptures from its memory, dropping them into oblivion, and blessing God for the
"consolations that, in His grace," He had conferred
through the "wonderful redemption," as it told Charles
VII, "of your good [capital] city." The doctors proclaimed
"loudly . . . our good loyalties and intentions," and at the
end of "our long afflictions" under the usurper, now allowed full expression to "the joy that is ours." At the same
time, however, the University made certain that its shouts
of enthusiasm and assurances of devotion contained one
little sentence in which it took the liberty of reminding the
King of the amnesty he had repeatedly promised since 1429.
It emphatically underlined the "need [*sic*] for fully supporting [meaning: fully reaffirming, fully applying] the general
abolition" of useless recollections.

Bouillé had but one idea: to show Charles VII that his
zeal knew no bounds. Having been through the Parisian
mill and familiar with every kind of compromise, he seems
to have thought that Rome would easily find a way to
satisfy the King of France while saving its canonical face.
And that was conceivable, however impossible it might
appear on the surface. But although the Holy See was

grateful to Charles VII for the part he played in evicting Felix V, Charles was now asking for a favor, and as long as the Pragmatic Sanction was not changed, Roman policy could only be to play hard to get—in other words, meet the royal request with sanctimonious religious reservations, the last thing that the ebullient Bouillé had ever expected in his unaccustomed naïveté.

Although he was a professor of theology, he was no diplomat, and he presented forthrightly what should have been only subtly suggested. He laid His Majesty bare, stressing that Charles VII had been humiliated and put upon. The least common sense should have told him that, as far as Rome was concerned, all that counted was the iniquity of the 1431 decision, Joan's virtues and irreproachable orthodoxy, and finally the vile toadying of Cauchon, who might be accused of felonious religious conduct. Oh, it was delicate, ultra-delicate, to start to attack Cauchon, for he did not stand alone; the University of Paris and the Inquisition were behind him, up to their necks in the same pot. So what had to be done was to allege technicalities, find errors of procedure in Joan's trial, which could be pinned on the Bishop of Beauvais to justify expunging the verdict from the record.

Anything of that sort might have worked, but not the heavy-handed approach that Bouillé used. He did not mention Joan at all, but almost exclusively the King: "The honor of the Very Christian King requires that silence not be allowed to bury this iniquitous, scandalous sentence, so offensive to the royal court, that was fulminated by the Bishop of Beauvais [and by the Inquisitor, too, sir!], an enemy of the King notoriously devoured by the wish to dishonor him. What a spot on the royal throne if, in the future, our adversaries were able to repeat that the King of France had kept a heretical woman in his army!"

Nothing could be more awkward! But his last words are

interesting and significant: he was not for letting anyone overplay Joan's importance in His Majesty's fate. Orléans? Reims? Skip that. This "woman" was "kept" by the King "in his army." No more than that: just another mercenary like all the others; Bouillé knew the tone that was expected. "That is why [the only reason why]," he continued in his bull-in-the-china-shop manner, "His Most Serene Royal Majesty is obliged to demand respect for the innocence of this Maid. Thus will the mouths of calumniators henceforth be shut, and inviolable faithfulness be assured in the royal house."

No one could say that Bouillé had not set it all out plain; the clerical servant might be a little dense, but he certainly was not lazy, nor was he wasting time. So now, on with the hearing! Bring on the witnesses! But some finesse was still necessary; these witnesses had to be sorted out. It would not do to go calling just anyone at all in this matter. If, as the good doctor said, it was important to "demand respect for the innocence" of the little soldier girl whom the King one day in his benevolence allowed into the ranks, there was also the question of respect for established status. Bouillé would feel it an imposition, for instance, to call Brother John Lemaître, currently preaching right there in Rouen, or the present Archbishop Roussel, even though he had appeared fourteen times at the 1431 trial as an assessor. Tact, above all. So the investigation, begun on March 4, 1450, heard none but small fry: Manchon the clerk, Massieu the bailiff, and those incidental monks (who remained incidental), Ladvenu, Isambart, and Toutmouillé.

Then suddenly, the very next day, March 5, stop! The Bouillé inquiry was over in less than forty-eight hours. What happened? Simply that a powerful personage, the great Beaupère himself, happened to be in Rouen, trying to get French confirmation of the canonicates he had been given by the English, and Bouillé therefore asked him to testify. Which he did, in remarkably direct fashion, not like the others at all, and showing no inclination to reverse his opinion of 1431. Short and direct in his deposition, he must have been more loquacious in his later off-the-record comments; and he pointed out to Bouillé the complexity of this matter he was rushing into like an innocent babe. Beaupère was a diplomat, and one familiar with Rome. He had little desire to see a reversal of a trial with which he had once been intimately associated; he was thus all the more anxious to make his scatterbrained colleague Bouillé realize the far-reaching implications of the matter he was blundering into. What about the canons of the Church? He was plain and simply trying to rape them. Did he think that the Pope, just like that, to be a nice fellow, would fall in line, one-two-three? Bouillé must have been joking—and, on this level, that was an unhealthy thing to do.

So Beaupère recommended to Bouillé that he cease and desist, and Bouillé could only bite his nails. He would have a few most uncomfortable moments, but he would have to convince the King to drop it (just for now, of course; later would be better). As far as Bouillé was concerned, he felt he had to obey; he dropped the matter, and resigned.

A fine start for whitewashing the royal lily!

Charles VII would have to wait two years before he could begin again.

During the summer of 1451, Nicholas V, at Philip's suggestion, decided to send a legate to France with the ostensible mission of helping to bring together the two Christian Princes of the West, the French and the English, who were still at war with each other. Charles could easily understand what the real intent was: Nicholas could not resign himself to the painful conditions that the Pragmatic Sanction had created for the Church; the unwelcome

visitor, while talking peace, would actually be getting in
recriminations on that score. But Nicholas thought he had
gotten hold of the best-qualified of negotiators, a real
Frenchman from France, one of Charles' own cousins, Cardinal d'Estouteville.

A letter of August 28, 1451, informed the King of d'Estouteville's coming, adding that he would be preceded by
the protonotary Seguin. The latter was received very un-
graciously by Charles VII, on September 28, and informed
that he would do well to advise d'Estouteville to spare
himself the trouble of the trip, as the doors of the Royal
Chancellery would not open to him, should he chance to
come and knock at them.

Did the Holy Father think that he could simply dispense
with established custom? What about "prior assent"? Since
when was inquiry not first made as to whether an ambassador would prove acceptable? Charles was not ready to make
such a break with custom. The King of France was not
disposed to welcome a legate so cavalierly accredited to his
august Court without his approval having first been sought
and properly given. Nicholas had better understand that
clearly!

There was consternation in Rome, "total confusion and
desperation" for d'Estouteville personally, as he wrote in
great distress to his cousin Charles on October 23. Everything would get straightened out, of course, for all Charles
intended from the outset was to make sure that he held the
upper hand. In 1451, he was no longer that humble "King
of Bourges" that Martin V in his day had been able to push
around at will. He explained this forcefully to Nicholas,
and thus gained the advantage in the discussions to come.
Nicholas made the proper request. The King of France
properly accepted. And a properly chastened d'Estouteville, put in his place along with the Holy Father, thus
arrived in February, 1452, in the proper frame of mind.

One can readily imagine the solicitude and deference he displayed in order to show how deeply he wished to please the King. So it was now or never for Charles to revive the question of reviewing the Rouen trial. And on May 2, 1452, d'Estouteville started the investigation all over again, from scratch; and once again came the Manchons, Ladvenus, and Isambarts, to outdo each other in repeating that Joan's trial, as staged by the English, had had but one goal: "to defame the lord King of France." And they did their best to prove that it was all tainted from the start: Cauchon was not empowered to operate at Rouen; Cauchon had erred in delivering the Maid to the English instead of to the University of Paris; Cauchon had violated the rules of the Church by allowing Joan to remain in a lay prison; and so on. There was a whole list of irregularities which were so serious that, *ipso facto*, they stripped the proceedings of any validity whatever.

But perhaps the King was not happy at having the matter tackled from this angle? For on May 6, d'Estouteville brought in Philip de La Rose, the treasurer of the Rouen church, who gave a different slant to the affair, no longer impugning the procedure, but attacking the basis of the charges. Once again, docile, indefatigable, there were the ever present Manchon, Isambart, Ladvenu, and John Massieu, now flanked by a few more.

On May 22, d'Estouteville declared the inquiry completed, and so informed Charles VII officially. Then, in order to make his own feelings crystal clear (and, of course, they had to reflect those of the Holy Father, didn't they?), on June 6, the Roman legate, *qua* Roman legate, conferred indulgences on all those who henceforth might take part in the annual procession of May 8. D'Estouteville was plainly exceeding his authority, rashly prejudging, in a word dictating, their decision to those who still had to pass upon the Maid's orthodoxy. Those? Or the one? For the decision was really up to the Pope alone, and in Rome some felt that d'Estouteville was going a bit too far.

So for all the efforts of that Good-Frenchman-Cardinal, nothing happened on higher levels. Despite all of d'Estouteville's good will, there was no progress. Rome turned a deaf ear.

At this point (on his own, or at someone else's instigation?), John Bréhal intervened. John Bréhal was a man of consequence, none other than the successor to Graverent, who had been so anxious at the time to make short work of the "witch." In 1452, Bréhal was Inquisitor-in-Chief for France; and if he took a chance this way (for, through him, the Inquisition itself was being "converted"), it is hard to imagine that the Holy See had not whispered an approval. Nothing out loud, certainly not. The Pope was merely suggesting a step forward, a shy little half-step, deliberate, hesitant, waiting to see whether the King of France would respond to this gesture of good will with some positive concessions on the application of the Pragmatic Sanction. And we can only conclude that the royal reaction was disappointing, when we see what little effect Bréhal's diligent efforts had on the Pontiff for more than a whole long year.

Thus Bréhal had taken d'Estouteville's place in conducting this operation, and we have a very strange letter of his, written to a Viennese monk, Brother Leonard of Brixenthal, on December 31, 1452. As forthright as Bouillé, Bréhal did not trouble to beat around the bush, but came out flatly:

"The King considers that his honor was gravely attainted by his English enemies [as if the Church had had no part in it]" who did not scruple "to prosecute a trial, on a matter of faith, against a certain simple maid, a virgin, who, at the instigation of God, as proven by evidence that

is almost irrefragable [that *almost* was really all that needed
to be erased], had fought earlier for him. . . . They burned
her meanly [*sic*] to dishonor the King [a repetition, but this
was the main point]. That is why [shades of Bouillé] His
Royal Majesty so ardently wishes to bring out what the
truth really is about that sentence," and "toward that end
[now putting his cards on the table], he did commission and
enjoin me [Bréhal was in His Majesty's service and making
no bones about it], the humble Inquisitor of this kingdom,
to seek the opinion of all doctors [whence, this letter]" so
as to repair this deplorable injustice. Bréhal's inquiry, it
went without saying, was purely religious and could be
concerned only with holy considerations; moreover, if he,
a churchman, had been chosen for this undertaking, it was,
he said, "so that it might be clearly seen [note the delightful
next words, in light of what has gone before about the
King's intentions and the reasons for the enterprise] that all
partisan spirit is excluded from the matter."

The King was looking for an efficient spot-remover for
his tainted crown. The theologians were the ones who
could give him the necessary ingredient, one of pure Catholic content. So Bréhal was mobilizing all the canonists. It
was a good idea, most high-minded, and as promising as
could be. Yet all of 1453 went by before it bore any fruit
where it mattered—at the Roman Curia. There, all was
sterility, silence, slumber. A meaningful gesture by the
King that would finally ease up on the Pragmatic Sanction
was awaited, but His Majesty made none. The situation
seemed hopeless, and Bréhal did not know where to turn.
He had been paid, yet, as a loyal if infrequent servant, he
was not at all pleased to take the prince's money for nothing.[3]

---

[3]He had, specifically, received one hundred *livres* at the start of the second semes-
ter of 1452, "to help him to cover the expense incurred in working on the matter
of the late Joan the Maid"; and in August he was allocated twenty-seven *livres*
more.

The King had no intention of allowing anyone thus to make light of a sovereign who, on July 17, 1453, had finally crushed the English at the battle of Castillon, regaining from them even the province of Guyenne which they had occupied for a century. So, in 1454, Bréhal once more went to Rome "to go before Our Holy Father anent the trial of the late Joan The Maid."

The key to the matter had been found at last, and word was that the one who came up with this salutary key was John of Montigny, one of the Parisian clerics. If what the King was after had run into obstacles for so many years, that was because it was too obviously a request of Charles VII. The proper approach was to leave the King out of it altogether so as to achieve the end he wished. A screen of fog had to be set up. Instead of the King, let the petition come from "the close kin of the Maid." That changed the whole aspect of the matter. Now it was no longer a political affair! Of course not!

The Vicar of Christ could never twist doctrine (which, it should be remembered, was one of immutability where the sentences of the Inquisition were concerned) for base opportunistic reasons. Even as the Bishop of Beauvais, all that "Peter's heir" ever had "before his eyes" was "Christ and the honor of the Faith." There was not one of his actions that was not motivated by and intended for the integrity of the "Mystical Body" and "the exaltation of the Faith." But, if he forbade himself ever and without exception to make changes for temporal reasons in the disciplinary rules of the Church, his heart, on the other hand, might certainly be moved to compassion for human distress. And Nicholas' heart almost broke when the appeal was presented to him by Joan's own family, those poor people, those true Christians, who for so long had been sobbing over "the offense committed against one of their own through the murder and lamentable suffocation [it

would be unseemly to mention the *stake* here] of the said
Maid."

Fine, fine! This was just what was needed. Joan's mother,
who had been forgotten until then, was unearthed; she had
made no earlier move, probably barely understood what
was wanted of her now, but she was alive and breathing,
and that was the main thing. The father was dead. The
brothers? Well, we know them: they would go along with
anything that might turn a profit. So a deeply moving
supplication was prepared, in the name of the family group
suffering the tortures·of the damned for a quarter of a
century (as had been made especially clear in 1436 and 1439)
due to the atrocious judgment that branded their beloved
Joan a heretic. Nicholas V's charity couldn't possibly say
no to that.

Or could it? Nicholas, in fact, remained cold as stone,
silently sulking; his heart certainly did not melt. But fortunately, his health was on the wane, and his timely disap-
pearance occurred at the beginning of the following year.
His successor, Calixtus III, a Borgia, more adept at working things out, signed the long-awaited decree.

On June 11, 1455, the Pope himself ordered "investigation
of the case" of Joan. Investigation? That had been done
long since. Remember Bouillé? And d'Estouteville? And
Bréhal? But no, in the eyes of the Holy Father, all of that
did not count. Since it had taken place without Rome's
official blessing, it was null and void. Only now, beginning
on June 11, 1455, did the sole valid investigation commence,
and if Calixtus ordered it, he made certain to clarify that
it was because "the Church must show compassion for a
widow." His rescript appointed three commissioners,
three Frenchmen, as was fitting—the Archbishop of Reims
and the Bishops of Paris and Coutances—and charged them
to "cause to be rendered, in the last resort, a just sentence."
As in Bréhal's remarkable letter to Brother Leonard, the

Pontiff's warning is disarmingly brazen. It was a religious matter, as everyone knew, a purely religious matter, and everyone must get this one basic truth into his head: "Nothing [herein] may be inspired by aught but pure concern for the Faith."

This was it at last; and none too soon. This third and final inquiry was preceded by a pathetic ceremony, on November 7, 1455, in the Cathedral of Notre-Dame in Paris. Poor old Zabillet, Joan's mother, who had been brought in from Domrémy, had to read (did she even know how?) to the pontifical commissioners the paper that the doctors had drawn up for her, asking relief from "the infamous and irreparable damage" (the latter adjective seeming most ill advised) done her family by the 1431 trial, a trial described as "perfidious, violent, and iniquitous, without the shadow of a right." The terms of this petition had been carefully weighed: the Inquisition was not named in it, nor was the Church nor any priest—not even the English (His Holiness would not stand for that). The whole fault was attributed to "certain enemies," which was vague and mild enough. The poor peasant woman, bewildered and half-suffocated by the crowd, could go on no longer after a few sentences. Unable to mouth the words prompted to her, she gave up and collapsed; she was carried out to the sacristy. Naturally, her broken heart was thought to have taken her breath away and buckled the legs under her; the whole nave of Notre-Dame echoed with excitement at the marvel of it.

This, of course, was not the only comedy of its kind to be witnessed by "that sanctuary of Notre-Dame of Paris, more loaded with history than any other, on our soil." There have been many more, from the *Te Deum* of 1420 in celebration of the Treaty of Troyes, that of Henry VI in 1431 for his Parisian coronation, and the one in 1437 when the same Parisians gave their enthusiastic welcome to

Charles VII, up to the *Te Deum* for the Concordat exacted
by Bonaparte. To say nothing of his consecration, as the
Pope himself came running when Napoleon whistled, so
the adventurer could declare himself "Emperor." And the
holy arches have not so echoed for the last time.

And so to work, on the prescribed rehabilitation. Most
of the testimony by witnesses who also appeared at the first
trial can only fill us with disgust. These people, called first
by Bouillé, then by d'Estouteville and Philip de La Rose,
now knew just what was expected of them: they had been
told, in no uncertain terms. The twenty-seven articles of
the questionnaire La Rose had drawn up were nothing
more than a literal *précis* of what each person called on to
testify was expected to say; each article ended, "Thus it
was, and that is the truth." One might have thought himself
in a totalitarian country (and not be wrong).

Each of them spoke his piece with relish: the English
exerted constant pressure on the tribunal; Cauchon did it
all; being threatened himself, he in turn threatened the
witnesses; Joan did not understand the words she mouthed,
when she recanted;[4] she was forced, irresistibly forced, to
resume her masculine clothing on May 27; she was always
obedient to the Pope, appealing to His Holiness, counting
on Rome alone to free her. (But no mention here of her
reservation: "God must be served first." That detail had to
disappear!)

Apart from Beaupère, who never changed his views, all
the others did a turnabout, remembered nothing of their
past, did their best to make it sound as if they had always
been for Joan. Canon William of the Desert, who had

---

[4]Bouillé's instructions specified that "one could not claim that the Maid had
recanted," since "she understood nothing at all" of what was on "the statement
that was read to her."

heaped accusations on Joan on May 29, and looked on un-
dismayed as she died, now had always held her to be a "true
Catholic." The monk John Le Fèvre, one of the most as-
siduous at the trial, in complete agreement with the higher
clerics in finding Joan a heretic, a schismatic, and a witch,
now delightedly became a "commissioner subdelegate" of
the rehabilitation tribunal, and Thomas de Courcelles, who
voted that Joan be tortured, had lost all memory of those
faraway things—he could recall only that he had "never
deliberated on any penalty to be inflicted on Joan." And
Manchon the scrivener, how he had stood up to that
bishop! How he had braved Cauchon's fury! Did they want
to know what he had done with the money he had been
paid for that trial? He had used part of it to buy a missal,
the better to pray each day for the soul of the poor dead girl.
And the Isambarts, the Ladvenus, God knew how they had
devoted themselves to Joan, compromised themselves for
her! Brother Isambart so admired her that he had held the
processional cross before the face of the dear little girl. He
had gotten so close to the pyre that, a bit more and, were
it not for Joan's warning to stand back, he himself would
have gone up in flames.[5]

These monks were the ones who furnished our easy-to-
please historians with the various quotations attributed to
Cauchon: the bishop, after the recantation, pacifying the
English with his, "Have no fear, we will catch her yet";
then "exulting" on May 28, after Joan had recanted her

[5] Gustave Rudler (*Michelet historien de Jeanne d'Arc* [Presses Universitaires de
France, 1925], vol. I, p. 104) smilingly notes that Michelet "was taken in by this
character's braggadocio, going so far as to treat him as a saint," and Quicherat
in 1850, prompted perhaps by Michelet, did not hesitate to characterize Isambart
as "the straightest man that Providence brought near the Maid during her martyrdom." To which Rudler comments, "Providence did not go to great pains!"
In 1456, with Isambart no longer there, Ladvenu quietly took over his near-heroic
role as crossbearer; and Massieu claimed credit for being the first to suggest the
idea.

recantation, and stating, "before everyone to Milord War-
wick, 'There! We've got her!' "[6] Joan's famous cry, "Bishop,
I am dying because of you!" was related, or invented, by
Toutmouillé (and immediately afterward confirmed by
Ladvenu), who had also, it will be recalled, described Joan
as "tearing out her hair" on the morning she died, which
would be quite a feat for a girl with a shaven skull. As for
Isambart, he claimed to have been so daring as to whisper
to Joan that she should make an appeal to the Council, and
Cauchon, with his sharp ear, hearing the whisper, was
supposed to have blurted, "Be still, in the name of the
devil!" It is hard to believe that the Bishop of Beauvais,
intent on having a "fine trial," and under the watchful eye
of the doctors from Paris, would run the risk of invoking
the devil at a time like that.[7]

Was Joan a rebel, who reverted to wearing men's clothing out of defiance? Not on your life, Bouillé advised, saying that if Joan put her leggings back on, it was "so as not
to provoke her warders to perverse lusts," and Peter Cusquel, on May 3, 1452, parroted that lesson. But Brother Isambart and Brother Ladvenu, with Manchon the notary and
Massieu the bailiff, teamed up to make the story even better: The truth was that "one of the guards had tried to rape
her" (Manchon); no, said Isambart and Ladvenu, it was "a
great English lord"; so "in order to be more agile in resisting," Joan again put on those masculine clothes which "had
been sedulously placed near her." But that was not it at all,
John Massieu embroidered: "Joan having retired," the English seized her female clothes and "took them from her
bed" (stole them, in a word) and left "on the bed her male
attire." As anyone could see, the poor girl was even more

---

[6]Isambart testimony, May 3, 1452.
[7]And if, indeed, Brother Isambart had thus incurred the bishop's ire, why did the
latter select him, along with his two colleagues of the same ilk, to participate in
Joan's final interrogatory on the morning of May 30?

innocent of any idea of rebellion! She had been forced to it, yes, absolutely forced. She would very much have liked to avoid thus looking like a criminal, but nature's demands were there; she had to get up and dress "to go to the privy, *ut purgaret ventrem.*" She pleaded in vain with her guards to return her dress; they refused, under orders. And that was how the English framed her as a defiant rebel.

Everything was grist to their mill, when it came to clearing themselves of guilt and daubing with the blackest of colors those before whom these same zealous witnesses had abjectly crawled in the old days. They were overgenerous in the details they added, asserting that Bedford had used Joan's examination for virginity at Rouen as a fine opportunity for a voyeuristic interlude.

And then, those witnesses from Domrémy! Obviously, Joan's native heath could be counted on to supply whatever answers were wanted: bouquets of flowers for Poitiers, 1429, or hodfuls of manure for Rouen, 1431. Now, in 1456, all the sentimental bleatings sounded alike, the tone having been set by Joan's mother's petition, as drawn up by the manipulators in charge. Now Joan, having been duly supplied by her good mother "with the sacraments of baptism and confirmation," was "brought up in the fear of God and respect for the traditions of the Church." Having "grown up amid fields and pastures, she went frequently to church and each month, at the end of confession, received the sacrament of the Eucharist." She "had compassion with all her heart" for the "great needs in which the people then found themselves," and she would have "never thought, conceived, or done anything whatsoever that went afoul the Faith." And each then added, in his own way, to this basic canvas; with delightful, if not too careful, embroidering, such as that of one Gérard who claimed to have seen with his own eyes in 1429 Joan "passing before her father's house with her Uncle Durand" and saying " 'Goodbye! I am off to Vaucouleurs!' " Or the audacious anecdote (that John Moreau took credit for) about Cauchon's fury when one of the 1431 investigators—Moreau did not name him, revealing only that he was "someone of importance from the Lorraine country"—had to confess to the bishop that nothing amiss could be found against Joan, either at Domrémy or anywhere else in the region. As a result, this good man "was unable to collect his salary" at Rouen, because Cauchon was so exasperated that nothing had been brought back to him from the Bar country that he could use to doom his victim. It is unlikely that in 1456 at Domrémy —where, at the presbytery from January 28 to February 11, all of these rustic witnesses passed before the delegates of the pontifical commissioners—anyone had read the transcript of the trial, which might have proved embarrassing in view of their assertions.

What about the brothers, and the old mother? Old shaking Zabillet had been called upon for a moment to get the matter going. Beyond that, she was useless. And yet should she not have been there in 1456, in the very front rank of "childhood witnesses"? As for the brothers, after their shady adventure of 1436 and the repeat performance in 1439, dragging them out of obscurity was totally contraindicated.[8]

One important document, which one might have expected to see appear, and cut some ice, in the affair, is the "Book of Poitiers" that Joan referred to several times at Rouen. All those clerics and bishops and learned doctors,

---

[8]Peter, in 1453, had obtained from the Duke of Orléans, finally back from his comfortable London exile, a modest reward: the exploitation (in fodder) of an island called Île-aux-Boeufs, near Orléans. John, who had at first latched on to the enviable job of bailiff of the Vermandois, had been demoted, and was now only provost of Vaucouleurs.

including Inquisitor Turelure of Toulouse, had interrogated her at such length at Poitiers about her background, her faith, her habits, and then finally found in her favor. Their opinions had been gathered in one volume containing all the questions that had been put to her, and all her excellent answers. That "Book of Poitiers" would have been a fine trump card for the 1456 operators. But where was it? Not to be found; no mention of it. Did the Roman chancellery not get a copy of it in 1429? And why was the original, which must have been in the King's possession, not brought out of the archives?

I believe that Rome had no wish for this document to be revived, whatever its significance. It would be indecent to expose the contradictions among theologians, according to whether they belonged to one side or the other. That was a sorry spectacle the Church would as soon do without. And as for the Poitiers examiners—of whom surely some must still have been alive in 1456—they would hardly have wished to have to explain publicly why in 1431 they unanimously stood mute, in absolute, shameful silence.

Bréhal, for his part, had gone a little far, being carried away when he had spoken of Joan as an instrument of God. None of that! Absolutely not! But now all these Ladvenus, Manchons, and company, were desperately trying to make Joan a Venerable, to place a holy halo over her. Her death now was just like that of Our Lord Jesus Christ, even to the "seven words" she spoke as she died (*seven* times she had cried out, "Jesus!"), and the awful sense of terror that overcame her executioner, once the deed was done, even as it had the centurion at the foot of the Cross. The man had come, that very evening, to the monastery of the Dominicans, to confess that he was "afraid of being damned" for having thus "burned a sainted woman." According to Cusquel, someone he described as the "secretary to the King of England" had stated in terror, "We are doomed! We have

burned a good and sainted person!" And just as Jesus had
wept for Jerusalem, so Joan had cried out, "Rouen! Rouen!
I fear me greatly that you must suffer for my death!"

Brother Isambart testified that Joan's heart[9] had proved
to be uninflammable, however they had tried, with coal and
oil, to reduce it to ash: "The executioner remained dumbfounded at this, as at a visible miracle." That was not all;
"many" highly reputable people asserted that as the fire
was crackling, they had been able to read "the name of
Jesus written in the flames" and that "an English soldier,"
"after dinner" on the night of May 30 in the presence of
Isambart, had revealed having seen, or at least thinking he
had seen, "a white dove . . . at the moment [Joan] died" rise
from the pyre and fly away in the direction of France. In
the direction of France! Toward the real King! They knew
what they were about, what words to use, at this rehabilitation trial so precious to His Majesty. That edifying incarnation of the Holy Spirit was indeed more royalist than celestial—or, at the least, celestially royalist!

They all had waxed indignant in 1452: Ladvenu against
the English who "tried to defame the King of France";
Isambart against the foreigners out to "defame His Royal
Majesty"; and Canon Miget against the enemy whose sole
aim in persecuting Joan was to "prove she was a heretic so
they could thereby defame the Lord King of France"! And
Manchon and his alter ego Massieu, on March 4, 1456, had
added this fine item: Joan, on May 24, hearing Master William Érard speak scandalously about the House of France,
had jumped up in fury and forbidden him to touch upon
her Lord King Charles, "the most noble Christian of them
all!" What a fine girl! How proper, in all respects! How
could they refuse to rehabilitate her?

Does this mean that all the testimony given in 1456 must

---

[9]And her "entrails," too, to be exact.

be disregarded? Nothing would be more stupid than to dismiss it *in toto*. Statements such as those made by Simon Charles, by d'Aulon, Dunois, and the Duke d'Alençon, on the contrary, deserve our greatest attention, subject, of course, to a check and comparison to other known facts. So all in all, the 1456 investigation, despite its irritating repetitions, does make a worthwhile contribution to historical knowledge, which is much more than could be said for the often painful tirades of 1450 and 1452.

The *dénouement* was approaching. Mistakes had been made, by Bouillé in trying to establish Joan as an infallible visionary,[10] and by Bréhal in endorsing the prophecies announcing the coming of the Maid.[11] The Holy See had no desire to let itself be carried down the path these enthusiasts were following. It felt it was doing a great deal in giving the King of France what he had so noisily been demanding for the past five years, while he had as yet offered nothing tangible in exchange.

Just as the French Army in 1906 was finally willing to agree to the cancellation of Dreyfus' conviction because there was nothing more to fear, all of the guilty ones now being safely protected by general amnesty, so in 1455 Calixtus III was finally ready to reverse the Rouen sentence, on the understanding that no one would be held accountable, no names would be incriminatingly mentioned. Inquisitor Bréhal took charge of drawing up the *Récollection* of the testimony and point by point refuted the twenty-five-year-

---

[10] "Joan foretold the raising of the siege of Orléans," Bouillé wrote, "the coronation of the King, the submission of Paris in less than seven years, the expulsion of the English from the kingdom, and peace with the Lord Duke of Burgundy [really?]. All of this came to pass as she predicted."

[11] Bréhal went into ecstasies over the fact that Joan was aged thirteen when she was visited by the angels for the first time. What a symbol! 13 = 10 (Commandments) + 3 (Trinity)!

old charges against the Maid. He denounced the slanders
without naming the slanderers. The "episcopal transcript"
of the rehabilitation trial emphasized the fact that the assessors were not to blame "since the articles presented to them
were false." Only "the judge and the promoter"—both
safely in their graves[12]—were derelict in their duty. "The
judge," the text reads, in the singular; even though there
were actually two, Bishop Cauchon and Brother John
Lemaître, the Inquisitor. In 1456, the latter was still alive,
but playing dead, as he had been advised to.[13]

And Heaven was to be left out of the girl's behavior
entirely. The church was careful to take no position concerning the so-called mission the Maid was supposed to
have received from the Almighty through Saints Michael,
Catherine, and Margaret. The Church preferred to ignore
this. There was nothing suggesting this legend in the pontifical rescript of July 4, 1456, which spelled the end of the
Joan affair. On the other hand, it had one ill-considered
phrase, it seems: "We," the Sovereign Pontiff solemnly declared, "sitting at our tribunal and having God alone before
our eyes, do pronounce and decree the said trial and sentences [of Rouen] to have been and to be null and void,
without effect, and expunged." "Without effect" is the one
that bothers me; "the said trial and sentences" were so little
"without effect" that by virtue of their existence, which it
is hard to "expunge," a girl was really and truly "delivered
to combustion." But then, we are dealing here only with
legal semantics.

---

[12]"Only the dead were punished [platonically]," says Father Paul Doncoeur, on
page 20 of his book containing the minutes of the interrogations of Joan of Arc
(1952).
[13]Despite everything, in the first sentence of his rescript, Calixtus III felt he had
to make a fleeting allusion to Joan's family's appeal against the bishop, the promoter, "and the Inquisitor of Rouen." The local Inquisitor, even though empowered by the Inquisitor of the Kingdom, "delegated by apostolic authority," could
always be said to have acted only on his own.

"Considering the appeal of Joan to the Holy See [good evidence of her orthodoxy; as for her deplorable reservation, 'God must be served first,' that too is 'expunged'], we do proclaim that she contracted no note of infamy, that she shall be and hereby is cleansed thereof, and, if need there should be [now what could that possibly mean?], we so do hereby cleanse her thereof absolutely."

I have spoken, the Pope is saying, *in petto.* Through my mouth, Peter has spoken: *Roma locuta est.* The case is settled. None may revive it again. What case? That of Joan-the-good-Catholic, recertified by the present act. But good words about her? Not one. A purely negative opinion.[14] It was false, it was forbidden to say this Maid was a heretic. Her police record, religiously speaking, had been wiped clean. Since the King of France was so anxious for it, all right, the Pope was willing. He now declared her a good Catholic duly patented and registered. Period. Rome rather drily let Paris have the certificate on Joan that it had requested, and the Holy See now hoped that Paris might express its appreciation of this gesture on a level of more tangible realities.

"Once more," says Father Doncoeur, "politics won out."[15] D'Estouteville and Bréhal were compensated by the King in the amount of five hundred *livres* each. Nothing munificent about the figure, but it would do.

---

[14] Régine Pernoud (*Jeanne d'Arc par elle-même et par ses témoins*, p. 322) says quite rightly, "One would look in vain in this rehabilitation decree for a single term that sounds laudatory"; it is "a purely negative act."

[15] *Op. cit.*, p. 21.

XIII

Beatification, Canonization, and Patron Sainthood

The royal house of France, to put it mildly, was never wild about Joan. Du Haillan, Charles IX's historiographer, was in no danger of incurring any displeasure in retailing Court gossip about the Maid. "Some," he wrote, "say Joan was the whore of the Bastard of Orléans, others of the Sire of Baudricourt, and still others of [Marshal Poton de] Xaintrailles." Only at the end of his digression did he seem a bit ashamed of having tarried perhaps too long over this matter, "more than became a History of France." This kind of anecdote about such a nothing of a girl seemed almost shocking in a story that ought to deal only with princes and the mighty. In Chapter II, we noted the opinions of Guillaume du Bellay and Pope Pius II (1458–1464). The latter closed with: Was Joan's adventure "the work of God or an invention of men? I would be hard put to express an opinion on this point." In the *Recherches sur la France* (Research about France) undertaken by Étienne Pasquier at the end of the sixteenth century, there are still echoes of the vile stories about Joan that were told in noble circles; Pasquier expresses indignation at such outrageous filth. At the death of Henry IV, in 1610, there were twenty-nine eulogies, but Joan was named only once, and then only in passing. True, Richelieu included a statue of the "good Lorrainer" in the gallery of the Palais Royal, built in 1633, but she was apparently not worthy of the notice of Louis XIV, not one of the glories of his kingdom. Bossuet, in summing up the history of France for his pupil the Dauphin, made mention of the fact that the Maid, once suspect as to orthodoxy, had been cleansed of all taint by the papacy itself. Thus the royal family need not blush—which was the main thing—for having made use of the services of the onetime barmaid.

The French Revolution respected Joan, without exalting her, and while it is true that the insurrectional government of Orléans destroyed the commemorative monument after August 10, that was because the King was shown in it; one of the cannons cast from the salvaged bronze was dedicated to the Maid. But then, in 1803, Bonaparte, deep in his struggle against the English, was to congratulate the people of Orléans for having put Joan back on her pedestal: "The illustrious Joan," he declared, "proved that there is no miracle which French genius cannot accomplish when national independence is threatened." This sentence entirely transformed Joan's posthumous fate, and we have yet to see the last of the results of that metamorphosis. Michelet was the prime impresario here. He wrote in 1839, a time of extreme tension in Anglo-French relations. It was he who invented Joan the patriot, indeed, Joan the very initiator of French patriotism.

Dumas *père* rang variations on the same chimes in his *Jehanne la Pucelle* of 1842. Joan was celebrated by Lamartine in 1852, as "the martyr of *la Patrie*." Then the historian Henri Martin rang it even louder: in his eyes, Joan was "the

Messiah of nationality, the very soul of France." This was
followed by other comparable acclamations by Henri-Alex-
andre Wallon (1860), Vallet de Viriville (1863), and Sépet
(1869). It was obvious what would happen after 1870, with
a beaten France dreaming only of *revanche*. The Prussians
now replaced the English as the "hereditary enemy." Luck-
ily, Joan, as the reader will recall, was a "Lorrainer," from
the province Germany had just stolen from France, making
her the ideal personification of the new crusade. Statues of
the "heroine" now popped up everywhere, and in 1876 Parisians, thanks to the sculptor Emmanuel Frémiet, could take
delight in their own golden Joan on horseback, in the Place
des Pyramides right off the Rue de Rivoli.

In 1884, at the instigation of Joseph Fabre, a devoted
partisan who had written a book called *Jeanne libératrice de
la France* (Joan, Liberator of France), 250 members of Parliament got together to demand a "national holiday" in honor
of Joan of Arc, to be observed on May 8. And a little later,
in the very year when young Charles Péguy, a new convert
to socialism but still an ardent flag waver, finished his first
· *Jeanne d'Arc*, Sarah Bernhardt, ludicrously costumed as the
Maid, was scoring a hit at the Porte-Saint-Martin Theatre
in Paris in Barbier and Gounod's "musical drama" on the
subject. Georges Méliès would soon be devoting one of the
earliest of films to the inspired soldier girl.

All of France, in 1893, was talking about the incident at
Chinon where two opposing views of Joan clashed, the one
Catholic and the other set up in reply by the freethinkers.
Raymond Poincaré, then Minister of Public Education, did
his best to get the two sides to join in the tribute to the great
Frenchwoman at Vaucouleurs. Nevertheless, Joan was in-
creasingly being taken over by reactionaries, and Péguy
wrote his play to try to win her back from them.

Péguy at that time was a faithful disciple of Jean Jaurès,
who, on July 1, 1893, in *Le Socialiste*, had called upon "the

capitalist bourgeoisie" to "stop wearing the armor" of Joan. "Emerging from the Stock Exchange where it has just underwritten the loans floated by the Triple Alliance," he wrote, "one would find it hard to take [this business bourgeoisie] for a new incarnation of the virgin of Domrémy."

But none of that did any good. The conservatives, shrewd in their estimate that the public had a short memory, those same "best people" who, terrified of losing their property rights, had allied themselves with Bismarck in 1871 to crush the Resistance and given the Germans all the French soil they asked for as long as they helped protect them from Gambetta and his "Red" friends, now were all for the most exalted kind of patriotism. And Joan became their emblem.

Félix Faure, blessed by the haves, unveiled the statue of Joan at Domrémy in 1896; and in no time the country was plunged into the Dreyfus Case. Toward the end of it, on December 5, 1904, the shock troops of these "good people," after hearing the diatribes and homilies of the pamphleteer Édouard Drumont and the poet François Coppée, ended their Paris mass meeting with shouts of "Down with the Jews! Down with the Masonic Republic! Long live Joan of Arc!" Henceforth the Maid belonged to the Royalist faction of *L'Action française;* each year, its youth group, *les camelots du roi,* would parade to Joan's statue in the Place des Pyramides.

Meantime, Rome, of course, could not remain unaffected by what was thus taking place in French public opinion, centered on a personage who had been condemned by the Church, it was true, but also rehabilitated by the Holy See itself, thanks to the coercion—now considered providential —of King Charles VII.

On May 8, 1869, the Bishop of Orléans, Monsignor Félix

Dupanloup, supported by eleven other prelates, called upon the Pope to canonize the onetime heretic. Dupanloup was not one for beating around the bush! Pius IX understood perfectly well that the subtle bishop, already known as the author of an impressive exegesis of the *Syllabus,* had another idea in mind: the Empire had shown itself to be "liberal," why should the Church not do as much? Would it not be fine proof of its desire for reconciliation, to make reparation by paying this signal honor to one of its own victims? The idea was worth pursuing, but deliberation and circumspection were the rule in the Roman Curia. Pius thought Dupanloup somewhat impetuous, but his need to make a decision was postponed: the catastrophe of 1870, by which Italy deprived—or relieved—the Pope of his temporal power (an event followed by endless lamentations), for years busied Rome with concerns much more immediate and pressing than the problem of Joan.

Leo XIII, in 1894, suddenly pulled Joan out of the closet. There was great excitement in France that year on the subject of Joan. Leo XIII had just launched his policy of *ralliement* (which brought many Catholics to support the Republic rather than remain royalists). Following the alarming elections of 1893 (in which 600,000 Socialist votes were cast as against a bare 100,000 in 1885), the Pope's proposals found a favorable response in what was then known, among "respectable" progressives, as "the new spirit," that is, a coalition of haves (whether for or against the Church) against the have-nots. The *beau geste* advocated twenty-five years before by Dupanloup might now be most happily appropriate. On January 27, 1894, the Holy See gave orders to "investigate the case" for eventual beatification of Joan.

But there was no reason to get excited. The idea at the moment was merely for Joan to become "blessed," the first step in the direction of "sainthood." Those words, "investigate the case," were exactly the ones, it will be remembered, that were used by Calixtus III on June 11, 1455. Moreover, the intention was still the same: to improve relations between the Roman Curia and the French government. Thérèse de Lisieux, who had composed a convent version of *Joan of Arc* as a "dramatic entertainment," was instructing her sisters in singing the hymn she had written:

> Come back, great-hearted girl,
> Liberating angel . . .

Liberating? Of course! France was now in the toils of Freemasons and "anarchists," you must realize. But at the same time, government ministers, professing belief in the once-new spirit of Voltaire while making solemn inaugural addresses at new statues of the Maid, lent a sympathetic ear to the other "new spirit" blowing in from the Vatican.

For beatification, some well-attested "miracles" are required. Now, the very word "miracle" is implicit in Joan's whole legend, and Bonaparte, using it in only a semi-religious sense, relied heavily on it in his strong seminal speech of 1803 to the City Council of Orléans. To the Church, a miracle is something more specific. Joan had always disclaimed any idea of performing miracles; she laughingly shrugged off those who asked her for some. But that was only while she was on earth. How about now, since she had been in Heaven? As the inquiry wended its way along the "investigation of the case," the necessary elements appeared, as later described in the beatification decree. For Joan did actually perform several authentic miracles from her abode on high. Since 1891, three miraculous cures were attributed to her: three nuns, one from the Congregation of the Holy Family, another from the Society of Divine Providence, and the third from the Sisters of Saint Benedict, all three suffering from ulcers—one in the stomach, one in the left breast, and the third on the legs—were "suddenly and completely cured" after praying to Joan to intercede for them. This wiped out the obstacles; everything was in order; Joan had her passport.

Still the distinction planned to honor the Maid was slow in coming. With Pierre Waldeck-Rousseau's premiership in 1899 in the wake of the detestable Eugène-Henri Brisson régime of 1895, relations kept worsening between France and the Holy See. In 1904, these disagreements led to the expulsion of the papal nuncio, and in 1905 to the separation of Church and state. Rome could expect nothing from the "radicals" now in power in Paris if it paid this tribute to Joan of Arc; to them, it would merely be more "Roman-collar business."

But *L'Action française* was very anxious for an ecclesiastical endorsement to upgrade its national heroine, and under Pius X Charles Maurras' royalists had considerable influence with the Vatican. Father de Clérissac organized a "monastic triduum" for the canonization of our soldier Maid, and he was delighted to see the Pope so well disposed toward it—"Saint Pius X," as we are now supposed to call him.

The papal bull of April 18, 1909, declaring Joan "blessed," sent the royalists into ecstasies. They were even more gratified when the following year, on August 25, Pius X (a real godsend; another Gregory XVI) made them the long-requested gift of condemning Marc Sangnier's periodical, *Le Sillon* (The Furrow), which stood for democratic, progressive Christianity. His illustrious predecessor Gregory had similarly condemned the liberal Catholic publication, *L'Avenir* (The Future), of the religious writer Félicité Robert de La Mennais seventy-eight years earlier.

Now Joan had only one last step to take: from "blessed" to "saint." This final promotion was to take place in 1920, again fitting in with Roman diplomacy of the period. Back in the days when young Bonaparte, who wanted to be Emperor, was ruling in France, Rome had considered whether it might not get him to make some territorial restitutions if it canonized some ancient member of his family. At that time, the papal legate candidly stated, "Canonization is always a favor granted by Rome."

France, in 1920, was a great victorious nation; no graciousness shown to her would appear excessive. And if German Catholics at the time could not properly appreciate the progress among the elect now made by a Frenchwoman, it was only because they were insufficiently attentive to the operational context. For this "favor" to France, the Holy See again expected some restitution: this time, the reestablishment of the nunciature in Paris. The "horizon-blue" (or veterans') Parliament, successor to the nonpartisan "sacred unity" (which had guided France's destinies through World War I), allowed French Catholics to entertain certain hopes; and, as it turned out, they were right. It must be said that everything was handled with skill, and so harmonized as to create a fraternization of the temporal and the spiritual. The flag-waving Catholic writer Maurice Barrès and the papacy worked along parallel lines: canonization on the one hand, national holiday on the other. On May 16, 1920, Rome canonized Joan; on July 10, the French enacted the law making May 8 the national celebration of *la Patrie*'s patriot *par excellence*. And to cap it all, as a result, on November 20, the Chamber of Deputies voted in favor of resuming diplomatic relations with the Holy See. Mission accomplished.

But what of the miracles? Additional miracles were required to justify promotion from one step to the next in the hierarchy beyond the grave. The Roman offices exhibited no concern on this score; it presented no problem. There was no fear that the proper materials would be missing. The papal bull of 1920 added to the three miracles mentioned in the bull of 1909 two new miraculous cures effected by Joan. The dates and places of these new wonders were vague, but the faithful were informed that one Miss Miran-delle, who had a "perforating plantar affliction," as well as a Miss Belin, with "peritoneal and pulmonary tuberculosis, complicated by an organic lesion of the mitral orifice," had, in a twinkling, been restored to perfect health through the intercession of the new saint. Once again, then, everything was as it should be; Rome could promulgate its promo-tional decree with clear conscience. It will be noted that Joan had widened her field of operations since becoming "blessed." She no longer dealt only with nuns (and their ulcers), but she did nevertheless concern herself exclusively with virgins.

The French were convinced that all this somehow made their heroine greater. Yet how many of them ever actually had the texts of the papal bulls before their eyes? There was no mention in them of Joan the soldier, nor of Joan the illuminate. Now in the twentieth century, Rome was far removed from what Inquisitor Bréhal had tried to get it to say in the fifteenth about the "irrefragable [well, 'almost'] evidence" of the Maid's divine mission. The Vatican adopted an attitude of pious and cautious silence on this point. Joan's "voices" were given no Roman authentica-tion. If Joan was canonized, it was, fittingly, only for her virtues. She was the young virgin with all the virtues: true exemplar of the good Christian woman incarnate.

Nevertheless, this was the signal for euphoria and di-thyrambic paeans of a quite different tone. Robert Brasil-lach, later shot as a collaborationist, and Thierry Maulnier, later a member of the French Academy, both as devoid of Catholicism as their royalist mentor Charles Maurras, rap-turously extolled the "angelical horsewoman," that "mas-terpiece of helmeted sainthood." A man named Baillat, officially representing the Department of Arts and Letters

of the Ministry of National Education, would gradilo-
quently say of her in 1956, as recorded in the *Mémorial*
(compiled for the fifth centenary of the rehabilitation), that
she had received "the highest consecrations of patriotism
and faith." Régine Pernoud was moved by the unique case
of this multiphased saint, "the only one to enjoy the appro-
bation of both Church and state [a fine combination]." And
Louis Jacquinot, Minister of State, speaking on May 13,
1956, at the Place du Théâtre-Français (the very spot where,
in 1429, Joan had unsuccessfully attacked the ramparts of
Paris), waxed eloquent about how Joan's compatriots must
be filled with happiness at the thought that each year, on
May 8, "all of the civil, military, and religious authorities
come together and meet around her memory."

She was a saint, yes; but be careful! Do not add "martyr"
unthinkingly. Jean Guitton is very forthright in explaining
this: "Joan cannot be considered a martyr, in the strict
sense of the term, by Catholic thinking, for it was a regular
Church court, in a regular trial, that condemned her to
death, . . . a court of the Inquisition canonically constituted."[1] Therefore, to add to Joan's religious qualities the
word that springs to mind would be committing, as far as
the Church is concerned, an egregious indecency; and
Guitton is quite right to put us on guard against such bad
form.

Hers was a "tattered memory" already in the century
following her death, according to old Étienne Pasquier. To
be sure! Shakespeare's *Henry VI*[2] was a polemical work, an

---

[1]Jean Guitton, *Problème et mystère de Jeanne d'Arc* (The Problem and Mystery of
Joan of Arc), 1961; p. 239.
[2]Actually a chronicle play by Robert Greene, "supposed to have been tinkered
by Shakespear," says Bernard Shaw in the "Preface" to *Saint Joan* (Penguin ed.,
1951), p. 11.

English act of vengeance in which Joan was shown as a shrew untamed, a daughter of the devil, who, at the moment of paying for her crimes, in order to escape her fate, confessed she was pregnant and ran down the list of her lovers. Pierre Ronsard, for one, bypassed her; in his very loyalist *Franciade*, she is totally ignored, even though Villon had saluted her almost a century earlier. The *précieuses* of the seventeenth century held her in esteem; their leader, Mademoiselle de Scudéry, proclaimed her admiration for the "chaste soldier girl." But then Jean Chapelain published his unfortunate rhapsody, in which Joan was divested of all mysticism and the author himself emphasized that Dunois was the "principal hero" of his epic.[3]

The haughty Montesquieu disdained the Maid; fairytales did not interest him. "Reason and philosophy," he wrote, "teach us to be wary of a thing [the story of Joan] which jars them both so strongly." Beaumarchais, in his *Lettres sérieuses et badines*, published in 1740, used a tone that antedated and foreshadowed Voltaire's epistle to Rousseau on April 30, 1755. Voltaire made fun of poor old Chapelain, who, he said, made "the mistake of taking seriously" a farcical story. Voltaire was barking up the wrong tree in thus writing to Rousseau, who, the year before, returning to his native Calvinist Geneva after a twenty-six-year absence and resuming his citizenship there, had presented the authorities with a copy of Joan's trial as a gift: surely he thought there was nothing farcical about it. But Voltaire had found himself a subject, and he gamboled on with it in his laughing manner—though his laughter had fangs in it. And yet, both Michelet and Anatole France have tried to convince us that Voltaire was really not so mean. He "did not really intend to dishonor Joan; in his serious books, he pays most brilliant tribute to her," wrote Michelet. Both

---

[3] *La Pucelle*, 1656, exactly two centuries after the rehabilitation.

these advocates, it must be surmised, felt that their prestige was such that we would take them at their words. But let us go back to Voltaire's text.

His innocent little satire on *La Pucelle* was a big hit in the salons of Geneva, and according to the banker Du Pan, provoked "great bursts of laughter from our ladies." In it, the Maid, daughter of the local priest, is a "fat chambermaid." After all kinds of adventures, she is exposed to the funniest of all "temptations" when confronted with the "amorous audacity" of—guess who! Her donkey, a magical ass, it is true, who has wings and is very loquacious. He has a mad crush on Joan and tries to seduce her; the Maid is preparing to give in: "Of her brown arse, the arches she raised up. . . ." But then—God be praised—Dunois arrives on the scene; thanks to him, the Maid keeps her maidenhood." As can be seen, this was delicate whimsy, harmless, respectful, and irresistibly funny!

Even Jean Jaurès later described as a "disgrace" what Michelet was willing to accept with a smile. And if Voltaire, in his *Essai sur les moeurs* (Essay on Manners), watched himself and hypocritically adopted a more fitting tone to deal with Joan, in his *Philosophical Dictionary*, on the other hand, he really let himself go. He invited his readers "carefully" to recall the detail we mentioned earlier about Joan being instructed by Brother Richard, along with other "devout ladies of the populace," in how to fake miracles; he said that at the Rouen trial "her judges thought her a witch, she thought herself divinely inspired; this is really a case of: 'Faith! judge and defendant are one as mad as the other!'" and concluded with his succinct opinion of her: "a sorry idiot."

Diderot's *Encyclopedia* (in the 1776 *Supplement*) was more moderate, but refused to be taken in by "fables invented by superstition. . . . Some authors, pious imbeciles," the entry (written by Turpin de Crisse) said, "have pointed out that, when living with her parents, Joan made a habit of seeking seclusion beneath an oak and concluded from this that she had long conversations with Saint Michael." The contributor to the great *Encyclopedia*, using the same logic as Michelet and Anatole France, assumed that no one would bother to check his "facts." The transcript of the trial clearly establishes that "pious imbeciles" had nothing to do with it, but that Joan referred to her "conversations with Saint Michael" many times on her own. As for her "habit of seeking seclusion beneath an oak," that is just plain forgery.

An eighteenth-century priest, Lenglet-Dufresnoy, made his own historical contribution, based on the unpublished, and precious, work of Edmond Richer, but unwilling to let people think him an easy mark, he wrote, "That this girl had visions, apparitions, revelations . . . is a pious belief that I leave to those with a mind less stubborn than mine."

In the nineteenth century, Chateaubriand overlooked Joan in his *Genius of Christianity*. He could distinguish "in modern times, but two fine subjects for an epic poem: the Crusades and the discovery of the New World." This, despite the fact that he was in England in 1794 at the time when Robert Southey, making amends for Greene-Shakespeare's old insults, paid tribute to Joan the pure, Joan the valiant, Joan the martyred. Schiller chimed in, in 1820, with his *Jungfrau von Orléans*, in which the Maid, in a daring fictitious set-to, got killed in battle, like a pre-Wagnerian Kriemhild. And there was still more to come, before Michelet: a *Joan* by Alexander Soumet, and after him, the previously mentioned *Joan* by Dumas. But, literarily speaking, nothing significant until Péguy.[4]

---

[4]Two contributors to the 1956 *Mémorial*, Pierre Marot and Thierry Maulnier, contended respectively that Victor Hugo never "mentioned her name" and displayed profound "indifference" to her. Again, a case of not knowing whereof they spoke. To my knowledge, Joan appears at least twice in Hugo's works, first in the

Overenthusiastic as he sometimes became when writing about Péguy, "the pilgrim of Chartres," the critic Albert Béguin felt his Joan of Arc was a "living portrait" of the heroic virgin, not only the most striking but also the most faithful image we have of her. Yet I for one wonder what could have led Péguy to attribute the opinions he did, to Joan, about rejecting the concept of Hell, about individual charity being tragically ineffective (what was needed was to change the system), and about how it was urgent "to kill war." It was Péguy, not Joan, who had been a member of the progressive *Groupe d'études sociales* of Orléans. The young graduate of the prestigious École Normale was putting his own dreams into her mouth.

Just before Péguy cooked up the second version of his *Joan of Arc*, which he called her *Mystery*, Anatole France had raised the hackles of the devout with his two thick volumes on the Maid. But he weighted his pages down with erudite footnotes and a whole apparatus of references (many of which lead nowhere), and it is not good historiography, as Edith Thomas writes, to "invent statements, mistake the imaginary for documentation, pass hypotheses off as certainties," to say nothing of making translations from the Latin whose "elegance" is matched by their "misconstruction." As for the heart of the matter, Anatole France was not content merely with wearing a good stage costume that might create the illusion; he put on kid gloves and here and there spotted a few smooth paragraphs, oozing with admiration for Joan. But Barrès' *Mes Cahiers* (My Notebooks) relate that during an informal conversation his colleague admitted to him that, all things considered, to his mind nothing more telling had been written about the

---

poem "L'Âne" (The Donkey), in which she is seen, "through the flame":
  Stark naked at the stake, twisting her arms sublime,
and then in the novel *Toilers of the Sea*, from which, a bit further, we quote the poet's moving words.

Maid than Voltaire's entry in his *Philosophical Dictionary.*
Which gives us the true measure of his intentions. And
Bernard Shaw was right in saying that Anatole France
should never have undertaken the job, since he was "funda-
mentally unable to believe that there ever was any such
person as the real Joan."[5]

Once again, friend Claudel must have been talking off
the top of his head, in the full flush of unabashed ignorance,
when he saw fit to trample on Shaw's *Saint Joan,* calling the
playwright "an absurd writer, who would have done better
to stick to his usual clowning."[6] To my mind, that 1923 *Saint
Joan* is what is best in all of the overabundant literature on
Joan that we have;[7] it is a fine text, grave, sensitive, intelligent, and profound. And it is a welcome relief from Péguy's vaporizings, from Barrès' nonsense about Joan's
veins filled with a mixture of "the blood of Veleda and the
Roman centurions [*sic*],"[8] Léon Bloy's demented ravings
(Joan was "the prodigy of the centuries, the greatest miracle since the Incarnation"), and Jean Anouilh's buffoonery,
which in *The Lark* shows us Charles VII torn between Joan
and Agnes Sorel, who when the Maid appeared on the
scene at Chinon was all of two years old![9]

---

[5]Shaw, *op. cit.,* "Preface," p. 32.
[6]Text of a lecture delivered at Basel in 1938, before the "première" of *Joan at the Stake:* Claudel did not work very hard to produce that commissioned "oratorio."
[7]Along with Delteil's *Joan of Arc,* which, of course, does not hold up; it is full of mistakes and falls apart every which way. But I still have a soft spot for that brutal and tender book, because of the very real love one feels in it. Ever since 1925, I have remembered the prayer that Delteil has Joan saying, that unexpected and poignant *Ave Maria:* "Hello, Mary! What grace there is on your cheeks! You, among all women, are really lucky; the Lord is your friend. And how beautiful your baby is, the fruit of your womb, Jesus!" After Anatole France's stuffy pages, that is like a breath of fresh air!
[8]Thierry Maulnier, of course, would later congratulate Barrès for sensing that "through the roots of the fairy tree [!]" Joan was connected with "the antique tradition of pre-Christian wonderment." Nor should we overlook Barrès' truly Bonaparte-like phrase about "the miracle of Joan, the eternal French miracle."
[9]*The Lark* (1951) was a fine title, but Claudel had written earlier (1942) of Joan: "that outcry, piercing as the song of the lark, of a child who believes in God."

Yes, her poor memory was "tattered"! Tattered and torn! Even as Dupanloup and his eleven acolytes were calling for Joan's canonization, Louis Rossel, a career Army officer turned Communard, awaiting death before a firing squad, wrote his adoring, albeit naïve pages, crediting Joan with strategic concepts of which she never had the slightest idea.

In 1936, young royalists continued to parade to Frémiet's statue to demand a return of the monarchy, while the extreme left raised banners in honor of Joan, that "daughter of the people, betrayed by her king, burned by her priests."

Brasillach, film historian and strange disciple of Joan the Warrior, collaborated with the Nazis in hunting down French patriots, while the onetime adolescent Communist, Claude Vermorel, wrote his *Jeanne avec nous* (Joan Belongs to Us) and worked militantly in the Resistance. Each in his turn, first Marshal Pétain, then General de Gaulle, made Joan the emblem of their causes, and Thierry Maulnier used his play, *Jeanne et les juges* (Joan and the Judges), as a vehicle to denounce the Moscow trials.[10]

The English and American writers! I almost forgot them! First, Mark Twain and Andrew Lang, of whom Shaw says that the one made Joan "into an unimpeachable American school teacher in armor" and the other "a beautiful and most ladylike Victorian."[11] Then, Mr. and Mrs. Butterfield, for whom it was very simple: Joan had tuberculosis of the brain; and Francis Leary, who felt that to fathom the mystery of Joan, a turn to the occult and secret cabalistic rites was required.

---

[10] In all fairness, I must say that, while the article Thierry Maulnier contributed to the 1956 *Mémorial* was an unfortunate performance, the same is not true of the long preface he wrote for his play, which includes some very penetrating observations.

[11] Shaw, *op. cit.*, "Preface," p. 33.

I prefer the simplicity of the Russian cosmonaut Komarov, who died on his space mission. His final reading (the book found open on his desk) was a chapter of history dealing with "Joan of Arc."

The "mystery" of Joan? The least ridiculous thing that Michelet ever wrote about her was the two words: "living enigma." However, let us be clear about it. As we have been tracing it, Joan's trajectory is in no way mysterious. The customary amazement about the alleged ease with which the peasant girl was welcomed at the King's Court fades away when we see that actually "ease" was the thing that Joan least met with at Chinon and that she was treated as suspect and quarantined for a long time. As for what followed, the freeing of Orléans, the Loire campaign, the consecration, and, even more, the events at Paris, there is not the slightest need to read "wonderment" into any of it. Joan's capture, her trial, and her death do not call for any supernatural involvement to explain them. One might rather say that they all cruelly underline its absence. And yet it is Joan herself who remains enigmatic. She is the only mystery, the real mystery, of her story. So let us, as we close, at least try really to get a picture of the person she was.

To begin with, three pieces of negative evidence: three things that have to be rectified. First. The joke, the great error, the violent distortion of the truth inherent in the classic theme: Joan created French patriotism. Michelet mainly was responsible for this accepted falsehood. Joan, in his words, "carried the whole people with her and they turned soldier with her. . . . She loved France so! And France, feeling this, in turn came to love her." Claudel fell right in with him: Joan "taught France once more [France having once known, but forgotten?] to turn its great store of available willpower and intelligence into a single con-

sciousness and a single desire." And then, Thierry Maulnier, inevitably as ever following behind Charles Maurras:
"Taking the helm of a people at war," Joan "revived a
nation from the grave of Lazarus"; Joan caused "the onset"
of the "collective consciousness of modern nations" in
Europe. This commonplace that turns up everywhere is
nonetheless a big lie.

Joan never had "a whole people" behind her. Joan never
"took the helm of a people at war." At Orléans, those who
followed her—enthusiastically, it is true—were not thinking of France; they were thinking of Orléans. They were
sick of the siege, the shortage of food, and the overcrowding
of their narrow city by all the refugee "suburbanites." The
King's army (which was never in any way Joan's army) was
not made up of patriots, but mercenaries, and when finally,
in April, 1430, Joan did for once go out on her own at the
head of a command, her troops were not natives, but two
hundred Piedmontese she had been able to put on the payroll. Never, not for one second, was there any "national"
impetus triggered by Joan. How indeed could it have been
possible at a time when the people of Marseilles as well as
those of Besançon were "Germans," those in the Bordeaux
and Landes regions of the Southwest were perfectly content to be "English," and a man from Brittany felt as alien
to one from Lyons or Lille as a Frenchman of today does
to a Chilean or a Papuan?

All those Pindaric odes about Joan and *la Patrie* are just
so much juggling, so much verbal fraud. Reread the transcript of her trial. Not once, as she faces those "English"
judges, do we hear a patriotic cry from her such as would
be uttered at the time of the French Revolution, or in more
recent days. Joan was not fighting "for France"! She was
fighting for her King, and, through the King, beyond him,
for God, for the Kingdom of God.

The nationalist right[12] has gone even further in its disfiguring of Joan. What is "nationalism"? It is the doctrine that puts the interest of the nation, whatever it might be, above all else. When a Péguy goes off on a tangent about God-Who-is-always-French because the French are always right, this is not too serious: it is just a kind of literary sideshow for a certain audience. And Péguy did not try to misrepresent Joan's principal concern. But when the people of L'Action française play with the memory of the Maid to the point of prostituting it to their own ends, it's hard to take. Joan was the opposite of a conqueror. She never hated the English as English. As Bernard Shaw wisely puts it in the preface to his play, "She objected to foreigners on the sensible ground that they were not in their proper place in France."[13] And strange as it may seem, Thierry Maulnier is the one who has the most pertinent things to say on this score: "In Joan's eyes, it was not as Frenchmen that God had chosen the French, but because theirs was a just cause, that of the invaded. If the French had gone to make war in England, they would have been in the wrong, and God would have been for the English. God was not for France; He was for justice."[14] Anyone trying to portray Joan as the originator of nationalism goes beyond verbal fraud to fraud pure and simple. Moreover, as Jacques Madaule so well stated it, Joan "had more to offer us than victories."[15]

---

[12]Do we ever stop to think how insane, how wildly ludicrous it is to couple that noun and that adjective? The right, as early as September 4, 1870, was working for Prussian victory over France; it prepared it, organized it, and obtained it. In the same way again, after having explicitly and openly called for the victory of Fascism in 1938 (see the article by Thierry Maulnier in the extreme-right magazine, Combat, for November, 1938), L'Action française went on to muster all its strength, in collaboration with the Nazi occupation authorities, against the French Resistance.

[13]Shaw, op. cit., "Preface," p. 29.

[14]Thierry Maulnier, "Un procès d'abjuration" (A Recantation Trial) (1951), preface to the play, Jeanne et les juges, pp. 29-30.

[15]Jacques Madaule, Histoire de France, vol. I, p. 208.

Second. The next thing to be swept out, just as completely, is another bit of nonsense, not as offensive to Joan as was the first, but equally false. To Jean Guitton, Joan's true greatness is her "purity." "Joan's purity," he writes majestically, was not only "her implicit glory" (which we must understand as: the thing that predisposed her toward canonization), but—now, get this!—"her reason for being."[16] That's some of the worst nonsense I've ever heard. For in the first instance, what does "purity" mean? Some people insist on taking this word in a vulgar material sense, as if virginity had anything to do with the "pure in heart" who are mentioned in the Beatitudes. But it is pure aberration to maintain in Joan's case that virginity was her reason for being. Joan expressed herself on the subject without the slightest ambiguity. Cauchon asked her whether her voices had told her that, if she ceased to be a virgin, she would forfeit her happiness and the friendship of Heaven, and her answer was that her angels had never told her anything of the kind. Joan had made no vow of virginity. Her attitude toward virginity was similar to her attitude on men's clothing. The Maid—meaning the Servant—held herself to be dedicated to a certain task; as long as that was not done, she had no time to think of anything else. She dressed as a boy, because she was doing a boy's job, and she remained a virgin because while you're involved in combat is not the time to get married. Later, if indeed there were to be a "later," which she did not believe, she would go back to women's clothes and her state of womanhood; she might love, she might marry, if her heart so desired. Because she would then be "liberated," because her work would be finished and she would again belong to herself. That was all. Joan was no nun; she was a guerrilla. She made neither a fetish nor a superstition of virginity. Physical continence was simply a temporary expedient she had adopted to allow

[16]Guitton, *op. cit.*, p. 188.

her to operate. Let us leave Jean Guitton to his pietistic academic foolishness.

Third. Quicherat, Shaw himself, and others tried to represent Joan as a forerunner of Luther and Calvin, an opponent of the Roman Church, calling for the right of free inquiry. But that is entirely wrong. Joan had not the slightest objection against accepted dogma. She was a born adversary of heretics and schismatics. Her painful personal disagreement arose out of just one point, a point of fact. Cauchon tried to get her to say she had lied and invented her "apparitions," but she could not agree to that, because it was a true fact that she had seen her angels, "as I am seeing you, with the eyes in my body," as she put it. Well then, he wanted her to admit she was wrong in saying these "spirits" came from a divine source, for the University of Paris had recognized them as demons. Demons, my angels? she retorted, furious. You must be crazy! And thus she was torn. Her loyalty was divided, and that was not allowed. She had either to renounce her "angels" or to be separated from the Church. Joan wanted desperately to remain within the Church, but she was horrified at the idea of betraying her divine companions. She died a Christian, a Catholic, without cursing the priests who killed her, for even now, in their crime, or their error, they were in her eyes priests of Jesus Christ.

Very well. Then just who was this girl? Which brings us face to face with the big question, brings us, if you will, to the last problem: Joan and God, Joan and her "voices."

I know very well that in order to retain the attention of a certain number of readers and avoid their pitying smiles, the best thing to do here would be to adopt a superior tone. This business of voices and visions is the really bothersome part of Joan's story, which is otherwise a fine and interesting one. Too bad to see the tragic tale compromised by such pathological details. For it is obviously quite impossible to give anything more than anecdotal value to this nonsense, is it not? And we would prefer it if this "nice" girl did not force us to.

For the Maid is certainly a case. Not a liar, to be sure. But unbalanced, probably a victim of frequent hallucinations. Yet we also have to take into consideration the period, its ambience, what country life was like in the fifteenth century, what could happen to a "mystical" temperament exposed to it. True, the word "mystical," suggesting a meditative creature lost in prayers, hardly fits Joan as we have seen her—healthy, strong, taking delight in open air and broad sunlight, not given to reverie, preferring action. But psychic troubles are stealthy, and one who seems most above suspicion may well turn out, all of a sudden, to be mentally ill. The derangement may be limited, but it is mental illness all the same.

Alain, so often perspicacious, invites ridicule when he begs us, in connection with Joan and her story, "Above all, don't get God mixed up in it!" He reminds me of the conscientious, hardworking, instructive Soviet scholar who pulled off the prodigious feat of writing a big book on Tolstoy without mentioning a word about his religious thought. Yet all of Tolstoy is contained within the long internal struggle which, in 1878, finally led to the peace of certainty that from then on was the determining factor in the conduct of his private and public life. Likewise for Joan. To cut her off from what she called "God," to place her "hallucinations" inside of parentheses for one condescendingly disdainful paragraph, is to condemn oneself to only a tangential discussion of her. Joan is Joan, indeed, only because God was "mixed up" in, guided, her life.

Belief in the "supernatural" is "the shame of civilization," according to Ernest Renan (*The Future of Science*). But where does the supernatural start? First, it would be necessary to define "nature," and Renan's rationalistic indignation seems rather childish. Étienne Gilson strikes me as more serious when he writes humorously, "Whatever surprises professors seems to them to lose its right to exist." I agree with the view expressed by Victor Hugo that nothing is more "puerile" than "to imagine that by blindfolding oneself against the unknown, the unknown is thereby abolished." He also added, "A certain type of scientific mind is no less narrow than the religious mind; error has only taken on a new look." Scientism can be obscurantist. A biologist such as Katavasov in *Anna Karenina*—and there are plenty like him—exactly fits the description Renan gives us of researchers who "pretend to be doing research" when in fact they "are trying to establish proof"; all of their totally open-minded "objective" tests are in reality only continually repeated attempts to demonstrate their own preconceived systems.

It was Hugo, once more, who wrote of "those encounters with the unlikely which, in order to save face, we call hallucinations,"[17] and he was not afraid to refer to the "transfiguring visions" which, he said, made "a camel drover into Mohammed, and a goat girl into Joan of Arc."[18] But, of course, Hugo's Catholic contemporary, the journalist Louis Veuillot, insisted that the poet was the original sucker of carnival fame, and André Gide sadly concluded that the "magnificent craftsman of language," the resounding gilded cymbal, was in the final analysis nothing but an idiot. Unfortunately, Bernard Shaw, whom it is hard to see as being gullible, shared Hugo's ideas. In his remarkable Preface to the printed version of *Saint Joan*, after considering all those impenetrable qualities that still remain around us, and all the powers that certainly are at our disposal although we are unaware of them (at least here in the "posi-

---

[17]Victor Hugo, *Les Travailleurs de la mer* (Toilers of the Sea), vol. II, ch. IV, p. 2.
[18]*Ibid.*, vol. I, ch. I, p. 7.

tivist" West), he wondered what reasons we might have to be proud of the limited world our "science" imagines, when we are surrounded by so much mystery which we repudiate the minute it appears before our closed minds.

André Breton wrote something I would gladly countersign: "It may be that life needs to be deciphered like a cryptogram." I am not sure the cryptogram of Joan's life is impenetrable.

Let us fully comprehend one thing, first of all: the thirteen-year-old girl, "that little bit of woman among the nettles and the buttercups, so amazed that she forgot all about eating her bread and butter" (that from Claudel), was the same one who, grown somewhat older, risked her life, yelled in battle, fought like a man, climbed ladders amid flying arrows and hurtling stones, burning pitch and boiling oil. She was the same little fury who called Gaucourt a "son of a bitch," and, arms akimbo as Brother Richard sprinkled his holy water, taunted him with, "Oh, all right! All right! I won't fly away!" They were all one and the same: the girl who, without the least sign of "hysteria," without even getting excited, calmly answered her judges at the trial, "The angels? Why, they often come among us. Others may not see them, but I do."

And there is a second important point: Joan described her visions only when she was forced to, when confronted with people who did not want to listen to her, who tried to make her out a liar or a witch. She knew very well she was neither liar nor demon; so she tried her best to convince them. And attempting to translate for them something that was truly untranslatable—for what happened to her was not the kind of thing that could be explained; it had to be lived—she relied on what they could understand, their accepted words and imagery. She started to talk about wings, fancy clothes, golden crowns, because that was how Saint Michael, Saint Catherine, and Saint Margaret were

shown in statues and on stained-glass windows and pic-
tures. The names she reeled off were the ones she knew, the
ones used in her presence by her mother, by the local priest
since childhood. And I am not in the least bothered by the
fact that in 1969 the Church dropped from its liturgical
calendar, along with forty-two other saints of both sexes,
"Joan's two saints," Catherine and Margaret, as being too
vague, having too little historical confirmation. At death's
door, when Joan was trying to be totally truthful (no matter what others might think), she confessed that sometimes
("betimes") "what came to her were very little things, in
huge multitudes." To which it is easy to hear the satisfied
rejoinders: "Of course! At last, it becomes clear. The very
characteristic of hallucination." And, in fact, one doctor
was even kind enough to draw me a sketch of the part of
Joan's brain, the lobe, that was undoubtedly affected.

But at the same time (I, too, must confess), I was thinking
of Ezekiel speaking of the angels: the phosphorescence and
shimmering of invisible creatures becoming visible to the
pure in eye, as in the shaft of a sunbeam where we had
thought there was nothing before, we suddenly see "a mil-
lion golden dots" dancing about.

The pure in eye? Who knows whether Joan was not
gifted with that purity of eye indubitably possessed by
Saint Jean-Baptiste Vianney (he *saw* into the secrets of
hearts) and also found in certain Mohammedan sufis, Tibet-
an priests, and Indian wise men, allowing them to perceive
what we cannot see, although surely it is there, present and
alive?

Most human beings exist in a state of incoherence. Most
often we are nothing but a bundle of organs, without unity
or conviction, dulled by habit, carried away by our desires,
or buffeted by circumstance. Joan, on the other hand, was

a person with substance, who held together, and knew what she wanted. A compact creature, made of a single drive, passionately obeying the pull exercised on her soul. What did she hear? A text without words. She put the words in herself. These were less "voices come from wind and space" (as Delteil says) than a summoning of her own substance.[19] She felt an appeal; contact was made. It was as if a great hand had taken hold of her little rough one, and she answered its pressure with her own confident, ardent pressure.

Did Joan have a vocation? Was she given "a mission"? Well, according to the view that she held of the world, each of us had his mission, we all had the same vocation of justice and love. However, there were those who listened and those who did not listen, or who refused to hear. Joan was one who had listened, heard, and answered, Yes, yes! Here I am! I am ready. I will do it. She stated, literally, "I believed it was an angel speaking to me, and I had the will to believe." A will to believe also means a decision to go along, to belong, a determination to participate intimately, vitally, springing from the very roots of one's being; the essential kind of understanding that is taken to be a revelation. And as Isaiah says of those who accomplish justice, something inside them becomes as the rising sun.

In that wild sense of belonging, that torrential unification, she found a whirlwind, a vertigo of happiness. Noth-

---

[19]To my mind, Joan did "hear," both inside and outside herself, an irresistible appeal, on which she herself set the meaning. As if she were Another, she immediately replied, without understanding, "I am the servant of the Lord." She was asked to give her all; she "gave her all." How? By action! Action for good, in other words, for God. And since a great injustice, a "great pity," was taking place, that was where she had to go. She felt magnetized, and threw herself, body and soul, into the path of the magnet. But magnetized means attracted, and to be attracted means to be loved ("To have faith is to believe one is loved"), and in response to that love she gave her own wild, boundless, absolute, sacrificial love. She was trying to prove (and that was her spring, her fervor, the ever-renewed source of her drive) that she loved, that she knew how to love—and how to love utterly.

ing else counted any longer. Nothing but this miracle of joy, innocence, and truth. That was what Joan was saying when she related, "When my angels came to me, oh, would that they had carried me off with them!"

Today Joan has become the subject for patriotic holiday bromides, marshmallow sentimentalities, but in her day she was a thorn in the side of the notables and prelates. When people like Joan appear, "society" tries them on for size, but quickly finds them totally unfitted to its safety. In this world of conformists, it is dangerous not to be like them. Upset them, and you must pay dearly for the privilege.

"It is far more dangerous to be a saint," says Shaw, "than to be a conqueror" and "many terrifying but quite comprehensible scoundrels die natural deaths in all the glory of the kingdoms of this world,"[20] while Tolstoy is excommunicated and left to die in a wayside railroad station, and Joan —Joan "of Arc," as she is called—is glorified in statues by the churchgoers and set up on their altars—but only after they have burnt her alive.

During the rehabilitation proceedings, some zealous witnesses tried to create a relationship between Joan's stake and the cross of Christ. On one point, at least, they were not wrong: both of them died unassisted, universally abandoned, even by Heaven. Christ and Joan were both killed by the priests of their day, and both because they insisted on saying, "God must be served first." Claudel, in a little-known piece of writing, described the Catholic University of Paris in Joan's time as "congested and taut as a tumor," its theologians furious with "this little person who dared say she was the daughter of God; and one could hear the

---

[20]Shaw, *op. cit.*, "Preface," p. 10.

echo of a certain shout that had been uttered fourteen hundred years earlier: 'Blasphemy! He says he is the Son of God! . . .' They would show her what they were made of on the Mount of Sentences,"[21] that sacred hill, that den of Pharisees.

So, in conclusion, we turn to Claudel once again, for a remark that tells exactly what the Church of the Martins, Eugeniuses, and Borgias was like in the world around Joan:

"From time to time, within the household of the Church, there is filth enough to make one vomit, . . . everything topsy-turvy, and everyone letting himself go; the House of God turned into a pigsty"; and yet, at the same time, within the depths of the people, "poor souls, with dirty faces, weeping in a corner . . . and others, with bloodied mouths, beating at the doors of the tabernacle with their exhausted fists, and yet others, up at the top of the steeple, astride the cross amid the stars," and calling on God for help.[22]

---

[21]Claudel, *op. cit.*; the figure of speech, in the French idiomatic phrase, is the gruesomely graphic "They would show her what kind of wood they heated with. . . ." *(Translator's note)*

[22]*Paul Claudel interroge le Cantique des cantiques* (Paul Claudel Examines the Song of Songs), p. 427.

Index